D1603733

American Mediterranean

American Mediterranean

 SOUTHERN SLAVEHOLDERS IN THE
AGE OF EMANCIPATION

MATTHEW PRATT GUTERL

HARVARD UNIVERSITY PRESS

Cambridge, Massachusetts, and London, England   2008

Library of Congress Cataloging-in-Publication Data

Guterl, Matthew Pratt, 1970–
    American Mediterranean : southern slaveholders in the age of
    emancipation / Matthew Pratt Guterl.
        p. cm.
    Includes bibliographical references and index.
    ISBN 978-0-674-02868-5 (alk. paper)
    1. Slaveholders—Southern States—History—19th century.
    2. Slaveholders—West Indies—History—19th century.
    3. Slaves—Emancipation—History—19th century.
    4. Slavery—Southern States—History—19th century.
    5. Slavery—West Indies—History—19th century.
    6. Southern States—Relations—West Indies.
    7. West Indies—Relations—Southern States.
    8. Cosmopolitanism—Southern States—History—19th century.
    9. Cosmopolitanism—West Indies—History—19th century.
    10. Pan-Americanism—History—19th century. I. Title.
E449.G98   2008
306.3'620975—dc22   2008001140

For Robert and Maya,
and for Sandi

Contents

Illustrations

American Mediterranean

Introduction

Faulkner's world is a frontier.

—EDOUARD GLISSANT, *FAULKNER, MISSISSIPPI* (1999)

What do we know of the "master class"? We know that the master class owned slaves; that they sought to profit from that ownership; that they understood power; that they fancied themselves to be the quintessential Americans; and that, in the end, their fevered dedication to slavery cost them national prominence, sparked a bloody war, and laid waste to everything they had built up. We know less, though, about their links to the wider fraternity of slaveholders in Cuba, in Brazil, and elsewhere, or about their place and their role in the hemisphere. The master class, I argue here, was connected—by ship, by overland travel, by print culture, by a sense of singular space, and by the prospect of future conquest—to the *habitus* and *communitas* of New World slaveholders, to institutions, cultures, and "structures of feeling" that were not contained by the nation-state.[1] Some of the masters of the Old South invested in a vision of the circum-Caribbean that included their own holdings, their own grand plantations. Their commitment to this broader slaveowning community did not fare well during and after the Civil War. But residues or memories of that worldview remained after the war and shaped Jim Crow. To tell the story in this way, one must approach the nation-state with a good degree of skepticism, peeling it up, peering underneath, and shining new light on the border-crossing social worlds of the long nineteenth century. As significantly, one must also set aside the conventional wisdom of the American Century—specifically, the Cold War conviction that the United States is a superpower because God willed it to be so—and remember just how fractious, how poorly formed, and how terribly disconnected the sprawling young republic and its component parts were in the tumultuous age of emancipation.

"He went to the West Indies." That was how the fictional character Quentin Compson remembered the story of one slaveholder's meteoric rise in the Old South. Compson's recollections are taken from William Faulkner's *Absalom, Absalom!,* a touchstone for anyone seeking to understand the pan-Caribbean master class. A threadbare child, Thomas Sutpen had listened when his teacher told him of "a place called the West Indies to which poor men went and became rich." After class, Sutpen had cornered the man, pressing him to tell the story of that lush and distant set of islands. The teacher seemed fearful, and Thomas thought briefly of striking him. He roughly grabbed the teacher's arm and compelled him to say more. Later, when Sutpen turned fourteen, and when his "design" required "money in considerable quantities," he remembered that the West Indies could be the wellspring of prosperity for a violent, dominating boy. And in doing so—in remembering it just this way—he assured his imminent ascent from poor white to slaveholder, from provincial to cosmopolitan, from insignificance to the mastery of slaves. Then, of course, he went to the West Indies, hoping to acquire the knowledge, skills, and capital that would allow him to dominate black slaves, to be powerful in the white world, and to control his issue. This was Thomas Sutpen's story. Or, at least, this was the start of it.

"I went to the West Indies," Sutpen had said. "That's how he said it," Compson remembered years later, "not how he managed to find where the West Indies were nor where the ships departed from to go there, nor how he got to where the ships were and got in one nor how he liked the sea nor about the hardships of a sailor's life." Sutpen's elliptical silences were as revealing as his confession. But the shortest route to wealth and power was well known in his day, and there may have been no need for explanation. As Sutpen put it, he had to "take whatever method that came to my hand." How else would a poor and callous white boy, born in the mountains of western Virginia, become fabulously and quickly rich, except through emulation of the most ruthless, grasping slaveholders of the Americas? Where else would he turn for knowledge of slavery on a vast, spectacular scale, except to the sugar plantations of the American Mediterranean? And how else would he learn to repeat their successes, and to elide their failures, except by hopping on a ship and following the easy, open routes that linked the bustling port cities of the South to the rest of the hemisphere? How else would he do this, except, in the end, by traveling

Thomas Sutpen, as depicted by artist David Tamura for the cover of the 1987 edition of Faulkner's *Absalom, Absalom!* Artwork courtesy of David Tamura.

abroad to learn the practical patois that he would need to purchase, control, and brutalize African slaves?[2]

For a long time, readers have focused on the significance of miscegenation in William Faulkner's portrait of Sutpen. "Creolization is the very thing that offends Faulkner," suggests literary critic Edouard Glissant, "*métissage* and miscegenation, plus their foreseeable consequences."[3] In the rush to transform his hopes into reality, Sutpen crosses a line he cannot uncross, unwittingly producing a mixed child. The whiteness of his aristocratic wife, Eulalia, is called into question, making their son, Charles, an abomination and a threat to Sutpen's dream of prestige and power. Sutpen flees, leaving this legacy of unhappy mixture—an embodiment of "the black legend"—behind. Arriving, some years later, in Mississippi, a wild frontier for slavery on the continent, and now more brutal and brooding, with a "quality of gaunt and tireless driving," Sutpen plants himself on one hundred acres, where he presides as a brooding lord of the manor and where he strives to reproduce himself, to make up for the errors of Haiti.[4] He has brought with him a fettered gang of "wild negroes" from the island, who speak the West Indian patois, and a tattered French architect. In the end, of course, the ghosts of Sutpen's past life (specifically, that of his son, Charles) return to haunt him, arriving on his doorstep, and—with the Civil War as a backdrop—all of Sutpen's hopes are dashed. He cannot find an appropriate heir. He fathers a child with a former slave. And after once again propagating racial mixture, he is killed by a long-time manservant. His estate, "Sutpen's Hundred"—where white would dominate black on a grand scale, echoing the hierarchy of the West Indies—proves to be a child's dream and nothing more. The manor house will henceforth be home to an impure mixture of whites, negroes, and mulattos. The "explosion of the curse," as Glissant described it, can be heard for generations.[5]

But there is more to the story of Thomas Sutpen than an unhealthy obsession with mixture or "creolization." Indeed, we cannot understand the slaveholders of the Old South—the subject of Faulkner's greatest analysis in *Absalom, Absalom!*—if we reduce the concept of "creole" to refer only to the result of interracial or intercultural sex. Sutpen is—in a detail that Glissant and others quickly gloss over—also a slaveholding *criollo*, a New World master, scrambling for power in one of the many messy, tropical dependencies that clung to the edges of the Caribbean. He is an archetype of the Old South in transition, a symbol of the slaveholding past, when the social networks and pathways that bound Mississippi to Guadeloupe and Haiti were heavily traveled, familiar, and unchecked. He is a white settler of European heritage, determined to carve civilization out of the New World and bound in self-conscious solidarity with his slaveholding fellows by shared tradition, by culture, and by the informal, border-crossing practices of translation, mediation, and appropriation. His creolism is, in this sense, a deliberate performance, and not just a sociological or biological process—a performance of consanguinity, of assumed sameness, of knowledge production across borders. More broadly, Sutpen is not alone in this story. His slaveholding fellows, the master class of the Americas, are not just Southern. They are Caribbean; they are West Indian; they are American. They speak Spanish, French, Dutch, and English. They, too, are relentless; they hunger for profit and power and have interests that cannot be reduced to empire. They have their own roots in and routes to the various histories of New World slavery. And, like Sutpen, they conceive of themselves, at certain times, as dramatically hemispheric and cosmopolitan.

Through the character of Thomas Sutpen, Faulkner brought to the surface a narrative of Southern history that exists outside of the nation-state. To continue and expand upon this excavation, *American Mediterranean* tells the story of a privileged and influential group of elite Southern intellectuals, planters, and former Confederate leaders, among them the West Indian Confederate Judah Benjamin, the transplanted Haitian James Achille de Caraduec, the Cuban expatriate Ambrosio Gonzales and his South Carolinian wife Harriet Elliot, the sojourner Andrew McCollam, and the exile Eliza McHatton.[6] They were hardly a single social unit or organized cohort, but their lives overlapped, intersected, and accumulated energy in important ways. Like the fictional Thomas Sutpen, these men and women were slaveholding *bricoleurs,* using a common vocabulary to make sense of and respond to the sweeping emancipations of the New World. As tensions between the North and the South escalated, these Southern masters turned their eyes further southward, to Jamaica and Haiti, where slavery had already been abolished with what looked to the Southerners to be disastrous consequences. They turned their attention as well to the few places where plantation slavery survived on a large scale, such as Brazil and Cuba. As they beheld this American Mediterranean with a mixture of horror and longing, the slaveholders came face to face with the great question of the nineteenth century: the problem of free labor.[7] When the time came to confront that problem in their native South, the master class had already thought long and hard about what kind of labor system could be reconstructed upon the ashes of its defeated slave society. Some packed their bags and headed for another place in the hemisphere, where they hoped to rebuild the world they had lost. But for the vast majority of those who stayed put, the positive and negative lessons learned from Haitian and Jamaican emancipations guided their legislative hands as they set about in 1865 to construct a new legal apparatus for the control of their own former slaves. They pondered once again the apprenticeship system the British had established with the emancipation of slaves in the West Indies. They experimented with the importation of Chinese workers, and they struggled to divert some of the swelling river of European immigrants into the South. Most of these experiments failed. But even in their failure, these slaveholders and their postwar descendants revealed how thoroughly embedded they were in a wider world that was being radically transformed by debates over freedom, abolition, and citizenship.

The Southern slaveowners at the heart of this story were not, then, just citizens of the United States. They were also citizens in a complicated tropical topography, *criollos* in a composite imaginary, and culturally hybrid philosophers of chattel bondage who could, when they wished, transcend the divides between the United States, the Caribbean, and Latin America. They were bound together as slaveholders in the New World, possessed of a shared "white Creole consciousness," marking them off from Europe and bringing their hemispheric identities into sparkling alignment.[8] They understood African slavery as a universal system of labor for the Americas and searched for best practices in other slave societies. They assumed that slaves everywhere had been poisoned by abolitionism and that the smallest slave rebellion anywhere could spark a massive uprising everywhere. They shared a belief in "steady, solid simultaneity through time," so that what happened to slaveholders elsewhere could also seem to be happening to them.[9] Like Thomas Sutpen, they saw versions of Haiti all around them, having "effectively loosen[ed] the first black republic from its moorings in place and in a certain kind of historical specificity" and allowing it to "drift," to become an elusive, mobile threat.[10] Despite their particular regional preferences, then, they believed that the fate of slavery in the South was closely intertwined with the fate of slavery elsewhere in the Americas, that the line separating master from slave could, if the circumstances were right, cut across the foreign policies and international debates of the various republics and colonies. They were, then, in some real and imagined sense, a part of the master class of the Americas. Their learned musings on the supposed problems of freedom were, to borrow from Faulkner, offered in a sort of slaveholder's patois. Their eager purchase of African flesh, whether in New Orleans or Havana, created a kind of "circum-Atlantic memory," the basis of slaveholding solidarity, and encouraged other cross-national cultural exchanges in the American Mediterranean.[11] As members of a pan-American slaveholding class, their apparently shared cosmopolitan interests could triumph, they sometimes assumed, over the various linguistic, racial, national, and historic chauvinisms that otherwise fractured the Hispanophone and Anglophone Caribbean.[12]

The term *cosmopolitanism* captures the acute awareness of global events and international affairs shared by these Southern creoles. It also references the familiar, everyday interchange between the global, the national, and the local. Few of the Southern slaveholders described here ever doubted or questioned their national citizenship or worried over their status as "Americans," a word they typically defined rather narrowly. But they were aware that there were other communities—specifically those marked by class, by race, and by slaveholding culture—that were far larger than the nation-state. And they sometimes keenly felt themselves to be linked by history or circumstance to those same communities. To make sense of this linkage, we need to consider race, nation, and class above and beyond the point of their most direct intersection and outside the physical confines of the United States. Whenever and wherever national histories of slaveholding and emancipation have deployed "race" and "class" as static, sociologically informed, analytical categories and focused them inward on the domestic narrative of "the coming of the Civil War" or "the emergence of Jim Crow," they have left out something important: the very meaning of racial identity and class consciousness—two of the "broadest divisions of mankind," both quite independent of national identity—to many slaveowners in the rambling nineteenth century. We need to refocus our energies on the far-reaching "hemispheric engagements" that shaped Southern slaveholding and, by extension, to scrutinize the labors of the most conservative, most powerful, and often wealthiest social class of the republic to forge stronger, politically useful connections to the wider world and, in the end, to join with men and women who were, it seemed, a lot like themselves.[13]

By the beginning of the Civil War, it was clear that the world of these cosmopolitan Southern slaveholders—this composite American Mediterranean—was shrinking. The age of nations and nationalism was solidifying borders across the Americas and in Europe, and the global process of emancipation was shattering the earlier New World consensus on the value of chattel bondage. Southern slaveholders with a personal or familial link to the American Mediterranean thus imagined the story of the master class in the Americas as a story marked by increasing loss and privation and by the threat of a looming apocalypse. Their actions in the Civil War constituted an attempt to redefine their cosmopolitanism, a gamble that failed in the face of the Confederate defeat. In the postbellum era, this fading Mediterranean ethos emerges most clearly in labor relations, in the solidarity of planters and politicians with other former slave societies, and in their efforts—through appropriation and reinterpretation—to mitigate the effect of emancipation. The great irony here is that the foreclosure of the literal hemispheric relationships—the economic associations, the presence of slaves and "coolies," and the shared histories and cultures of cash crop agriculture—did little to bring an end to the imagined ones, to the *communitas* of masters and the "mystic chords of memory" that bound the Old South to the slaveholding past of the Americas. After the war— after slavery—the masters of the Old South reacted to the freedom of their former slaves like cultural amputees, bewildered by the phantom sensations of something lost and by the failure to recognize, or believe, in the permanence of its removal. For those few who left the postwar South, and for those great many who stayed behind, the nostalgia for the past, the melancholic pathos of the present, and the determination to shape the future were thus suffused with the ghostly remembrance of the American Mediterranean.

Some of the Southern slaveholders described here would be utterly mystified by contemporary historical portraits of the Old South, by the comparative charts and quixotic algebras of oppression purportedly proving that the Southern states were unique or that they witnessed "the triumph of a racism more insidious than any other in the New World."[14] Histories of slavery and emancipation have long described an increasingly parochial Southern planter class that had grown disconnected from its once-close Caribbean cousins, setting the stage for the impending fratricide of the Civil War. "Southerners," Kenneth Stampp wrote, "were among slavery's last apologists. . . . Theirs was a 'Lost Cause' even before they took up arms to defend it. Being culturally isolated, living in an unfriendly world, was a frightening experience, which made many of them angry and aggressive. Outside of Africa itself, they could now look only to Brazil, Cuba, Porto Rico, and Dutch Guiana for societies, which, like their own, contained masters and slaves. The rest of the world was full of strangers."[15] As a partial consequence of this "new [and] sharpening divergence" between the nineteenth-century South and the Americas, the argument goes, the region grew increasingly, provocatively, defiantly separate from the United States.[16] As historians sought an explanation for the Civil War and Reconstruction, the South was situated, by and large, in a national context, as a "distinctive" region, its history and personality scarred by "frustration, failure, and defeat," suffused with "evil" and "tragedy," defending an "un-American adventure in feudal fantasy."[17] It was distinctive, then, in a dual sense: nationally and hemispherically. Secession, Eugene Genovese argued, epitomized the South's role as the "greatest paradox in a subject overflowing with paradox" and reflected a unique sense—unique in the Americas—that the planters populating that band of states from Texas to Virginia had become "the self-appointed guardians of a way of life." "The slaveholders

of the Old South," he concluded, "thereby came closer to forging themselves into a distinct—or, if you will, pure—slaveholding class than any
others in the New World."[18] But the core group of slaveowners and
planters discussed here routinely steps outside of these ambitious historiographical claims of distinctiveness and peculiarity. They certainly
imagined the Southern slaveholder to be a superior type, but they did so
by locating the South in a global historical context, by emphasizing a
common past of bondage and mastery, and by worrying over a shared
future of emancipation. They may well have loathed their Cuban colleagues, for instance, but they shared some strong sense of solidarity
with them, too.

Internationally minded, comparatively positioned and self-aware
within a larger pan-American master class, and remarkably mobile and
restless, the slave masters of the Old South were a unique group, even
among planters. Few other slaveholders in the hemisphere developed a
"proslavery argument" that relied on scientific racism. No other
planter group was, for lack of a better expression, so doubly national
or as committed to the republican fraternity of the United States as it
was to the growth of Southern nationalism and, in the end, to political
separatism. None, in sum, enjoyed the disproportionate wealth and political power of the slave masters of the Old South.[19] And yet, some in
this rarified master class were also inspired by a common history of
racial bondage and the gloomy prospect of a shared future of emancipation to create, or imagine, a collaborative community across the Caribbean for those whose fortunes were also bound in some fashion to
slavery. The "problem of freedom," as historian Thomas Holt calls it,
and the postemancipation "labor problem" were pan-American concerns, presenting a clear and present danger to these members of the
Southern planter class, giving them good cause to follow the travail of
apprenticeship in Jamaica, to look at the emerging labor regime of
Cuban sugar cultivation, or to conceive of a new life in Brazil.[20] We
make a mistake, then, when we look only at the domestic context to
understand slaveholding congressional politics and when we ignore the
creole cultures of influential slaveowners, along with their adaptive
bricolage, their selective readings of hemispheric history, and their elaborate social connections to the broader Americas.

American Mediterranean is not, however, a work of comparative history. Indeed, the more general presumption that the U.S. South was
different from the rest of the Americas is an unintended consequence
of our reliance—as a discipline and as a community of intellectuals,

academics, students, and policymakers—on comparison. Over the past forty years, a handful of discipline-breaking works have compared the U.S. South with what historian Peter Kolchin calls "other Souths"— with South Africa, Brazil, Cuba, and elsewhere—and have noted remarkable parallels and divergences while probing the singularity of the U.S. experience, especially when it comes to race.[21] Once again, the South is always portrayed as different. George Fredrickson, for instance, concluded that the ideology of egalitarianism (the "American Creed") limited the role of the federal government in the establishment of Jim Crow and expanded the role of the states. Carl Degler, in considering the "Mulatto Escape Hatch" in Brazil, pointed to its supposed absence in the South as a proof of difference. And Herbert Klein's *Slavery in the Americas,* adroitly jumping back and forth between Virginia and Cuba in successive chapters, stressed the "uniqueness" and "fundamentally different" qualities of Southern slavery, which was, he argued, the purest caste system in the New World.[22] Works like these relied on a careful method: isolating a few stories that shared some important features, they laid them alongside one another, picked out some significantly distinctive qualities, and then sought to explain them. Because of such work, we have a much richer understanding of race relations in the United States than we did fifty years ago. Still, in isolating two cases (e.g., Virginia and Cuba), even to emphasize general similarities, these comparisons relied on some clearly understandable, easily marked border between each place, each story, each unit. They emphasized, even if unintentionally, the power of the local, the strength of tradition, and the boundaries of the nation-state, or of place and location. Comparisons, no matter how well conceived, can hide connections.[23] Comparative history can be landlocked; but in *American Mediterranean,* the history of the South is pushed offshore.

The creole travelers, statesmen, and slaveholders profiled in this book remind us that the power of the nation-state to delimit experience, meaning, and influence was, in the nineteenth century and in the Americas, both limited in scope and contradicted by alternative identifications, experiences, and communities. But the more specific historical significance of this American master class is most dramatically revealed at the close of the war, when the Anglophone planter class of the South was thrown into deep, profound crisis. Desperate for a solution to their "labor problem" and reaching for severed connections to the Caribbean, the response of these cosmopolitan planters to emancipation would have made perfect sense to any other planter in Jamaica, Cuba, or

British Guiana: legislate compulsory labor; create a new judicial machinery to control and punish those who would not work; attempt to import coolies and "white" immigrants as supplemental labor; use violence to control those marked as "black" and "yellow"; and, if all this fails, flee to somewhere else, to some other island, republic, or colony where slavery still survived.

To understand how all of this happened, we need to understand the master class in diaspora, in exile, and in empire. We must follow the Thomas Sutpens of the Old South to the "West Indies" and back again to see how this group of slaveholders made sense of emancipation. Doing so can add new details—like a transparency laid over a familiar map—to our most obvious assumptions about the postemancipation period and can draw attention to the willfully itinerant and globally informed master class. It can remind us that the Civil War is not just a great divide for the various historiographical traditions of Southern history and U.S. history, but also that it utterly transformed the place and role of the South in the Americas. It can gently recast the nineteenth-century U.S. South as a messy, complicated borderland of sorts between North America and the Caribbean, a transitional region of the hemisphere with conflicting and overlapping political, economic, social, and cultural identities. It can transform our dominant comparative perspectives into what Rebecca Scott, whose recent work has evolved into an exploration of connections, calls "something else."[24] It can, finally, help us to see that what has long been imagined as a stark, uniformly "U.S-centered" dialogue about the coming war between "the North" and "the South" was originally staged as a pan-American production, with rich and meaningful backdrops, global plotlines, and multiple angles of spectatorship. It took place, in short, in the American Mediterranean—the extraordinary network of rivers, seas, and waterways that served as the lifeblood of the New World, where longstanding currents and flows shaped the deeper history of slavery and freedom.

CHAPTER ONE

The American Mediterranean

A line from the Delta of the Orinoco to the east end of
Cuba is but a thousand miles long; and yet, to the west
of it, lies this magnificent basin of water, locked in by a
continent that has on its shores the most fertile valleys
of the earth. All and more, too, that the Mediterranean
is to Europe, Africa, and Asia, this sea is to America
and the world.

—MATTHEW F. MAURY, "GULF OF MEXICO" (1854)

Octavia Walton was a classic "Southern belle." She was also widely regarded as "one of nature's cosmopolites, a woman to whom the whole
world was home."[1] The granddaughter of the Virginian George
Walton, who was a signer of the Declaration of Independence, Octavia
had been raised in the polyglot surrounds of Pensacola, a frontier naval
port in the Florida territory, and had been schooled in a half dozen languages and literatures by an "old Scottish tutor." She grew up with the
children of Anglophone colonists, Spanish settlers, Haitian exiles, mulattos, slaves, and Seminoles, and earned great fame in the South for her
internationalist orientation; her "linguistic versatility" in Spanish,
Italian, and French; and her "sympathetic and assimilating faculty,"
which allowed her great rapport with others and enabled her to find
comfort in any location or cultural setting.[2] Henry Clay, the Marquis
de Lafayette, Washington Irving, and Fredrika Bremer—a varied group,
to be sure—found her utterly enchanting and marveled at her social
dexterity and her global wit. As a young woman, Walton was an ex-
citing object, it seems, largely because these "talents" accompanied her
maturation at that place along the Gulf Coast where the residues of
French, Spanish, and British empires were blended. She was, people assumed, a reflection of the near future of the American South, as former
colonies and tribal lands were subsumed into the expanding slaveholding region of the United States, and as various cultures and languages and races came together in new and unpredictable ways. She was
famous enough to have a song written about her, the tropically titled

"Beautiful Isle." And she made a lasting impression on those who surveyed her wardrobe, fashionably juxtaposing her "lemon-colored satin
gown" with a "wreath of coral on her dark braids, and coral morocco
shoes."[3]

In 1836, after moving to Mobile, Alabama, another port city
drawing ships, people, and commerce from around the world, Walton
married Henry S. Le Vert, a young French émigré and surgeon, and
thereafter styled herself as "Madame Le Vert." As the quintessence of
Southern cosmopolitanism, she possessed an extraordinary measure
of "social sovereignty" and became, as her contemporaries remembered it, the appointed arbiter of high culture along the outer rim of
the Gulf of Mexico.[4] Her carefully orchestrated sitting room "Mon-
days" were sophisticated affairs, drawing weekly visits from the most
polished sorts of people in Mobile, as well as guests from Europe,
from the West Indies, and from across the South. In between social
appointments, Le Vert labored to translate Cuban poetry into English,
corresponded with poets and politicians, and traveled the world.[5] She
was, in sum, a peerless exemplar of the hemispherics of the mid-
century South—at home in the world of ideas, fluent in myriad languages and literatures, and a literal product of the slaveholding world
of the American Mediterranean.

In 1857, after two decades of aristocratic prominence, Le Vert collected her intimate letters—most of them written to friends and family
while she was abroad—and had them published with the unassuming
title of *Souvenirs of Travel*. Produced in Mobile, *Souvenirs* was a rare
Southern travelogue, and it offers a precious glimpse into the antebellum travels of elite white women. The book was well received, or at
least Le Vert's considerable vanity allowed her to claim such a reception. Her missives, when arranged in sequence, provide a rich portrait
of her two trips to popular historic sites in Europe and demonstrate
her familiarity with European literature and culture and her personal
friendships with continental glitterati. Madame Le Vert, it seemed,
knew all the right people. In its efforts to document this intimate
knowledge of important things and royal personages, then, *Souvenirs*
reveals itself to be part of the pronounced nineteenth-century Southern
effort to redefine the South as intellectually serious and cultured, with
stronger links to Europe than to the literary nationalism of Emerson,
and to overturn its reputation as a crude and uncivilized backwater
through the establishment and promotion of ornamental soirées and literary circles. Southerners imagined themselves, Michael O'Brien writes,

An 1833 portrait of Octavia Walton, or "Madame Le Vert," by Thomas Sully. From the Historic Mobile Preservation Society Archives.

as "the custodians of empire" and drew deeply from European history and culture to provide "order" for their world and to establish their place in it.[6] Le Vert's manicured Monday salons thus offered a regular opportunity for the display of the stylized performance of Europe's old imperial "project" in the hybrid New World and for the deliberate translation of European styles to match the authoritarian and expansionist aims of the master class in the Americas.

On her way to Europe for a second trip, Le Vert paused for a few weeks at "the brilliant city" of Havana, a familiar destination for many Southerners of her particular social class. A visit to Europe "back then," Eliza McHatton recalled, writing of Le Vert, was "like taking a trip to

Mars."[7] If Le Vert's visit to the Old World had been "the dream of [her] life," this stopover in Havana was something else—a brief and necessary sojourn at a familiar way station.[8] Le Vert had a deep appreciation for the efforts of the *filibusteros* to liberate the island from the cruelties of Spanish domination.[9] She knew the place well and could imagine it as an integral part of the South. She was greeted at the dock by a childhood friend and was speedily conveyed to Sarah Brewer's Hotel Cubano. After a brief respite, Brewer escorted Madame Le Vert to promenade at the *Paseo Tacon,* which they circled in a *volante,* an ornate horse-drawn carriage, driven by "an intensely black negro, with immense boots . . . ornamented with silver." In her commentary on the "big-booted postillions" and the jubilant frolics of the local slave population and in her repetitious appreciations of the "gallant-looking" lighter-skinned Cubans, Le Vert countered the prevailing abolitionist portrait of the gruesome sugar industry and of Cuban creoles as untrustworthy, less civilized "off-white" people.[10] She provides, in other words, a very Southern and very feminine imagining of the island: sympathetic to slaveholders, replete with risqué and comic "darky" portraits and whispered gossip about the neighboring island, volcanic Haiti, and lacking any in-depth consideration of *el ingenio,* the grim sugar factories of the Cuban countryside. Like many of her slaveholding contemporaries, she may well have assumed that Cuba would inevitably become part of the South. When she left the island for Europe in early February of 1855, she described it, tellingly, as "our last day in America," as if the distinction between Cuba and the South was far less significant than the difference between the Old World and the New.[11]

The extraordinary and exemplary Madame Le Vert was, in many ways, a product of her time, her place, and her social position. Taking her cosmopolitanism as a starting point, this chapter explores the antebellum South's relationship to the Caribbean, with special attention paid to Cuba, Haiti, and Jamaica. It emphasizes, with broad strokes, the mirrored attractions and repulsions offered by the wider Americas, assessing the South as it reached out to the Americas, wrangled with the North for control of the republic, and established itself—intellectually, culturally, and socially—as an independent nation-state. With secession and civil war looming, debates in the U.S. South about the futures of slavery, emancipation, freedom, and citizenship were structured not just by internal political disputes, but also by the "failure" of Haiti and Jamaica, and by the chance that Cuba might become a slaveholding state or, conversely, home to the largest "free" population of former slaves in the New World. Throughout this period, the Caribbean, the Gulf, and the Mississippi often appear in the imaginings of Southern slaveholders as a singular American Mediterranean, as a profit-rich and danger-filled region "curtained," as one writer put it, "on the east, by a chain of fruitful islands, stretching from Trinidad to Cuba. . . . On the north and the south and the west, [it is] land-locked by the continent, which has bent and twisted around the sea, so as to fold it within its bosom."[12] Southerners, as this use of a Mediterranean metaphor shows, were fond of classical allusions. The antebellum South, here, was Rome, with all its vices and appetites, its fears and possibilities, and its fortune and magnificence. In the face of powerful parallels and connections, Southerners labored to distinguish their own world as superior to the rest of the Americas, all the while critiquing the "cold" North as equally and disturbingly alien. They had an interest in describing the South as *primus inter pares* in two contexts, in both the United States and the Americas: they were bound to slavery, they were inordinately proud of their system of government, they favored the racial politics of the Old South, and they were fearful of the changing world around them. In order to understand the impact of the Civil War and the melodramas of the postbellum milieu, then, we must first come to know the Old South as a half-hearted part of this American Mediterranean.

Dreams and Nightmares

In the spring of 1856, sixteen-year-old Harriet Rutledge Elliot and thirty-eight-year-old Ambrosio Gonzales were married at Oak Lawn, her family's plantation in Beaufort, South Carolina. "Hattie" and "Gonzie" had spent much of that summer at the sulphur baths and springs that could be found at that time across the upper South, where the younger elite men and women of the planter class often gathered— along "Nullification Row," the string of homes owned by South Carolinians in Salt Sulphur Springs, West Virginia, for instance, and in Sweet Springs, Virginia. The couple fell in love, according to Gonzales's able biographer, after Gonzales's sustained visit in September of 1855 to Beaumont, a summer residence in Flat Rock, North Carolina, belonging to Mary, Hattie's older sister. In the months between their engagement in early December and their marriage in April, Gonzales— not atypically in such unions—sent regular, prescriptive advice, encouraging his future wife to "practice sewing," to work at her "hairdressing," and to refine the other skills that, as he saw it, would enable her to master her proper "dominion": the home.[13] A narrow, fit-looking man with thinning silver hair who, many would later say, looked a bit like Confederate General Pierre Gustave Toutant Beauregard, Gonzales was a temporary clerk in the U.S. Patent Office, earning "ten cents per hundred words."[14] Harriet was the youngest daughter of a socially prominent planter and sportsman, William Elliot, himself a former member of the South Carolina House who had resigned in the early 1830s rather than vote against his colleagues in the Nullification Crisis and who later penned a series of essays on slavery under the pseudonym "Agricola," a name that evoked—as Tacitus would have it—a character of such refinement that "to speak of uprightness and purity in such a man would be an insult to his virtues."[15] Harriet and Gonzales's engagement was not without its peaks and valleys, and the much older Gonzales labored to keep up with her, reminding her of his exotic nature and using his background to excuse a range of verbal gaffes: "I am a foreign thing," he wrote, "and never lost my native tongue."[16]

If Gonzales, a product of the Hispanophone Caribbean, offered his discomfort in English to Harriet as explanation for the occasional romantic gaffe, he was nevertheless a fluent, native speaker of the only other language that mattered to the Deep South: the language of slaveholding. The son of a well-pedigreed mathematics teacher from Havana, Gonzales was educated as a child in New York, where his closest friend was the young Louisianan Beauregard, before returning to the University of Havana for a law degree. He spoke four languages and was, by the time of his engagement, a naturalized American citizen. He was a firm believer that the annexation of Cuba by the United States would extend constitutional protections to slavery on the island, ensure the perpetuation of sugar production, and dispel the chance of a slave rebellion. He was, more importantly, one of the most prominent *filibusteros* of his day, a trusted confident of General Narciso Lopez, the leader of one of the most dramatic "expeditions." Gonzales was also an aggressive lobbyist and fundraiser who pushed John C. Calhoun and others to come out publicly in favor of the acquisition of slaveholding Cuba (a move that would be matched, it was theorized in the late 1840s, by the annexation of free Canada).[17]

Following the example of Texas, where white settlers from the United States had eventually forced a war with Mexico and the incorporation of a slaveholding republic into the union, Lopez, Gonzales, and their Southern allies raised funds to organize private companies of men from the polyglot South into military forces, to purchase ships and weapons, and to illegally send these forces to Cuba to inspire a revolt against Spanish colonialism. As Gonzales explained it, in terms that would generate sympathy in the heart of any Southerner, "white" Cubans lacked the right to assemble peacefully and to voice their grievances with the government and so could only watch in horror as the prospect of a race war dawned. "While slaves and Asiatics are . . . introduced," Gonzales wrote sadly, "white colonization is discountenanced, that the threat of a colored population may be held to the Cubans while 24,000 bayonets are pointed at their breasts."[18] Gonzales, as one *filibustero* remembered him, was an "ardent soul," a "noble Creole" struggling against "a foul, foreign dominion" that threatened to arm and "turn loose" Cuba's large African population at the first sign of any independence movement.[19] And Gonzales turned, quite logically, to the larger fraternity of slaveholders for help, offering the island as a fully developed and economically vibrant state that would walk in lockstep with the Old South and the planter class, which faced its own "foreign" adversary.

Ambrosio Gonzales's concerns about Cuba resonated in the South. As mapmaker and entrepreneur Carlos Butterfield imagined it, the Gulf South was the literal gateway, through Mobile and New Orleans, to the Caribbean, and it was the logical staging ground for the martial demonstration of the Monroe Doctrine. Butterfield's 1859 map, drawn to demonstrate the potential of a U.S.–Mexico mail connection, had revealed a rich network of steamship routes and rail lines that traversed national borders and natural divisions. The pieces were all in place, Butterfield argued. All that was required was the completion of the "entire circuit," which would stimulate "commercial intercourse" between New Orleans, Mobile, Galveston, Veracruz, and any number of other ports.[20] The elaborate connections across the region, Butterfield and others assumed, would thus enable the widest range of economic and political penetrations, bridging the Americas and, perhaps, pushing out meddlesome European powers.

For many in the South, the rest of the hemisphere was destined for American domination, enabled by an expanding slave population, technologically superior agricultural methods, and superior Anglo-Saxon stock. Advocates of this inevitable consolidation of the continent under the control of the United States included a wide range of people, among them the brightest lights of the leadership of the future Confederacy. In the Civil War, for instance, Matthew F. Maury, whose thoughts on the Gulf of Mexico serve as the epigraph for this chapter, would earn great

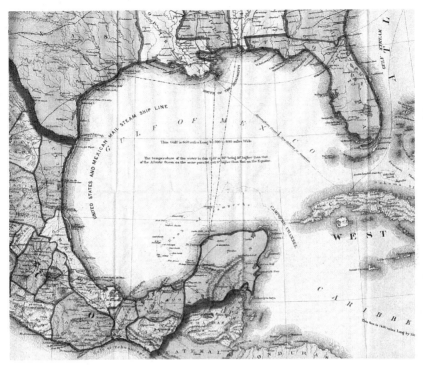

Detail from Carlos Butterfield's Map of North America, including Mexico and the Caribbean. From his *United States and Mexico Mail Steamship Line* (orig. 1859), courtesy of the Latin American Library, Tulane University.

fame as one of the most daring, innovative naval officers of the Confederate States of America. But in the years prior to the war between the states, he served as the architect of a plan to export enslaved Africans from the American South to Brazil, which had abandoned the transatlantic slave trade in 1853. Such a plan, Maury hoped, would change the dangerous demographic calculus of the Deep South, where "too many slaves" predestined a race war and the end of white settlement. Of course, Maury's plan would also ensure the hemispheric survival of slavery itself; Southerners could invest the profits from the sale of their slaves at home even as their cousins in Brazil could once again procure cheaper, more reliable, and "seasoned" chattel from a dependable, legal source. To send off "excess" slaves to Brazil, Gerald Horne notes, Maury had to rely on an expansive interpretation of "the internal slave trade" and to treat Brazil as if it were a sister society, as "a sort of American colony," and as a state-in-waiting, with significant ties to the slaveholding South. "Maury's bold schemes," Horne concludes, "were indicative of an era when citizenship was blurred and territories were being seized promiscuously."[21]

Cuba and the South had long enjoyed a special relationship as two of the largest, most profitable, and physically proximate slaveholding societies in the New World. Southerners—alongside some New England families—owned plantations in colonial Cuba, ran hotels, and operated businesses in Havana. Southerners were not only slaveowners in Cuba (Nicholas Trist, the American counsel in the 1830s, owned the Flor de Cuba plantation), but also businesspeople there (James Robb, president of the New Orleans Gas Light & Banking Company, established a sister company in Havana). The overlap and cross-pollination is so broad as to defy quick summary, and the resulting "binding familiarities" were hardly limited to the South. The railroad cars, sugar boilers, and locomotives brought in to modernize Cuban sugar production came from American companies along the Atlantic seaboard, and New England mechanics proliferated on the Cuban *cafetals* and *ingenios* that were so often visited by Southerners. The U.S.-born population in Cuba doubled in the two decades before the Civil War, and the Cuban-born population in New York was the largest, and most significant, in the country. But if Cuba, as one historian summarizes, "entered the North American imagination as the 'tropics' . . . as the opposite of what the United States was," it appeared in the mind of the Southerner as something else: as a racial problem and as a future state in the slave power bloc, with nettlesome social dynamics that were destined to be absorbed by the supposedly predestined advance of the United States into the global South.[22]

By the 1850s, the decade of Harriet and Ambrosio's courtship, travel to the Caribbean was quicker and more frequent than ever before, and Havana sat at the center of the strengthening network of port cities, of trade and travel.[23] As the capital of an enormously important Spanish colony, the imperial port city was often described as the "finest in the West Indies, or, perhaps, the world." At mid-century, it was the second most important commercial hub in the New World behind New York. A deep, narrow channel on the north side of the island was overseen by the formidable Castle Moro before opening into "a magnificent bay, capable of accommodating 1000 ships."[24] Sugar and slaves, coffee and coolies, all passed through that narrow channel, coming and going, turning the harbor into a switching point for global trade between the New World,

Africa, and Europe and for hemispheric trade among settler societies and colonies. The island's safe berth, its location relative to beneficial trade winds and currents, and its role in the slave trade had long given it a reputation as "the *boulevard* of the New World," a phrase coined much earlier by the Abbé Raynal and repeated in the enthusiastic antebellum literature of the filibusters.[25] Trade with the United States, one popular reference claimed, had "increased threefold" in the decade prior to 1855, making the United States the largest economic partner with the island colony.[26] A warm climate and reputed health benefits lured many travelers from all over the world, while its brutal slavery and tragic indentured servitude made continued sugar cane and coffee production possible and drew, as if by hypnotism, the rapt attention of all visitors. Images of the Havana harbor, lush with tall ships, are a common staple of mid-century newspapers and travel literatures, and the Castle Moro may well have been one of the most written about New World locations in the nineteenth century. Cuba, a kind of dream world for the South, could even expel the hellish, otherwise absorbing memories of Jamaica and Haiti; "Hayti and Jamaica," William Henry Hurlbert remarked upon his arrival in Havana, "loomed large upon the horizon of my purpose when I wandered here, but they have gone like a vision of sails."[27]

Visitors often came to Havana through New Orleans, a sister city of sorts, which is located about six hundred nautical miles north and west of the Cuban city and which styled itself as a rival twin. A bustling sugar town near the mouth of the Mississippi, the multinational, "imperial" history of New Orleans was captured in Charles Pike's 1847 "Coast Directory," a survey map of the plantations along the river between New Orleans and Baton Rouge, some of them owned by the descendants of French settlers, some by St. Domingo exiles, some by Spanish families, and, scattered throughout but concentrated farthest upriver, some by planters from the continental United States.[28] New Orleans, as Walter Johnson describes it, was a brick-and-mortar manifestation of myriad "tiny connections" of the global economy, bringing together paddlewheel steamers so overloaded with cotton bales that it was hard to see the frame of the boat; great cane planters, creoles, and cotton kings; travelers from around the world; and vast numbers of enslaved Africans.[29] It was also, as resident Thomas K. Wharton noted with disgust, one of the "dirtiest" and "sickliest" cities in the Union, "a simple but most unpalatable truth" for a city where quarantine regulations often conflicted with the drive for profit from trade.[30] By the 1850s, New Orleans was the keystone city in the "great nation of futurity," a "grand emporium of all the vast tracts traversed by the Mississippi and the Missouri," as well as a rich trading port with notable national and international connections to New York, Boston, Havana, Vera Cruz, and Liverpool.[31] The city was a vision of what the South might become, but it was also a site of separation, a staging ground for efforts to distinguish between what was "American" and what was "creole"—a word with a complicated history in Louisiana, a marker of the Francophone past, of older European settlements, and, as the nineteenth century progressed, of a baroque, morally suspect Catholicism.[32] Indeed, in an age in which New Orleans was increasingly connected to the world on a greater scale than ever before, debates about the proper place of the *ancienne population* and the best future for New Orleans were, in some real sense, evidence of an internal debate about the city's status in the life of the Caribbean.

New Orleans and Havana were knotted together in a quickening connection, and travelers and *filibusteros* who sojourned to either port could simultaneously blur and clarify the difference between the South and the Americas. George Williams of Charleston, for instance, began his account of a trip to the "Queen of the Antilles" by noting his alienation: he wandered amidst the "luxuriant verdure" of the island as a "stranger in a strange land." Writing to his family, Williams described Cuban civilization as inferior to that of the slaveholding South; its technologies of agriculture were, as he saw them, closer to those used in ancient Egyptian slavery than to those one might find in and around Charleston. Only the island's natural abundance, he assumed, made it possible to produce a profit from sugar and coffee cultivation. The frequency of American travel and the preponderance of *Americanos* in supposedly backward Cuba encouraged in Williams a sense of national chauvinism, but it was a nationalism with limits. "We *Americanos*," Williams wrote proudly, "stick together like brothers."[33] At least, they did until the discussion turned to the slavery question and the chance of annexation, both of which were "wedge issues," splitting antebellum Southern travel accounts from those authored by enemies of "the slave power." The planter class, no stranger to *el miedo al negro*, feared that Spain (or, even worse, Britain) would emancipate the slaves of Cuba nearly as much as abolitionists feared the annexation of the island by Southern slaveholders. Southern portraits of Cuban slavery, not surprisingly, could thus be somewhat sympathetic.[34] Williams's letters, written in the 1850s, take a deeply appreciative tone when the subject turns to the life of slaves: "The negroes," he summed, "have many more privileges

E. H. Nelson's portrait of busy New Orleans, along the Mississippi, for *Frank Leslie's Illustrated Newspaper* in 1860. From the Prints and Photographs Division, Library of Congress.

than with us." And he reserved special venom for the coolie trade, long described as a "liberal" solution to the labor problems posed by emancipation. "I am surprised," Williams wrote, "to see so many Chinamen scattered throughout the Island. They are brought here by the cargo, in English and Yankee ships, and sold into ten years more slavery!" "Oh, for a Harriet Beecher Stowe, to write a Chee-Chow-Wang romance upon the cruelty to this deluded people," he continued with tongue firmly in cheek. "It is a horrid thing, according to modern philanthropy, to steal wild Africans, but a blessing to kidnap the educated Chinaman, and sell him into slavery. Consistency is a jewel."[35]

But when Williams turned to the question of annexation, his prose became heavy, pressing, and romantic, as if he were crudely ticking off the attributes of an attractive bride. The United States would soon, he hoped, "put this garden of Spain into our family group":

The planters are getting one hundred per cent more for sugar and molasses this year than last. Sugar-cane is king here. The tobacco crop is next in value. It is estimated that the productions of Cuba this year will be worth one hundred millions of dollars! The population is fifteen hundred thousand. The island is capable of supporting ten times that number of inhabitants. The annual exports amount to six hundred million pounds of sugar and eighty million coffee. The export of coffee is about ten millions, partly in the leaf, besides three hundred millions manufactured cigars. Railroads are being built in every direction; some six hundred miles are already completed. Steamboats also are constantly running on the northern and southern coasts.[36]

Here was a list of qualities that any Southern planter could appreciate: an island and potential state capable of matching or exceeding—dollar for dollar, pound for pound—the manufacturing hubs and immigrant way stations of New England. With an eye toward a public audience, it was a list compiled without any reference to slavery and without any mention of the island's tropic breezes and healthful winter climate.

The careful forensic accounting of Cuba's economy by Williams and other Southern travelers (and their Northern critics) was, in some ways, a residue of the filibustering age, itself a reflection of the nation's expansionist tendencies. For several generations, privateers along the frontier's edge had chafed at the power of the nation state and had, through gradual settlement or force of arms, stolen away territory that by treaty belonged to France, Spain, Mexico, Canada, or some other foreign government.[37] New land meant new opportunity and less chance that an enslaved population would reach dangerous concentrations. Texas, then, was "politically and economically sublime," and its acquisition was pursued and accomplished by Anglo *filibusteros* who were tired of waiting for manifest destiny to catch up with their desire for a land rich in slaveholding promise.[38] Success in Texas—measured by the official appropriation of territory and expansion of slavery—encouraged other efforts elsewhere throughout the Southwest and the Caribbean. But despite the mythic images of gamblers, drunks, and washouts popularized in movies and novels about the Alamo, the *filibusteros* and those who followed them in the 1850s were not mere bandits or pirates or simple homesteaders, but men with dreams of power. John Quitman, for one, was the governor of Mississippi when he tried to assist Narciso Lopez and Ambrosio Gonzales in their plans to conquer Cuba. "We claim the right of expansion," Quitman argued, "as essential to our future security and prosperity. . . . [We] require more elbow room, to guard against the possibility that a system of labor now so beneficent and productive might, from a redundant slave population confined to narrow limits, become an ultimate evil."[39] New land, Quitman and others believed, would keep the demographic ratio of the Deep South at an acceptable level and would forestall the chance of any slave rebellion. If these men were able to line their pockets along the way or were granted executive authority over a new Cuban republic, all the better. For men like Quitman, then, filibustering was high politics conducted through private, unofficial means.[40]

The history of the South had, at this point, no permanent limits. There was no reason, then, to doubt that Cuba might eventually become part of the Union. For three generations, the "peculiar institution" of slavery had become increasingly common across the Deep South and the Southwest. Transience, one historian writes, was "a normal part of existence in the Old South."[41] Local populations of wealthy slaveholders moved across and beyond the South—with slaves and capital in tow—at a rate equal to or greater than the migration patterns of poor immigrant workers in New England. Plantations changed hands regularly, as the rootless planter class moved west to Texas and the Southwest, where land was cheap and slavery could expand rapidly, mirroring the expansion of immigrants across the upper Midwest. Along the way, the planter class gathered in the great port cities of the Atlantic seaboard: in Charleston, Mobile, Savannah, and New Orleans. If most continued on to greener pastures in the Southwest, others took advantage of the short two-day journey from New Orleans to Havana. Some went there to survey a possible future state, assuming that Cuba would soon be annexed by force or by treaty. Some simply went on business, to manage an estate, to visit with friends, or to investigate the methods of sugar production. Either way, there were a great many slaveholders—or those who shared some interest with slavery—who ventured, as it were, farther southward. "We have had a charming trip to Cuba," Callie Elliot, the daughter of William Elliot, wrote to her sister. "It was only too *short,* the country is magnificent, the climate delightful, the people (the Cubans) the nicest in the whole world."[42] For Southerners like Callie, a trip to Cuba was, in some ways, a journey into a possible, a better, future, offering larger profits, better health, and greater numbers of enslaved Africans. "Should you meet any Cubans," Callie Elliot wrote to her brother, William, "do try & get all the information you can respecting the price of lands in Cuba. *I have a cough!*"[43]

Cuba was, then, the next Texas, but with greater short-term promise.[44] Literature produced in the South almost invariably surveyed it as both a contemporary competitor and a future acquisition, marrying a hard-edged economic appreciation with the usual proslavery romanticism. John S. Thrasher, a longtime advocate of annexation, suggested that Louisiana sugar production, lacking "the superior cheapness of labor" found in Cuba, competed at a great disadvantage and that the appropriation or purchase of the island would bring labor costs there in line with those of the South. Hoping to increase the sense of peril and speed up the debate, Thrasher also noted that Cuba was just then seeking "at all hazards" to bring larger numbers of Chinese coolies and to install a "system of African apprenticeship."[45] Cuba, another such report began, was a "valuable island," only "a few days sail from the Atlantic Ports of the U.S. and only two and a half days steaming from New Orleans." With the realization of telegraph communication across the continental United States, the island "will become," Thomas Wilson enthused, "a grand manufactory and depot of sugar, to which orders for sugar may be sent from the most distant parts of the U.S. and which by steam may be filled, in less time, than a little affair could have been accomplished between N. York and Philadelphia, in old times." Southern travelers could, at times, claim to have special "insider" knowledge of the island, a product of their lengthy history of economic and social relations with all levels of Cuban society. And they could be dismissive of those with abolitionist credentials who hailed from New England and dallied in Havana for only a day or two before painting grimmer portraits of the island's future. "Now any person with the least experience," Wilson continued, "knows that it is impossible to gain much knowledge during a few months spent . . . flying through a vast territory. I have seen many of these gentlemen in their travels, and it appears to me that their time is spent principally in pleading at the bar, and in discussing politics with some funny old quiz, who engaged them in conversation, or in discussing the merits of the os flesh of two countries."[46] Aside from the suggestion that short-term "Yankee" travelers were more interested in drink and sex than anything else—the word os is an anatomical reference to an aspect of the vagina—Wilson's account of the island assumes that Southern interest in Cuba was financial before it was anything else, even if the island's supposed desire for annexation by the South was very often styled as a matter of seduction and conquest by a comely suitor.

Visions of a Cuba that was "longing for annexation" were an expression of this Southern version of manifest destiny, but they could also be an expression of something else.[47] The "Southern dream of a Caribbean empire" would erupt into periodic attempts to wrest control of Cuba (among other locations) by physical force, as privateers from Louisiana, Mississippi, and Alabama would board a few ships in New Orleans or Mobile and, accompanied by expatriate Cuban allies, venture to gain surreptitious entrance to the island and eventually overthrow Spanish control.[48] But these "expeditions," as Rodrigo Lazo and others have noted, were, in some fashion, joint missions and not simple reflections of imperial energies. They included both Southerners and Cubans and often blurred the difference between the two groups. After departing New Orleans or Mobile, the voyage would often pause in the international waters of the Gulf of Mexico, a presumed safe place to hold elections and appoint officers. This was a sign, perhaps, that the friendships and partnerships forged in New Orleans and New York—the two sites of Cuban exile—produced a movement that was as much about conquering Cuba as it was about joining the island, as much about dominance as it was about a potential union of equals. For advocates of filibustering, Lazo concludes, "a disjunction emerged between the hemispheric ambitions of the U.S. government and what *filibustero* writers believed America as a hemisphere meant for liberation writers."[49] The same might be said for Anglophone planters or Southern advocates of filibustering. If, for instance, Ambrosio Gonzales and Narciso Lopez approached John Quitman for support in their efforts to free Cuba from Spain and Quitman acted on their behalf, were his actions an expression of Southern imperialism alone, or did they also include a measure of sympathy and solidarity? It was—and still is—often unclear in this political exchange where the interests of the South ended and where those of Cuba began, a marker of the locational conflation that could reign over the outer edges of the Caribbean and the Gulf of Mexico.

Not everyone, of course, agreed that the expansion of the South into the Caribbean would be advantageous for the United States. Even as others looked toward the Caribbean for new territory, some Southerners went to great lengths to distance themselves from the racial or cultural effects of expansion into the troublesome colonies and republics that lay southward. To support his argument that frequent racial mixture—an assumed fact in every slaveholding society in the Americas—was dangerous, Josiah Nott, a Mobile physician and advocate of polygenesis, arranged for the translation of the scientific theories of Comte de Gobineau, a French scientist who linked civilizational decline with miscegenation and racial essence. Pointedly contrasting the two sides of the island of Hispaniola, Nott's translation emphasized that the mulatto class of "Dominicans" were "modified" Europeans, their blood tainted by mixture with "the nature of the Africa" and their chance of intellectual advancement stymied by the presence of larger numbers of "negroes" who, though several generations removed from Africa, "are the same as in their native clime"—prone to "idleness" and, more disturbingly, "murder." Haitian history, in slight contrast, was only "a long series of massacres," and the egalitarian ideals of the late eighteenth century slept "undisturbingly and impotently upon the paper on which they are written." But as Nott's biographer notes, the Southerner cleverly "omitted Gobineau's suggestion that the United States had no great future and his conclusion that slaveholding presented a major problem." There would be no mention, in Nott's repackaging of Gobineau, of the grim *horizon de tombes* found throughout the Americas—the Frenchman's moral critique of slavery was displaced in favor of his focus on the relationship between "race," place, and the survival of New World political institutions. There would be, as well, no estimation of the effect of slavery on the "great nation of futurity."[50] The South, in the end, was half-tropical in some real sense and utterly dependent on slavery. It was also completely convinced of its own superiority. Instead of latitude and longitude, then, the master class used the purity of "race" to position itself in the hemisphere and to stake a unique claim to the future greatness of their nascent nation. But in doing so, and in devoting so much effort to the loud and angry repetition of this exact message, the master class also revealed just how liminal it feared the South had become. Absorbing Cuba or any other Caribbean place would not resolve this liminality, though it might accomplish certain short-term political goals.[51]

Northern critics, echoing these fears, often pointed out just how supposedly tropical the South had become. Portraits of the South that emphasized its Caribbean flavor were, implicitly or explicitly, drawing conclusions about its location in relationship to "the tropics," conclusions that could often emphasize the relationship between hot temperatures, immorality, violence, and sex, applying a North American version of *leyanda negra*, or "black legend," to the slaveholding states. To label the South racially impure or emotionally volatile was to highlight its histories of slave punishment, rape, and race mixing; to focus on the moral consequences of those histories; to make the South seem "Latin"; and to suggest, as generations of ethnologists and climatologists would do, that civilization could hardly survive let alone prosper beneath a certain latitude. Even the more sympathetic depictions of the South would go to great lengths to note just how "civilized" the place was before the inevitable disclaimer that, given the humidity, the heat, and the need for cheap labor, the edifice of Southern civilization would necessarily be built on an unstable racial "mudsill." Southern efforts to shore up the color line, to legislate racial purity, and to trumpet the purity of white Southern womanhood were, then, framed against the assumption of mixture elsewhere in the Americas and were based on a denial of the sameness of the South in this regard. Antebellum Southern views of the Cuban future sometimes featured a rejection, after annexation and reform, of Catholicism, miscegenation, and the draconian punishment of slaves, which would redeem the new territory for the South in the eyes of the republic or the world. One also finds a level of desperation present beneath the surface, as if the future of slavery itself was utterly dependent on the prewar South absorbing other slaveholding societies—no matter how foreign or different—in order to preserve slavery in the hemisphere.

Much of New England was opposed to the expansion of the South on antislavery grounds. Richard Henry Dana, one of the most popular travel writers of the day, offered his own assessment of slavery in Cuba, a presumption, it seems, of every single Northern person who visited the island as a self-styled "traveler" during the era of the *filibusteros*. "Shall the industry of Cuba go on," he asked, or "shall the island be abandoned to a state of nature?" If the answer were the former, he concluded, then "the blacks must do the hard work or it will not be done." Perhaps, he mused, there was a free labor alternative, but he had not seen one that would work in Cuba, where the labor was long and hard and would not keep a wage worker contented. He was hardly convinced, either, that coolies were the solution. "Their presence in Cuba," he noted, "adds another distressing element to the difficulties of the labour question, which hangs, like a black cloud, over all the islands of the West Indies."[52] (Dana's "vacation voyage" did not include a trip to the slaveholding region of the United States—where the same ominous rumbles emanated from that same "black cloud"—but he was very much concerned about the South's fate.) *To Cuba and Back* represented a distinctly unique genre of literature and was at once a form of social critique, national puffery, and amateur ethnology. "We had been talking high patriotism,"

Dana recalled, remembering the return voyage to New York from Cuba, with all of the comparisons between the U.S. and Cuba "favourable to our country."[53] Dana, Rodrigo Lazo reminds us, was an opponent of slavery who "simultaneously held racist views about Cuban blacks, Spaniards, and Cuban creoles" and who "looped" Cuba "into a southern region of slavery with the U.S. South so that an opposition emerges between New England on the one hand and Cuba and the U.S. South on the other."[54] From this vantage point, it was quite clear that Cuba should never become a state in the republic: "you cannot reason," Dana had sniffed dismissively, "from Massachusetts to Cuba."[55]

But could you, in 1859, still "reason" from Massachusetts to Mobile? From New England to the Deep South? Much of the lower South, it seemed, had already slipped into the Caribbean abyss. New Orleans, in particular, was often explicitly set in a racially troublesome hemispheric context. Hispanophone sojourners often found New Orleans to be far more familiar than New York.[56] Anglophone travelers noted a similar, somewhat sultry or Catholic tone. Sweeping through the city on his way to the Caribbean, New Englander J. Milton Mackie noted that the city was "sufficiently *bizarre*" and "full of incongruities and irreconcilable contrasts." "Here," he remarked, "are half a dozen different races, and half a dozen different colors of the skin." Mackie was struck by the proliferation of language—the "various foreign accents of every quarter"—and by the extraordinary cosmopolitanism of a port city filled with Americans and Creoles, Germans and Jews, Spaniards and Chinese. Above all else, Mackie was curious to find so much ambiguity, so little certainty about whether he was in the tropics or in the United States. Of "the Creole ladies," he wrote that they were "lovely creatures . . . French in dress, manners, and ideas, and pleasantly transitional between the women of the tropics and those of the States." Describing a typical dinner party, he pointed to "the gentleman sitting opposite, with such an imposing confidence, with hair artistically combed back, with so grand an air, so much deference to the lady sitting by his side. Is he a cotton lord, or a sugar lord, or some foreign potentate on his travels?" New Orleans, for Mackie, was a city of "most marked contrasts" and ambiguous identities in a region that was itself already a cultural and economic link to the Caribbean, with its histories of mixture and slavery and emancipation.[57] If "the Creole ladies" were "pleasantly transitional," as Mackie described them, so, too, was New Orleans and, by extension, the Old South, captured here as a liminal geographic region and confusing racial jumble.

"Havana," Anthony Trollope wrote cleverly, "will soon become as much American as New Orleans," a statement that says much about both places.[58] Another traveler could not help but note that New Orleans shared with Martinique the dubious distinction of preserving, in a "driftwood destination," the fading, chivalric qualities of the ancien régime.[59] For others, New Orleans quite simply looked like many other port towns and cities in the Caribbean. James Phillippo, for one, noted that the "general air and *tout ensemble*" of the Crescent City brought forth "a confused remembrance of some of the best Spanish and French West India towns." Phillippo could not help, moreover, but focus on "the varied character of the inhabitants," from the "Southern Planter" to the "unpolished Irishman" to "Chinamen," but most especially including the local slave population, "exhibiting almost every variety of shade of colour, from the jet black through all conceivable transitions to white almost as pure as that of Europeans." This topsy-turvy, mixed-up society was most obviously marked by endless "peculiarities": "No city in the world," he concluded, "presents greater contrasts of national manners and languages."[60] The "Creole population," wrote Briton Amelia Murray, having just arrived in New Orleans from Havana, was "an influential ingredient, and give[s] the tone to manners and customs; so that New Orleans has more of a Southern air than even Charleston or Savannah."[61] "In the southern portion of North America nature is a great poet," Fredrika Bremmer summed up, "in the northern a great human being."[62] The poetic, pensive South might not be sunny Cuba, with its *dolce far niente,* but neither was it cold New England, with its obsessive rationality and industrial fetishes.

As critics noted the enhanced tropical feel of the South, they also worried about the consequences of such a climate. John Abbot's antislavery work, *South and North,* found him in Havana for just six hours, long enough, apparently, for him to confirm his worst suspicions. Abbott's first ride in a *volante* was thrilling, but his attempt to pay "the negro drivers" a "proper fare" turned into a comedic farce requiring the intervention of a third party. Cuban slaves, Abbot concluded, had sunk "to the very lowest state of human debasement"; Chinese coolies were doomed to a life worse than slavery and were generally suicidal, a fact that would, he confessed, "haunt my mind . . . till I die." While enjoying a long lunch, he grew more and more fearful of Havana's annexation, of the chance that the slave power would grow and that "we should probably see a stampede of slaveholders, with their slaves, to

Cuba, as the world has never seen before." Disaster would result. "The sugar plantations," he augured,

> without exceptions would be abandoned. Carolinians and Georgians would forsake their worn-out fields, where "fanatics" annoy them, for this new, more inviting, and safer realm for the institution. Slaves would be in greater demand than ever before. The slave-breeders on the border states would sell off their stock with a rapidity hitherto unparalleled, impelled by the double motive of increased price, and increased danger of escape by the "underground railroad." . . . None would go to Cuba but determined slaveholders. The continental states would be greatly drained. There would be an immense accumulation on the island; and then, alas! Might come the catastrophe—the reënactment of the tragedy of St. Domingo!

By midafternoon, the *De Soto* had pulled away from Havana, with Abbott aboard. "The dim outline of the Island is still visible," Abbott wrote, "and will soon be lost in the approaching darkness." Still, the memory of what he had seen in Cuba—and what it meant for the South—would linger, forcing Abbott, as he later gazed at the mouth of the Mississippi, to wonder how long it would take the river to deposit enough sediment for a land bridge to Cuba. "I hope," he shuddered, "that the awful tragedy of time and sin will be brought to a close long before those ages should have rolled away."[63]

If the very idea of "the South" was, at mid-century, trussed in one fashion or another to the Caribbean, the region itself was also increasingly engaged in a war of words with the North, a great and angry debate that drew the hemisphere's most powerful slaveholding interest group into a closer, rougher embrace with its unhappy partner. Few in 1850 might have been able to predict that slavery would soon be gone from the United States or that the planter class of the South would in a few years be prostrate before the North. After all, only a small handful of presidents had failed to support slavery; and the Supreme Court, under Chief Justice Roger B. Taney, had long worked to strengthen the constitutional right to own slaves, a shameful result of the classification of human beings as "private property." The prevailing hope was that within some small measure of time Cuba would become a Southern slaveholding state, followed, perhaps, by Mexico. And within a global context, the planter class of the Old South was far wealthier and more powerful than its siblings in the West Indies (who at least had been able to dictate the terms of emancipation), far more politically powerful, and far more likely to shape the future in its own best interests. Despite these reassuring certainties, some in the planter class nevertheless recognized, as historian Steven Hahn writes, that they had been "drawn into the swirl of a revolutionary age."[64] Haiti sat just off the easternmost end of Cuba and was a symbol of the most dangerous kind of revolution. The abolition of slavery in the British West Indies—"one of the sublimest moments in history"—was, too, a bell that could not be unrung. "The slave of today," *De Bow's Review* noted, "the slave of antiquity, the slave born amid the burning sands of Africa, the slave upon some distant tropical isle of the Indian ocean, and his fellow slave some fifteen thousand miles away in the West Indian archipelago, all felt alike the magic shock communicated by that royal decree."[65] If the slaves of the South should remember that shock and, taking note of the determination of the North to stifle the growth of slavery and remembering Toussaint L'Ouverture's liberation of Haiti, rise up against their masters, all would be lost.

Southerners thus viewed the American Mediterranean with a mixture of fear and excitement. The problem, as concerned planters saw it, was that the institution of slavery was, in the 1850s, in mortal peril, threatened across the hemisphere by a cascading set of emancipations, slave rebellions, and humanitarian movements that labeled "the Slave Power" as both sinful and dangerous. By mid-century, the abolition of slavery in the British West Indies appeared to have been a disaster (though the truth of it was far more complicated). Cuba, the source of so much Southern enthusiasm, had staved off a number of slave rebellions—or illusions of such—through military violence and the strictest planter authority and through supplemental labor from China, providing a vision of the future that seemed uncomfortably alien to most Southerners. The deepest, most frightening nightmare for the Southern planter class was the prospect of another "St. Domingo," or Haitian revolution, another cathartic upheaval pitting the angry black masses against their former white overlords. "A sleeping wake or waking sleep," as black provocateur Martin Delany put it, "a living death or tormented life is that of the Cuban and American slaveholder. For them there is no safety." Slaveholders, he continued, were like a "criminal in the midst of a powder bin with a red hot spigot of iron in his hand, which he is compelled to hold and char the living flesh to save his life, or let it fall to relieve him from torture." In either scenario, the impending freedom of the slave was impossible to forestall. "Of these two unhappy communities," Delany concluded, "the master and the slave, the blacks have everything to hope for and nothing to fear. . . . Their redemption from bondage is inevitable. They must and will be free; whilst the whites have everything to fear and nothing to hope for, 'God is just, and his justice will not sleep forever.'"[66]

The decades prior to the Civil War were ones of extraordinary crisis and anxiety. The growing animus of the planter class and its political allies toward *les amis des noirs* was exacerbated, not soothed, by the acquisition of new territory from France through the Louisiana Purchase. The subsequent debate between "the North" and "the South" over how much of that land should be devoid of slavery, a debate that culminated in the Missouri Compromise of 1820 and that established a northernmost latitudinal limit on chattel bondage, increased the friction between proslavery and antislavery positions. The resulting state of perpetual emergency in the South assumed that the dangers of slave rebellion were omnipresent. The publication of Garrison's *Liberator* in 1831 and Nat Turner's Virginia rebellion in the same year were, then, watershed moments in Southern history. "Reason," Thomas Roderick Dew remembered, "was almost banished from the mind, and the imagination was suffered to conjure up the most appalling phantoms, and picture to itself a crisis in the vista of futurity, when the overwhelming numbers of blacks would rise superior to all restraint."[67] The argument that slavery was a "positive good"—as South Carolinian John C. Calhoun put it—was even more finely sharpened, as well, by the ensuing debate in the Virginia legislature over gradual emancipation, by the "gag rule" debate over antislavery petitions in the House of Representatives, by the Nullification Crisis and the establishment of the bedrock principles of Southern nationalism, and by the increasingly radical efforts of abolitionist groups to ferret their literature into the Deep South and, it was hoped and feared, into the hands of slaves. Efforts to expand the territory of the slaveholding South through annexation or filibustering were, with all this in mind, responses to the pervasive fear of enclosure (any limit on slavery was unacceptable), the fear of slave rebellion (new territory would scatter growing slave populations), and the fear of prostration before the North (new territories would become new states, with new senators and new representatives). These fears channeled Southern intellectual interests into one of the deepest, most conservative streams of Western intellectual history: the defense of racial superiority and the permanent enslavement of supposedly inferior peoples.

For the mid-century defense of slavery, Southern intellectuals turned to a number of sources, including the Bible, emerging "racial" science, and classical history. The South had not long served as a font of great regional literature nor was it seen as a center of scientific investigation, so the growing list of essays, compilations, and pamphlets that justified racial bondage is doubly notable; "We must wonder," one historian writes, "at the enthusiasm with which southerners explored the scientific defenses of slavery in an age when the section's other principal interest in science was in discovering how best to apply manure."[68] The eminently practical South—though it had just "discovered" the importance of science to its efforts to preserve staple production and slavery—had also long been committed to the study of historical context, and history writing was a feature of its arguments in defense of an emerging police state. Thomas Roderick Dew's aforementioned lament for the consequence of Turner's rebellion at Southampton was preceded by a summary of the events at St. Domingue, where "the bloodiest and most shocking insurrection ever recorded in the annals of history" had "stript" France of "the fairest and most valuable of all her colonial possessions."[69] The regular reflection on the meaning of Caribbean history hinted at a deep, thoughtful concern by planters and proslavery apologists for the long-term economic consequences of emancipation elsewhere and at an awareness of the parallel circumstances that were affecting other slaveholding societies. Portraits of lawlessness and bloodthirstiness outside of the South were also a justification in themselves for a tightening or quickening of the siege mentality of the South. Indeed, many of the most hard-edged elements of mid-century Southern slaveholding—the increasing use of fear instead of "kindness" to control slaves, the use of brinksmanship and saber rattling in diplomacy with the North, the concern about locating a "safety valve" in the West or the Caribbean to reduce the largest concentrations of slaves, the high-wire opposition to all forms of abolitionism—were drawn from the experiences of slaveholders throughout the Americas. One sometimes gets the perverse impression from the regular use of this dystopian material that much of the New World was a sort of topsy-turvy slaughterhouse, where slaves butchered slaveholders, and that, by the 1850s, only the South, Cuba, and Brazil were still breathing.

Jamaica and Haiti were the Scylla and Charybdis of this darker American Mediterranean, the latter freed by force and racial bloodshed, the former freed by soft-hearted liberal reform. In both cases, internationally oriented cash-crop agriculture—the life's blood of the planter class—failed completely after slavery. This simple "fact," as it was understood then, was very important to those who were concerned about the future of other slaveholding societies. When we frame the literature on Cuba and the South from this perspective, centering the hemispheric qualities linking both, we call attention to the roiling, uncertain backdrop of the period, which featured the past precedents of Haiti and Jamaica. Cuba, Richard Henry Dana suggested, might be the key to the Gulf of Mexico, but it was just as likely to be the key to Pandora's box. "Close upon her," he wrote, "is the great island of Jamaica, where the experiment of free negro labour in the same products is on trial; near to her is Haiti, where the experiment of negro self-government is on trial; and further off . . . yet near enough to furnish some cause for uneasiness, are the slave states of the Great Republic."[70] "The two islands of St. Domingo and Jamaica," wrote Benjamin Hunt, an "expert" on the West Indies, offered "to the choice of the present slaveholder a sample of the different fruits, one or the other of which will probably compose the final harvest of all slavery which is not timely uprooted." "In St. Domingo," he concluded, "the French have been destroyed by the blacks; in Jamaica, the English are being peacefully absorbed by them."[71] Haiti and Jamaica were, by and large, object lessons in failure, the stuff of nightmares, not dreams; they were not so much travel destinations as they were bleak stopping points, future-tense reminders of what might come next for slavery, the planter class, and the much ballyhooed "civilization" of the Old South.

Proslavery advocates would routinely list the contrary "examples" of Haiti and Jamaica as proof that chattel bondage should continue, lest the world's demand for sugar, cotton, rice, and other staples be unmet. "The world furnishes no instances of these products being grown upon a large scale by free labor," J. D. B. De Bow noted: "The English now acknowledge their failure in the East Indies. Brazil, whose slave population nearly equals our own, is the only South American State which has prospered. Cuba, by her slave labor, showers wealth upon old Spain, whilst the British West India colonies have now ceased to be a source of revenue, and from opulence have been, by emancipation, reduced to beggary. St. Domingo shared the same fate, and the poor whites have been massacred equally with the rich."[72] "Remove the restraining and controlling power of the master," the distinguished Southern jurist Thomas R. R. Cobb argued, "and the negro becomes, at once, the slave of his lust, and the victim of his indolence, relapsing, with wonderful rapidity, into his pristine barbarism." "Haiti and Jamaica," Cobb added, "are living witness to this truth."[73] When George Fitzhugh, an iconoclastic and influential proslavery writer, penned his most famous condemnation of the unnaturalness of "freedom," titled *Sociology for the South,* he set the words of Ecclesiastes on the title page: "THE THING THAT HAS BEEN, IT IS THAT WHICH SHALL BE; AND THAT WHICH IS DONE IS THAT WHICH SHALL BE DONE."[74] Here, ripped from the Old Testament, was a warning that what had come to pass in the rest of the American Mediterranean would come to pass in the South if the age of slavery should come to a close and the age of emancipation should dawn on the Old South. There was, Fitzhugh noted, "no remedy" for the postemancipation societies of the West Indies; there would, therefore, be no saving the South if it, too, should be forced to give up its slaves. In this context, the planter class sought stability and safety in expansion and control and in the study of what had happened elsewhere under supposedly similar circumstances.[75]

Of these two reference points, Jamaica, where emancipation and labor flight had reportedly brought Britain's largest sugar-producing colony to its knees, was slightly less sensational. Most of the well-educated traveling class would have known something of the so-called Great Experiment of 1834: legislated emancipation, which was followed by the temporary cruelties of apprenticeship, among them the whip, the treadmill, and the penal system. A generation later, the fate of the island was still unclear, its productive potential offset by the frustrating refusal of former slaves to work for their former masters or on gruesomely familiar plantations. Abolitionists universally proclaimed the success of individual former slaves on the island, showing far less concern for the exploitive sugar industry. But all in all, the island was still very much an experiment. "Will the growth of sugar pay in Jamaica or will it not?" wondered the traveloguer Anthony Trollope. Not if the white man made it, he concluded, nor even if the brown man did, so long as slavery existed somewhere else. But "the 'peculiar institution,'" he noted, "will not live for ever. The time must come when abolition will be popular even in Louisiana. And when it is law there, it will be the law in Cuba also. If that day shall have arrived before the last sugar-mill in the island shall have stopped, Jamaica may then compete with other free countries. The world will not do without sugar, let it be produced by slaves or free men."[76] For any visitor to the American Mediterranean, the lure and loathing of this prophetic place, this once-rich and now-poor laboratory for African free labor, was impossible to ignore. "The downward tendencies of the island," wrote John Bigelow, after returning to Jamaica for the first time in sixteen years, "cannot be more rapid than they are at present." If, however, "Jamaica was an American State, she would speedily be more productive and valuable than any agricultural portion of the United States of the same dimension."[77] American initiative—the soft compulsion of consumer goods and the energies of what would today be called "development"—could ensure, he believed, extraordinary progress.

Haiti, in contrast, inspired almost universal fear, loathing, and rage. Three generations earlier, Haitian slaves had infamously taken the expressed universalism of the French revolution at face value and then engaged in what was remembered—rightly or wrongly—as wholesale racial slaughter. For much of the 1850s, the tiny, diplomatically unrecognized republic on the eastern end of Hispaniola was governed by Faustin Soulouque, a former slave freed as a young man by the decree of Léger-Félicité Sonthonax in 1793 and a soldier in the revolutionary army, who was proclaimed emperor in 1849. "King Soulouque is a black man," Trollope wrote pointedly, conflating skin tone and civilization: "One blacker never endured the meridian heat of a tropical sun."[78] In the decade that followed his ascension as emperor, or "king," Soulouque gained an international reputation for barbarism, for the murder of presumably more civilized "mulattos," and for deep-rooted corruption. Haiti had long been a reminder for all Southerners that the "labor question" could not be resolved easily where slaves were in the majority, but near universal disdain for Soulouque meant that even liberal-minded, presumably sympathetic persons lamented the state of the republic.[79]

The new world's only free black republic served, in short, as a fascinating visual backdrop for contemporary debates about the future of slavery in the Americas. "We ran down the North coast," Nicholas Trist's wife wrote on her way to Cuba, "within 15 miles of the island all the way. As my ill luck would have it, the weather was very hazy: so as to see the mountains plainly, but only just enough to make me wish for clear weather, when the sight of them would have been a great treat. The mountains rising *up out of the sea,* higher than our blue ridge. What a combination of climate and scenery, land & water! And to think that such a Paradise should be in the hands of such animals!"[80] Tropical health specialist Nathaniel Willis noted the "mountain tops of Hayti visible off the starboard bow—their bases and the main stretch of the isle of Negro-cratic dominion hidden by the cloud-mist of morning." Arriving at Jacmel, Willis suggestively noted that they were greeted by "a negro clad in a suit of black—the suit he was born in—standing erect, shiny and unconscious, on the end of the pier."[81] At its best, Haiti could serve as a possible repository for emancipated Africans from the United States, expatriated or "colonized" on the island; at its worst, Haiti was a racial nightmare, embodying fears of rape and rebellion, signaling the seriousness of all debate about slavery.[82] Such was the portrait of dark "Hayti," at least until 1859, when the coup d'état led by General Fabre Nicolas Geffrard—described, in at least one newspaper, as a white man—returned some measure of "stability" and "progress" to the island, leading abolitionists and liberal New Englanders (and even some Southerners) to propose Geffrard's republic as a new home for freed Southern slaves.[83]

The revolt in Haiti was a peculiarly significant memory—or social construct—for antebellum Southern slaveholders.[84] In the late summer of 1791, inspired by the egalitarian rhetoric of the French Revolution and the brutality of slave labor in sugar cultivation, slaves on the French, western side of the island of Hispaniola had taken up arms against the master class. Some hoped for the seizure of their rights as full citizens, while others simply wished for a chance to be free of the lash. Sonthonax, sent to manage the revolt, first cultivated an alliance with the free mulatto population and then, somewhat to the surprise of his new allies, emancipated the colony's African slaves by decree. Toussaint L'Ouverture, an aging ex-slave, emerged as the Cincinnatus, or George Washington, of the revolution, turning away from his retirement to become the leader of the ragtag revolutionary army and a skilled statesman, parlaying the competing desires of England, France, and Spain into some measure of independence for the island's majority population, before he was captured by trickery and brought to France, where he died. The final stages of the revolution—right up to its end in 1804—produced little beyond death and sadism, as French soldiers, dying rapidly from yellow fever, struggled to kill the largest number of Haitians as quickly as possible. Contemporary and historical accounts of the revolution—including some written in the twentieth century— regularly emphasized the barbaric violence of the former slaves against their former masters and framed the uncivil revolution as a preface to the island's desultory postemancipation financial state. In proslavery thought, then, the idealism of the abolitionist movement in the 1850s was understood to be historically parallel to that brief moment in the early days of the French revolution, when Brissot, Condorcet, the Abbé Grégoire, and "all that brilliant band" lobbied for the end of slavery in the West Indies and freed Africans were subsequently incorporated as citizens in the republic.[85] Every subsequent mistake flowed from that first error in judgment. New England abolitionism, much like the antislavery fulminations of *le société des amis des noir,* was, at best, thought to be based on a serious misjudgment of the capacity of Africans for civilization and self-government and, at worst, at cross-purposes with the will of God.

Such parallels were hard to ignore, especially when the most determined forces of radical abolitionism were, at least as some saw it, quite literally and openly searching for an American Toussaint and hoping to encourage the same sort of bloodshed on Southern soil. In late 1859, broadsword-wielding Kansan John Brown hoped that his occupation of the federal armory at Harper's Ferry would be the beginning of a massive revolt against slavery, something rather like the rebellion at St. Domingue. In the wake of Brown's execution, some measure of financial support came to his widow from Haiti, a reflection of the larger pan-American meaning of his "meteor-like" life, "flashing through the darkness."[86] In a public letter, Brown's surviving son expressed his gratitude to "all the good Haytians" who grieved at the loss of "Capt. John Brown, and his companions in arms." He went on, moreover, to invoke the patronage of the saint of the St. Domingue revolt and to hope, as well, for that man's strength of spirit to awaken the South. "It is only the body of Toussaint L'Ouverture which sleeps in the tomb," he concluded, "his soul visits the cabins of the slaves of the South when night is spread over the face of nature. The ears of our American slaves hear his voice in the wind-gusts which sweep over the prairies of Texas, of Arkansas and Missouri; his voice finds an echo in the immense valleys of Florida, among the pines of the Carolinas, in the Dismal Swamp, and on the mountain-tops, proclaiming that the despots of America shall yet know the strength of the toiler's arm, and that he who would be free must strike the first blow."[87] For the planter class, there could be no stronger proof of the dangerous mix of abolitionist idealism and the treachery of slaves than the idea, offered repeatedly by Wendell Phillips and others after Harper's Ferry, that John Brown's raid marked a veritable second coming of Toussaint L'Ouverture, with the worst, as the South saw it, yet to come.[88]

If the symbolic reverberations of Brown's raid and his subsequent execution were far in excess of the real chance of widespread revolt, it was, in large part, because enslaved and free Africans in the United States and slaves in the South were already dangerously attuned to the legacy of Toussaint. Indeed, a wide array of pamphleteers, rebels, novelists, and former slaves—among them David Walker, Denmark Vesey, William Wells Brown, Henry Highland Garnet, and Gabriel Prosser—had already found strength and authority in the violent success of the Haitian revolution. In noting the "divisions and consequent sufferings of *Carthage* and of *Hayti*" in his famously provocative *Appeal to the Coloured Citizens of the World*, first published in 1829, and the "butchering" of blacks by whites, David Walker, for instance, invoked Toussaint as a vengeful Old Testament messiah for enslaved African peoples: "The person whom God shall give you," Walker advised, "give him your support and let him go his length, and behold in him the salvation of your God."[89] A "war against the tyrants," William Wells Brown concluded, joining the revolution of slaves to the ideals of the American Revolution, would be sparked by the "indignation of the slaves of the south," and would "kindle a fire so hot that it would melt their chains, drop by drop, until not a single link remained; and the revolution that commenced in 1776 would then be finished."[90] "To black Americans," historian Alfred Hunt notes, "long starved for real heroes, Toussaint . . . showed them that freedom could be won and how it could be done," an object lesson of extraordinary value in the antebellum age, when it often seemed as if the slave power would last forever. Across the color line and throughout the American Mediterranean, Hunt continues, "Toussaint was the most powerful black symbol of his time."[91] Some proslavery apologists and Southern planters might well have been eager to laud Toussaint for his imposition of martial law during the revolution, and for his farsighted—as they saw it—concern for sugar and coffee production on the western side of Hispaniola, but none would have wished for a Southern version of the man to appear in the Carolina low country or along the Mississippi River.[92] It was all too easy, they charged, for opponents of slavery to describe these actions, as Frederick Douglass did, in terms of racial uplift and postemancipation "development" or to affirm that the labor and land reforms enacted in the wake of the bloodshed had been nobly aimed at "the improvement of the negro race."[93]

As common touchstones in antislavery protest and as objects of fear and desire, Haiti could sometimes become dangerously confused with Cuba. In 1859, the *Anglo-African Magazine* published the opening chapters of a new novel, titled *Blake, or the Huts of America*, by Martin Delany, a renowned antislavery activist of radical temper. *Blake* was a response, in some sense, to Harriet Beecher Stowe's exquisitely sentimental *Uncle Tom's Cabin*, which featured light-skinned protagonists, much melodrama, and great tragedy. In contrast to Stowe, Delany featured a global cast of characters, including a dark-skinned revolutionary named "Blake," and diverse and representative figures for all aspects of the slavery question. Tellingly, *Blake* begins in a Southern port city, Baltimore, where the Natchez planter Colonel Stephen Franks has come to negotiate with his partners, including Captain Juan Garcia, who is from Cuba. They are, as Delany describes it, "little concerned about the affairs of the general government" and "entirely absorbed in an adventure of self-interest."[94] They have gathered together to discuss their plans to transform a merchant ship into a slaver and to debate the relative merits of Baltimore and Havana as the site of this transformation. By the time the sprawling novel is complete, the travels of "Blake" across the South, throughout the Caribbean, and everywhere in the Atlantic world have enabled him to formulate an internationalist or "Pan-African" response to such men and to the slave power. Among slaves, he has a unique or "uncommonly broad view of the problem of slavery in the Americas," which enables him to sow the seeds of rebellion and exile and to claim a civilized black manhood. Blake shares the planter's sense of slavery, recognizing it as cosmopolitan and global, primarily self-interested, and prospering, at times, outside of the authority of the nation-state. Beginning the novel with that meeting of slaveholders and their partners, Delany suggested, in contrast to Stowe, that slavery was not contained, that it was borderless and cosmopolitan.[95] The novel played on the dreams and nightmares of the Old South. "Few people in the world," Delany editorialized at one point, "lead such a life as the white inhabitants of Cuba, and those of the South . . . [a] dreamy existence of the most fearful apprehensions, or dread, horror and dismay; suspicion and distrust, jealousy and envy continually pervade the community; and Havana, New Orleans, Charleston or Richmond may be thrown into consternation by an idle expression of the most trifling or ordinary ignorant black."[96]

None of this was lost on the planter class, which repeatedly moved—over the long history of the half century before the Civil War—to stave off the prospect of "another St. Domingue." Fear of mulatto refugees from the former slaveholding colony led Charleston officials in 1803 to arrest one man for distributing a Haitian "Declaration of Independence," the first step in the South's erection of "an intellectual blockade against dangerous doctrines." Concern that Denmark Vesey's 1822 planned (or imagined) insurrection, supposedly scheduled for Bastille Day, had sought support from Haiti prompted the South Carolina legislature to impose new restrictions on the movement of free black sailors, who were presumed to be agents of the revolutionary contagion, and to have them jailed while in port. Haiti was a vital cornerstone of colonization efforts—the relocation of freed slaves to Africa or the Caribbean—that aimed, at the very least, to reduce the largest and most densely concentrated populations of black bodies and, even more ideally, at the detropicalizing of the South and the establishment of white settlement. Southern politicians, planters, and proslavery intellectuals, some of them schooled by white planters now exiled from St. Domingue, labored to produce a consensus on all matters relating to emancipation and to thus minimize what was seen as an omnipresent threat either through the removal of freed slaves and free blacks or through the complete foreclosure of the very idea of emancipation. Nearly every single proslavery effort aimed at proving that African peoples in the New World were incapable of self-government, of slow tutelage toward some measure of civilization, or even of the most basic kinds of trust used Haiti as a touchstone.[97] Long before the civil rights movement, with its disgust for the role of "outside agitators" and "federal men," the slaveholders of the Deep South styled themselves as latter-day versions of the French West Indian planter class, as "southern colonies" pinned between the sharp-elbowed empire of the North and the resentful, untrustworthy slave population.[98]

Revolution and War

A good many of the *grand blancs* of St. Domingue had escaped north to the American South, either directly from the Caribbean or through Cuba. Having been displaced by the revolution on Hispaniola, they sought refuge and a return to their previous status in Charleston, New Orleans, or Baltimore. They wielded tremendous influence in the early 1800s, especially in the lower South and even more particularly in such port cities as New Orleans and Charleston. James Achille de Caradeuc, to name just one, was a successful South Carolina planter who, like Faulkner's Thomas Sutpen, hoped to use knowledge gleaned from the Caribbean to better his chances in cash-crop agriculture in the Deep South. James's family had settled in South Carolina some fifty years earlier, after the great rebellion in Haiti had sent streams of "exiles" or "refugees" to Charleston and New Orleans. James's grandfather, Jean Baptiste, had left St. Domingue in the wake of all of this, in 1792, in a small boat, carrying only his family, about "six or seven" slaves, and a "cargo of sugar." Jean Baptiste was no minor player in the Haitian Revolution, and the removal of his family to Charleston was not an insignificant event; he was, indeed, the "Marquis de Caradeu," a wealthy sugar planter whose brother, Laurent, owned La Caye, a large sugar plantation. Jean Baptiste was also the general commandant of the French military in St. Domingue, a man for whom "hanging would settle everything" and who—as C. L. R. James once put it—"earned the admiration of his fellow slaveowners for his vigour and ingenuity as a hanging propagandist." To demonstrate his talents in this regard, Jean Baptiste publicized one mass execution by having the heads of revolutionists "fixed on pikes along the hedges of his plantation, palm tree style."[99] Leaving Haiti for the American South, Jean Baptiste's exile was proof that the violence on that island could not be contained, that there could be no lasting peace among whites, mulattos, and blacks, only race war and barbarism.

The Caradeuc family settled near Aiken, South Carolina, where their various plantations became homes away from home for Charleston's St. Domingue refugee community. "All poor French from St. Domingue," James remembered later in life, "or poor refugees from the French revolution too poor to return were welcome at the Cedar Hill home," a largesse that was greatly facilitated by the presence there of "about 18–20 St. Domingue negroes, old and young."[100] These regular gatherings were occasions of haunting recollection, where the once rich held onto battered silver and china, surrounded by something rather like Thomas Sutpen's "crew of imported slaves," clutching to the receding memories of privilege and abundant wealth.[101] James's grandfather, the Marquis, died in 1810, and his father passed away in 1820, and so young James was sent off to France for his education, where he, his brother, and his mother orbited in the same, smallish West Indian exile community that imagined itself, as the Normans had once done, to be more French than the French themselves. James returned in 1839 to the family plantation in Aiken with a greater fortune, his family coffers now fuller from indemnities paid by France to the planter class of St. Domingue, reparations for slavery that were now funded by Haiti as a price for its international recognition. The arrival of "the French money," as it was called, was cause for family celebration, as James and his mother distributed some small amount to each family member each month, a regular reminder of what had once belonged to the family. James continued to be, in all ways, a transnational soul. He married a daughter of the exile community who had been schooled at Madame

Talvande's Academy in Charleston, owned and operated by one of the city's most famous refugees from the French West Indies. He also renamed his family plantation Montmorenci, after a hereditary estate in the Old World. In all things, he divided his loyalties equally between the Old South and monarchical France, even seeking out the simplest of French goods—for instance, garden shears and scissors—for home use, preferring them to anything made in the United States.[102] At Montmorenci, he experimented with viticulture, importing "French vignerous," hoping to produce a fine French wine in the slaveholding South, an experiment that would have foundered were it not for those indemnities from France. "With all the facilities we possess at the South," he wrote to the small community of grape growers in the Deep South, "with our soil, climate, and more particularly our slaves, nothing can prevent ours from becoming the greatest wine country that every was."[103]

For these descendants of the *grand blancs,* civil war meant a return to the nightmare of black rebellion. When Aiken was captured and garrisoned by "Negro troops," James complained that these soldiers, whom he presumed to be former slaves, were "arrogant and impertinent to their former masters" and believed "that they are equal in every respect to the white, and should now own the land and the property." The occupied South was on the knife's edge, fearing the chance of slave rebellion as much as a future without slaves. One Sunday, James remembered to his diary in the summer of 1865, "these soldiers" tried to forcibly integrate the local churches in Aiken, an action that led to their eventual replacement by "a company of Germans, who were quiet and well behaved."[104] Only a few months later, the "signs of the times" were, in his mind, "gloomy and portentous of evil!" Now James prophesized a massive black rebellion on the scale of the Haitian insurrection, leaving the Southern countryside littered with dead bodies, black and white, and with no labor save that which could be forced to serve. The end result of the "mighty negro insurrection," James opined, would be that "they will be subjugated, and their status changed: they will not become slaves for that name is abolished for ever, but apprentices, who will be compelled by severe legislation to labor, and to become useful members of the community." Freedom, James continued, would "dwindle down" the "negro race," and "immigration will set in the South: Germans, Poles, Swedes & Frenchmen will settle our farms: Irishmen will supercede negro laborers in Cities."[105] Here, then, was a vision of the near future of emancipation that was, in

some ways, as much Haitian as it was Southern, colored by family, regional, and hemispheric histories of bloodshed and uprising, a product
of the increasingly interconnected network of waterways and port
cities, histories and memories, that had led Anthony Trollope derisively
to describe St. Thomas—as much a part of this network as Charleston,
Havana, or New Orleans—as a "Niggery-Hispano-Dano-Yankee-
Doodle place."

CHAPTER TWO

The White Republic of the Tropics

Slavery was . . . the common recognized institution of
the New World.

— JUDAH BENJAMIN, *SLAVERY PROTECTED BY THE COMMON
LAW OF THE NEW WORLD* (1858)

The Old South's dazzling antebellum hybridity was transformed and constrained by the wartime creation of an independent slaveholding republic. "The new Empire is at last fairly launched," announced the *New York Times* in early 1861, after the congressional delegations of a handful of Southern states had, with extraordinary formality, resigned their service to the United States and removed themselves to Montgomery, Alabama, to draft a new constitution for their "Slaveholding Confederacy." "The seceding States," the *Times* continued, had "assumed the attitude of nationality." But in the midst of this haphazard creativity—this "assumption" of nationalism—some of the South's peculiar borderland culture and Caribbean complexion were elided. In sifting and separating what was "Southern" from what was "Northern" or "Mexican" or "Cuban," a warring state brought greater clarity to the map of the Americas, snapping it into sharper focus. For a brief moment, the slaveholding South was its own nation, standing with Brazil and Cuba as the largest remaining societies committed to chattel bondage. It was also still claimed as a part of the United States. The "paradoxes" of the moment were, the *Times* admitted, "the most extraordinary ever exhibited in history." "Of the thirty-four States," it noted, "twenty-eight are still represented in the National Congress . . . but within this empire is *another*, assuming equal dignity and power."[1] To stifle the fledgling nation within a nation, the *Times* recommended the stationing of well-armed ships of war outside of the most important Southern ports and the redirection of trade through seaboard cities like

Boston or New York.[2] Commercial publisher J. B. Elliot, hoping to capture the encirclement of the South—its forcible separation from the Caribbean—in a single, popular image, drew a vast black snake sprawled around the old United States, with its thickest part cutting straight across the American Mediterranean. In Elliot's vision of the encircled South, everything was turned upside down: in New Orleans, slaves slept on barrels filled with sugar and exclaimed "Can't ship now!" while in Mississippi, small black figures defiantly burned down a plantation home.[3]

In its defiance of the Union, the South walked a very fine line, earnestly desiring to retain slavery, with its Mediterranean echoes, while refusing to drift too far away from the powerful faith that the states were collectively distinct from and fundamentally superior to their neighbors in the Americas. Like the North, the South was deeply invested in the prevailing belief that the states had defied history and were uniquely capable of transcending the historical cycles that had killed off other significant civilizations. The Confederacy could not easily have given up the sense of hemispheric superiority that sat at the core of the doctrine of manifest destiny. During the war, it shamelessly aped the very same republic it fought on the battlefield, taking its constitution with little adjustment and claiming its revolutionary heritage, its governmental structure, and even a good measure of its classically inspired heroic iconography. It appropriated the very history of the union as its own, tracing its leadership back to George Washington, Thomas Jefferson, and John C. Calhoun. Indeed, it imagined itself as the true heir to the revolutionary generation. It labored, as well, to stave off the charge that it was becoming "Latin" in any meaningful way, even if it sought, above all else, to preserve slavery—a supposedly tropical institution. The war thus forced the South, if briefly and incompletely, to focus on the triumphant nationalism of the fledgling Confederate States of America and to transform the long-standing cosmopolitanism of the master class. This was no easy task. Even in the midst of a war that featured unparalleled destruction, generational suicide, and widespread social mayhem, the leadership of the Confederacy struggled mightily to synthesize the image of the South as an Anglophone "city on a hill," looking down on its fellow slaveholders in the Caribbean, bringing together its "Latin" ethos as a vast slaveholding empire with its future as the greatest of the tropical republics, the impending lord and master of the warm, blue waters of the American Mediterranean.

"The Lower South by 1860," Allen Tate once wrote, "was a distinct nation."[4] Hamilton Eckenrode, writing a few years earlier, in 1923, described the Deep South as "African jungle in part; medieval Europe in part; American democracy in part," and offered Jefferson Davis as a "Tropic Nordic," a racially distinct and advanced species of European capable of surviving and prospering below the cooler latitudes.[5] Tate's argument is a keystone of the antimodernist "Lost Cause." And Eckenrode's bizarre formulation is a eugenic echo of nineteenth-century logic. Both, in their own way, are right. But neither image, strangely enough, matches our current consensus that the Confederacy was a dreamy and fictive thing, an imagined place dreamed up by people who are best understood as "Americans."[6] Despite this dissonance, the slaveholding region's appeal to the revolutionary republican tradition, the lust for Caribbean territory, and the location of the South in a pan-American context were all vital components of a worldview in which the slaveholding states, like the Roman Empire, imagined themselves as the superior civilization in a singular, maritime system of economic, social, and cultural exchange. The Confederacy brought new light and air to these ideas, allowing them to grow in unpredictable ways. And the defeat of the South permanently extinguished this new light, changing its role in the American Mediterranean. It brought an end to slavery. It drew the region even more tightly into the Union and answered any lingering questions about the supremacy of federal power. It halted any chance of Southern expansion into the Caribbean, where slavery persisted and flourished and where sugar and coffee still offered the prospect of unlimited profit. It further sharpened the division of the pure from the impure, the civilized from the backward, the perfectly white from the imperfectly off-white. It pulled the South even further away from the Americas. Were it not for the war, the Confederacy might have claimed Cuba or annexed even more of Mexico, and the South's decision to adhere to the republican traditions of Jefferson and Calhoun might have resulted in even closer parallels to Rome, with its commitment to slavery, trade, and empire. Were it not for the war, New Orleans might well have matured into the next great world city of the Caribbean, supplanting Havana. Were it not for the war and its aftermath, gradual emancipation in the South (when and if it came) might have featured coolies and apprentices or some other novel modification of the world's histories of bound labor. But the war did come. To make sense of what came after it, when the South, like vulgar Rome, lay in ruins, we need to shed new light on the creation of the

Confederacy's mise-en-scène, its mixture of neoclassical pretension and "tropical Gothic."[7]

Slaveholding Diplomacies

In early March 1858, nearly one year to the date after the *Dred Scott* decision, Judah P. Benjamin, a senator from Louisiana, stood up in the Capitol building to offer a hemispheric context for the debate about slavery. Benjamin is best known as the man who wore three hats in the Confederate government: "Attorney General, Secretary of War, *and* Secretary of State." It was a political juggling act that, when seen in light of his religious background, has earned him notoriety as an ethnic trailblazer.[8] In the midst of the Civil War, he was either derided as "Mr. Davis's pet Jew," to borrow Mary Chesnut's coarse summary, or lauded as a "Delphic oracle."[9] In 1858, however, Benjamin was a well-known U.S. senator, respected for his oratory and legal acumen, for his early ambition as a sugar planter (before the flooding of the Mississippi ruined his much loved plantation), and for his success in the turbulent, bruising world of New Orleans politics. As such, Benjamin had listened carefully to the complaints of his fellow senator, William H. Seward of New York, who had invoked the *Dred Scott* decision and charged that the president and the slaveholding chief justice had conspired to weigh down the people of Kansas with the "millstone of slavery." It was Seward's attack that led Benjamin to rise on that one-year anniversary of the decision that rendered African slaves as noncitizens, to clear his throat and claim his right to speak, and to unfurl, once again, the proud and angry banner of the proslavery defense.[10]

The argument Benjamin presented that March was both simple and profound. Much of the debate over slavery, he said, rested on a "radical, fundamental error," a presumption that "slavery is the creature of the statute law of the several States where it is established." A related falsehood, he continued, was the belief that "slaves are not property beyond those limits; and that property in slaves is neither recognized nor protected by the Constitution of the United States, nor by international law." "I controvert all these propositions," he noted dismissively, as if everything that had been said before were rubbish. And so, indeed, he did. Slavery, he suggested, was built on a solid, global foundation of common law—built, in other words, on historical precedent traced back long before the thirteen colonies of the Atlantic Coast broke away from England. After commenting on how regularly courts named

A portrait of Judah P. Benjamin in 1856. From the Prints and Photographs Division, Library of Congress.

Africans as "merchandise, chattels, [or] just as much private property as any other merchandise or any other chattel," Benjamin offered a sweeping historical account of the rise of slavery in Brazil, in the Spanish colonies of the Americas, and in British North America, much of which would have been familiar and perhaps even boring to his fellow senators, before concluding that Southern slaveholders might well enjoy the protection of the U.S. Constitution and could surely justify slavery through the rights of the states, but they could also even more assuredly rely on other, more global and traditional justifications for enslavement and purchase. "The European continental powers," he concluded, "which joined and co-operated with Great Britain in the discovery and establishment of colonies on this continent, all followed the same views. . . . The legislation of all of them was the same. . . . Slavery was thus the common recognized institution of the New

World."[11] The institution was not "peculiar" at all but "common" and, as such, fairly benign. Southern slavery was but a phase of New World slavery, and the master class of the Old South was but an aspect of something far larger—an American Mediterranean peopled, like the great sea of classical antiquity, with slaveholding societies who shared common parentage, connections, and ways of knowing. Such an argument, as historian Don Fehrenbacher put it, reveals the grim "proslavery potentialities of the *Dred Scott* decision," potentialities that would soon be cut off by the Civil War.[12]

The man styled as "the South's Disraeli" was also a perfect representative, of sorts, for New Orleans, one of the principal port cities of the American Mediterranean. As such, he was hardly an outlier in the South.[13] His father, Philip Benjamin, was born on the tiny volcanic island of Nevis in the West Indies and moved to London to find a bride. After Philip's marriage to Rebecca, the daughter of a Sephardic merchant, the Benjamin family returned to the New World, settling at Christiansted, St. Croix, where they lived with their two slaves in a two-story wooden house, facing north on a hillside. "In a day's sail among close-lying islands," an early biographer writes, "one might meet people of half a dozen races, representing a medley of colors, religions, and nationalities."[14] The Benjamins' life was not easy, and they soon pressed themselves into the bowels of one of the hundreds of small sailing ships that regularly traipsed across the Caribbean and up the Atlantic coast of the newly independent U.S. republic, removing themselves first to the port city of Savannah, Georgia, and then to Wilmington, North Carolina, before settling at Charleston, South Carolina. Judah Philip Benjamin was eleven years old and had lived only a few months in Charleston when Denmark Vesey, a free African, was accused of planning a massive slave rebellion, complete with the burning of the city and a proposed escape by ship to Haiti, the island republic where slaves had once freed themselves by force of arms and had set out to exterminate, rumor went, the white planter class. Vesey's public execution was, in a word, a spectacle— his body and those of others were left to hang for days. Those dark, swinging bodies, accompanied, no doubt, by the city's forbidding, carrion-eating birds, surely left an impression on the young West Indian boy who had so recently arrived in the Atlantic coast's most bustling tropic seaport.

At the age of fourteen, Benjamin entered Yale, leaving behind one of the largest centers of the slaveholding South for the puritanical chill of New Haven. He proposed, at one youthful debate, that the United States should "take possession" of Cuba, foreshadowing his adult yearnings for the conquest of the Americas. He left Yale early, at the age of sixteen, for New Orleans, the conduit of cultural exchange between the East, the West, and the Caribbean, where, to borrow again from his biographer, "he absorbed [the city's] point of view—cosmopolitan yet very Southern, commercially progressive yet politically conservative."[15] Then, rooting himself to the place, he married the creole daughter of a Saint Domingue exile, set himself up as a "Sugar Master" at Bellechase, a plantation a few miles downriver from the city, and spent his time experimenting with the modernization of sugar production, plotting the proliferation of railroad lines, and dreaming up the means by which Louisiana could provide the world with sugar, all of it cut by African slaves and all of them bound to the land by law.[16] Some of this personal history surely factored into his argument before the Senate on that March day in 1858.

The immediate political stage for Benjamin's address was shaped by the remarkable hemispherics of the Old South in the years just before the Civil War. The increasingly fractious dynamic between free states and slave states, or between the self-styled North and South, was bound, in many different ways, to the question of westward and south-ward expansion, whether that new land was incorporated by treaty, purchase, or private filibuster. More narrowly, the five short months taken up with the debate and passage of the Kansas–Nebraska Act were, as historian David Potter once catalogued, also marked by the fil-ibuster William Walker's annexation of a large chunk of Mexico into his Republic of Lower California, by President Pierce's announcement of the purchase from Mexico of what is now southern Arizona and New Mexico, and by Mississippi Governor John A. Quitman's barely secretive preparations for a liberation of Cuba by force of private arms.[17] In the prelude to war, the need for new territory for slavery— where dangerous concentrations of presumably rebellious slaves could be exported—had been closely coupled with two parallel nationalisms (that of the United States and, increasingly, that of the South), a cou-pling that encouraged a sense of the republic as potentially limitless, fraught with internal peril, and unquestionably righteous.[18] The 1840s and early 1850s were the high-water mark of this intertwined argument in favor of expansion and conquest, and these decades stand as one of the country's most unilateralist epochs, at least in spirit, where viola-tions of the Neutrality Act, or calls for its complete abolition, could be a useful addition to one's résumé on an application for diplomatic ser-vice. Benjamin himself was a rather well-known champion of a New Orleans-centered version of "Gulf Coast Imperialism," hoping that an ambitious railroad scheme cutting across Mexico, a southward plunging semicircle that ended in California, would girdle the region, making the conquest of Central America a fait accompli and enabling the South to grasp the riches of "the Eastern World" without interference from Northern ports or commercial interests.[19] "That commerce belongs to New Orleans," Benjamin maintained; it "makes empires of the countries to which it flows."[20] In the end, all of the saber rattling and scheming only made civil war more certain, as the thirst for a geographic expansion of slavery across the plains of the lower Northern hemisphere and, indeed, across the Caribbean strengthened the resolve of the antislavery advocates.[21] When the war finally came, with the departure of the Southern senators from the Capitol building, the establishment of a new Confederate capital in Richmond, the writing of a new constitution, and, finally, the firing on Fort Sumter, it would be staged in this same hemispheric context.

At first, there were hopes for imperial expansion into the Americas. "For the future," the new president of the Confederacy, Jefferson Davis, announced in Atlanta in early 1861, before the rough edges of Confederate diplomacy had been sanded off, "we are to be embraced in the same moral category as Brazil and Cuba." Unconcerned with the sanctimonious "moral" algebra of the abolitionist North, Davis advised the public not to be concerned about the prospects for future growth. "There were the West India islands," the reporter's summary of his speech reads, "which, under the old Union, were forbidden to us, and there were the Northern parts of Mexico." Agriculture and slavery, Davis continued, "furnished indissoluble cords for binding together, in a grand homogenous Union, the States now making common cause with us."[22] "The North has wanted Canada and the South wants Cuba, the expansion of both may be restrained by the narrow views of each, let them be left freely to grow casting their branches widely."[23] The establishment of Confederate nationalism, Davis initially hoped, meant expansion into the Caribbean and closer economic and cultural solidarity with other slaveholding societies; to remain in the old union of states, to eschew expansion, to ignore "St. Domingo with its bloody teachings, and Jamaica with its silent monitors of pauperism and decay," was to resign the South to "Africanization."[24] In terms of its labor system and the "institutions" that accompanied it, the South—a society based on cash-crop agriculture and slavery—no longer shared anything social or economic with the industrial, manufacturing, immigrant cities of the North. It shared far more "morally" with the Hispanophone and Lusophone slaveholders who managed the *cafetals* and *ingenios* of Cuba or Brazil. Both slaveholding societies were, at least at first, potential acquisitions of the republic. Neither was the equal—in any real sense—of the new empire.

Very quickly, however, the Confederacy had to set aside its fanciful desire for future conquests. Instead, it was forced to more aggressively press its claim to be a nation-state righteously engaged in foreign policy. Along the Gulf coastline, the "paper blockade" of the South— "this monstrous pretension of the United States," Jefferson Davis called it—forced the Confederacy to deploy small, fast boats, often using Caribbean ports and relying on friendly local officials, to sneak through with commerce or hamstring the larger, stronger Union navy. This rather practical naval strategy had been conceived by one of the few capable men in Davis's cabinet, Stephen Mallory, who had been born in Trinidad before moving, as a young boy, to Key West, a port, one writer suggests, that "was to the Gulf of Mexico what Gibraltar was to the Mediterranean."[25] Following Mallory's approach to naval combat, Confederate blockade runners used some of the same off-the-map locations that had once launched the *filibusteros*. The blockade runners also frequented Havana and Nassau as free enterprise zones and homes away from home. Sitting low in the water, their decks heavily laden and squared off by cotton bales, side-wheel steamers like the *Caroline* and the *Denbigh,* or the Spanish ship *Havana,* relied on guile and bravado but also on old friendships, familiar locations, comfortable surroundings, and well-traveled contraband routes along the Gulf coast and across the West Indies and the Caribbean.[26] They relied, in other words, on the very nature of the old hybrid South for their every success. Old partnerships and collaborations did not vanish in 1861 but persisted through the war. When Mallory looked for aid in Havana during the war, he was able to rely on these same networks, on old friendships and family rooted in his younger days in Key West and Pensacola, and on his wife's abundant family connections in Cuba.[27]

In the American Southwest, various Anglo, Caribbean, and Mexican partners likewise exploited the old informal networks of exchange that had long prospered in the borderlands between the two nations. Prior to the summer of 1863, when the Union army captured Vicksburg and with it the Mississippi River, the Confederate armies had drawn a significant portion of their munitions and supplies through the trans-Mississippi and, ultimately, through the Matamoras region of Mexico.

Confederate agents would place orders for a wide range of vital goods and war material in various English cities, and those goods would be shipped to the Mexican side of the border, near enough to the Rio Grande for easy transfer to the South. With so much profit to be had, Matamoras quickly became a busy commercial hub for an illicit trade that transcended national borders and international disputes over recognition. The significance of this trade was not lost on the U.S. government and the Union army. "Where is Colonel Hamilton?" one breathless consular communiqué, dispatched from Monterey, read. "If in New Orleans, tell him that the rebels are buying up everything here that can be eaten, worn, or that can be used to kill Union men."[28] "Can a few men, provided with arms and ammunition and authority to recruit be sent to Point Isabel, and protected by a light draft gunboat?" one officer asked. "If so, thousands can be saved. The rebel trade with and through Mexico would be broken up, and you little dream how important it has become."[29]

In the formal diplomatic realm, the Confederacy struggled to synthesize its ambitions as an empire in the Caribbean with its day-to-day effort to survive in a desperate quest for recognition. The region was, from the first, poorly suited for diplomacy. Southern diplomats were generally misinformed, rough-hewn, inept, and often offensive to their hosts—they were, in short, earlier versions of Joe Bing, the archetypal "failed" diplomat of the Cold War era.[30] Bridging cosmopolitanism and hubris, the Confederacy took an early and fatal disinterest in foreign policy, relying instead on abiding faith in "King Cotton" and a belief that the European market, which was deeply dependent on Southern cotton, would, in the absence of the precious fiber, compel Britain and France to intervene in the Civil War. Blithely withholding cotton from Europe and "building on the logic of the embargo and enforced scarcity in Europe," the Confederacy also lobbied against planting across the South (fearing, as well, that Northern armies might come into possession of it) and burned the annual crop. Not surprisingly, the annual cotton yields during the Civil War plummeted.[31] The unpopular association of the South—and cotton—with slavery and empire also surely did not help. Pointing to the obvious dangers posed by "the new Republic," John Stuart Mill asked: "Are we to see with indifference its victorious army let loose to propagate their national faith at the rifle's mouth through Mexico and Central America? Shall we submit to see fire and sword carried over Cuba and Porto Rico, and Hayti and Liberia, conquered and brought back to slavery?"[32] It is not surprising, then, that efforts to secure diplomatic recognition or some form of European intervention routinely failed.

Relations with Mexico—the southwestern switching point—were equally troublesome. The independent republic had long been an obsession of expansionists seeking a "safety valve" for a growing slave population, an obsession that would continue through the Civil War.[33] But Napoleon III had recently occupied Mexico City and had installed—through a dubious plebiscite—an Austrian archduke, Maximilian, as the emperor of Mexico. For a brief time, the fates of Maximilian's Mexico and Jefferson Davis's Confederacy were inextricably intertwined, though Judah Benjamin rightly feared that Napoleon had his own plans for the eventual reconquest of Texas.[34] "Southerners assumed," one historian writes, "that French recognition of the South would assuredly accompany the Confederacy's protection of the puppet emperor."[35] Some, too, worried that the Confederacy might be split in half by the war, absorbed, in part, by the empire of France. And one of Davis's adjutants wondered whether Napoleon—"a proslavery man himself"—might want to "join forces with the South?" Though France, itself, was suffused with "strong abolition feeling," Napoleon might, the letter continued, be willing to express solidarity with the Confederacy while also "insisting upon emancipation as the price of recognition."[36] Spain, too, might recognize the Confederacy. In any case, the European powers were once again meddling in New World politics, with consequences for both North and South. "Our revolution has emasculated the Monroe Doctrine," wrote Confederate Colonel John Thomas Pickett (who had precious little respect for Mexicans) to the Mexican minister of foreign affairs. He continued, "the Spaniards are now become our natural allies, and jointly with them we may effect a partition of this magnificent country." "Revolutions," as Pickett put it dryly, "bring us into strange company."[37] One Frenchman, urging recognition of the Confederacy, even suggested that an independent, triumphant Southern nation—if recognized by the power behind Maximilian's Mexico—would ensure an end to filibustering, to "the adventurers" who would "fling themselves into Mexico."[38] Even as the old "routes" and "roots" of the Southwest and the Caribbean brought dwindling trade to the port cities of the Gulf South, the establishment of Maximilian's empire and the increasing strength of the blockade put limits, or borders, on the South where before there had been next to nothing.[39]

Confederate diplomatic efforts were likewise constrained by the steadfast commitment to slavery in the new republic. Southern expansionists had so regularly lobbied for the annexation of Cuba, for instance, that Confederate diplomats, seeking support or recognition from Spain, were forced time and time again to disclaim any interest in the island.[40] In private, Jefferson Davis might assume that Cuba would eventually be a new territory in the white republic, but in public the official line was different. "The Confederate States," instructed Robert Toombs, secretary of state in 1861, hoped that "Cuba shall continue to be a colonial possession of Spain." The Confederate States were "desirous . . . of no extension of our boundaries," Judah Benjamin wrote assuredly in 1863; the Confederacy instead sought "safety and happiness solely in the peaceful development of our own ample resources."[41] This constant demurral reflected a changed reality. Once the "independence of the Confederate States" had been achieved, one savvy diplomat suggested, "the South would deem it its interest that a great country like Spain should continue a slave power. The two, together with Brazil, would have a monopoly of the system of labor, which alone can make intertropical America and the regions adjoining it available to the uses of men." Spain and Brazil should be driven to recognize the Confederacy, Robert Hunter urged, because he hoped that "they would observe with pleasure the growth in power and influence of a State bound to them by this tie of a great common interest, and they would earnestly desire to see the nations thus bound together armed with the means to protect their common social system."[42] In some real sense, the establishment of the Confederacy clarified the political place of the South in that "intertropical America" and highlighted the hemispheric significance of that "common social system."

The Confederacy's reliance on this universal memory—on the shared past of the slaveholding New World—appealed to many others in the circum-Caribbean. Most famously, over seventy Cubans, historian Antonio Rafael de la Cova reminds us, fought in the Confederate army, a number that includes the heralded "Cuban Rifle Company" of New Orleans. One much-debated postwar blockbuster—the narrative of Loreta Janeta Velazquez—told the story of a Cuban woman who chose to dress as a man and pass as an American so that she could fight for the South in the Civil War. (Jubal Early later thought the book was a fake, but he chose to reject it because of its unflattering portrait of Southern manhood, not on account of its description of Velazquez's entirely believable border crossings.) It is hard, in these narratives, to know where patriotism starts and slaveholding solidarity ends. In April of 1861, the Cuban exile Ambrosio Gonzales appealed to General P. T. Beauregard for service in the army of the Confederacy. Gonzales, now married to Harriet Elliot, the daughter of a prominent South Carolina planter, had been touring the South, giving demonstrations of the "Maynard Breech Loading Rifle" to excited crowds. Caught up in the fever of secession, and wearing a "military uniform" and carrying a sword, he rushed to the Charleston harbor to watch the bombardment of Fort Sumter. Quickly, he wrote to remind his old schoolmate Beauregard that he had served as "Adjt General" and "second in command in 1850 to the Cuban force," a reference to the failed filibustering expedition of Narciso Lopez. It was enough to earn him a position as an artillery chief under Beauregard's command and the rank of colonel. He would serve through the war, and his family would stay at their Oak Lawn estate until Sherman's march forced them to flee. Even as the Confederacy established itself as a discreet political unit, its enthusiasm for the common social worlds of slaveholders lent it a broader, international appeal.[43]

Bonds of Affection

The composite slaveholding Confederacy was a unique thing, even amidst the diversity of American nations, colonies, and settler outposts, and its cultural nationalism deserves some careful scrutiny. The nineteenth-century Caribbean, as historian Franklin Knight notes, struggled through "a long period of social disintegration and reconstruction . . . [in which] the aging structure of the rigid, cruel, plantation societies yielded to the impatient emergence of a new set of polyglot societies of free, but distinctly not equal, peoples."[44] The Confederacy does not easily fit this narrative. There were, for instance, no other models in the Americas for a slaveholding republic (none, that is, except for the United States). Cuba and Puerto Rico were still colonies of Spain. The British and French West Indies had been emancipated years earlier. Inspired by the ideals associated with Latin American liberator Simón Bolivar, Mexico, Nicaragua, Costa Rica, Guatemala, Panama, and San Salvador had also abolished slavery. Farther south, Brazil, a vast slaveholding country with long-standing strong links to the Old South, was a baroque, Catholic monarchy. Haiti, to continue down the list, was a dreadful, frightening parallel. On the other side of Hispaniola, Spanish Haiti was in complete disarray; lacking any advanced plantation-scale agriculture, the *caudillo* government of Buenaventera Báez was even then clamoring to rejoin the Spanish empire in the Caribbean, just as it would later plead for annexation by the United States. And Honduras, a rough and tumble frontier port, was on the verge of becoming a colony of the British Empire. By 1861, in fact, almost every other independent republic in the Americas had already brought an end to slavery or was preparing (in the case of the United States) to do the same. The Confederacy, then, was the only white republic with an expanding commitment to chattel bondage.

Despite its uniqueness in the New World, the Confederacy nevertheless was, in some strange fashion, the nearly perfect embodiment of nineteenth-century nationalism. For well over thirty years, the region had stressed the importance of "the journey" to the North, noting the vast distances—social, temporal, cultural, and economic—between the slaveholding states and the so-called free states.[45] Southern newspapers, magazines, and literary societies promoted, to paraphrase Benedict Anderson, provincial reflections on "the metropole"—Washington, D.C., the center of federal power, imagined by some as imperial—as well as covering local and regional news, such as the marriage of an influential slaveholder to the daughter of an important merchant, the price of sugar cane or cotton in this port and that port, and the activities of "the North" against the shared concerns of "the South." One essayist in the *Southern Literary Messenger* offered New Orleans as the new "Athens of the South" and located an emerging Southern literary tradition in existing local institutions, including universities and colleges, newspapers, monthly magazines, and literary circles. "We must . . . give to the literary productions of the South, the patronage which has heretofore been given liberally to the works of Yankee writers." Southerners, the magazine suggested, must take up the "noble ambition" to render New Orleans, the pivot of the trans-Mississippi frontier and a focal point of the slave trade, "the intellectual focus on this new CONFEDERATION."[46] Across the South, newspapers, monthly magazines, and pamphlets, engaged in the popular task of nation-building, focused their attentions not on roads, railroads, and ships, but on reading groups and songs, on public performances of national identity, and on private commemorations of allegiance—the intimate display, for instance, of one state's secession ordinance alongside the Declaration of Independence. New primary school textbooks were written, setting the South in opposition to the North. One woman, historian Drew Gilpin Faust tells us, "procured locks of hair from a dozen Confederate generals and fashioned them into a sculpture that she intended to put on public display."[47] The new flags of the Confederacy—the "stars and bars" and the "Southern cross"—were greeted with great reverence across the South as literal symbols of the emotional and sentimental attachments, or bonds of affection, that connected new citizens to their new nation.[48] The print culture of the South had "created an imagined community among a specific assemblage of fellow readers," for whom these defining issues were of paramount importance.[49] It was logical, in the age of nationalism, that political independence—marked by secession and state formation—should eventually follow the creation of an independent culture and social identity. It was just as logical, as members of the slaveholding South withdrew from Congress, that the emerging Confederacy, utterly dependent on bound labor, should drape itself in the most unrepentant racial hierarchies, deliberately confusing race, class, and nation.

The figurehead of this new nation-state had to be a determined slaveholder with the disinterestedness of a Roman patrician—a white patriarch of impeccable "blue" or "white" blood. And he had to come not from the upper South, but from the lower frontier region, where slavery still seemed limitless. Here, the Confederacy turned to Jefferson Davis—Mississippian, slaveholder, war hero, traitor to the union, and cause célèbre of the conservative tradition. Long styled the "the representative man of the Southern Confederacy," Davis was the owner of Brierfield, a vast plantation on nearly nine hundred acres on the east bank of the Mississippi River, just south of Vicksburg. It had been carved out of the hard, wild Mississippi frontier by African slaves, much as Thomas Sutpen's famous "hundred" had been.[50] As a younger man, Davis had returned from the Caribbean—from a brief trip to Cuba, where he had traveled to recover his health—determined to become a planter, a master, and an owner of slaves. Working alongside his slaves, it took him eight years, his biographer notes, to tame the wilderness and bring the idea of Brierfield—shaped by his fellow slaveholders and his vision of slavery in the Caribbean—to life. "His sense of humor was keen," his wife, Varina, wrote in 1890, with no irony:

> He was a keen observer of everything. Every shade of feeling that crossed the minds of those about him was noticed, and he could not bear anyone to be inimical to him. Nothing could be more winning than his efforts to conciliate even his servants when he thought they were annoyed with him, and he had his reward, for to a man they loved him, and were willing to bear any little impatience on his part cheerfully. . . . Whenever he went to the quarters the twelve or fifteen little toddlers that could walk would run from the plantation nursery calling out "Howdye, massa," and stretch out

their short arms for a handshake sometimes, in imminent danger of the horse treading upon them.[51]

This, at least, was the quite common delusion of the Southern planter and his wife, seduced by slavery's social role as "capitalism in feudal-aristocratic drag."[52] The Brierfield "big house," an isolated "cane brake," as Davis called it, was a single-story affair, modest when compared with some of the grander palaces erected along the lower Mississippi, but still possessing a series of fluted Roman columns and a wide front porch. As Davis became more and more involved in state politics, life at Brierfield was a welcome retreat, offering Davis the constitutionally rejuvenating experiences associated with slaveholding, racial privilege, and aristocracy. When news reached Brierfield that Davis had been elected president of the new Confederate States of America, the messenger found him cutting roses in the garden. "He assembled his negroes," Varina recalled, "and made them an affectionate farewell speech, to which they responded with expressions of devotion."[53] Invoking popular notions of Roman history, Davis had rushed back to Brierfield after his "retirement" from the Senate, so that he could be "called" back into service as the new leader of the breakaway slaveholding republic. In February of 1861, having hastened to Montgomery, Davis climbed into an ornate carriage, accented with saffron and silver and drawn by six horses, and headed off to become the new president of the new Confederacy.[54] The whole of the Deep South, as Mary Ashton Rice Livermore recalled, "gave itself up to a very intoxication of delight."[55] And Davis himself later remembered a "universal feeling" in those early days, a sense of "common cause and destiny," and a fusion of "local interests" with "the common welfare."[56]

He was the right man for the job, or so it was thought at the time.[57] Before his selection as president of the Confederacy, Davis was a well-credentialed imperial Southerner, not some provincially minded rube. He had fought in the Black Hawk War, been a minor hero of the Mexican War, and served as a capable secretary of war in the Pierce administration. He was a leading, if occasionally temperate, figure in the proslavery movement and was well versed in the history of slavery in the hemisphere. Although publicly opposed to filibustering, his sincere desire for the acquisition of Cuba was obvious enough to warrant the courtship of the *filibustero* Narciso Lopez, who hoped that Davis, a hero of the Mexican-American War, might join him in his ill-fated

A. R. Waud's sketch of Brierfield, for *Harper's Weekly* in 1866. From the Prints and Photographs Division, Library of Congress.

attempt to "free" the island from Spanish rule. (Davis was promised $100,000 and a coffee plantation, but he demurred.)[58] Like Benjamin, most of his fellow Southern senators, and a host of others, Davis was an advocate of slavery's expansion into the new territories and a propagandist for the dreams of the master class.

As an icon of the new republic, Davis was supposed to link the South to the generation of the founding fathers. In each of the various crises that marked the path to civil war, the antebellum South had fantasized that it was the true heir to the American Revolution. Not surprisingly, then, the Confederacy was imagined as "the consummation, not the dissolution of the American dream."[59] Davis had pressed to keep the "old" flag" but failed to persuade his comrades, who were swept up in the "flag passions" of the Civil War and who yearned for a new symbol. He "insisted," Varina Davis recalled, "that a different battle flag would make distinctions enough between combatants; but he was overruled."[60] The "old" U.S. Constitution, "which our fathers bequeathed to us," was borrowed and transformed into a Confederate constitution with very few modifications. "We have changed the constituent parts," Davis said, "but not the system of government."[61] "All of the essentials of the old constitution," Davis's vice president, Alexander Stephens, noted to

Alexander H. Stephens, vice president of the Confederacy. From the Prints and Photographs Division, Library of Congress.

applause, "have been preserved." "Some changes have been made," the Georgian admitted, but these were "great improvements." The president of the Confederacy served a six-year term and could not be reelected. And "the old thorn of the tariff," he continued, "a cause of so much irritation in the old body politic, is removed forever from the new."[62] For Stephens and for Davis, these minor modifications were simply a return to the original intent of the founders, for the "old" constitution was, "at first, mainly the work of Southern men." "But for the South," Stephens wondered, "what would have become of the principles of Jefferson, Madison, and Washington?"[63]

The emerging Confederate aesthetic featured a certain kind of "martial religiosity" that suffused the rich debates over flags, national seals, military portraiture, and the divine mission of the South. Davis's first presidential portrait, an 1861 lithograph by J. C. Hoyer and Charles Ludwig, titled *Jefferson Davis, First President of the Confederate States of America,* emphasized his military experience, his bearing, and his manner. Davis stares balefully, manfully, off to the right. In a subsequent effort to capture Davis's martial prowess, Hoyer and Ludwig mistakenly suggested that the "First President" had taken the command at Bull Run, an inaccuracy that only assured the Southern public that the Confederacy was in good hands.[64] Another icon of U.S. history, George Washington, also regularly appeared in the debates over a Southern style. Indeed, Washington was a part of Jefferson Davis's carefully choreographed story line. Like Washington, Jefferson Davis had to be summoned "back" to service. Like the great general of the Revolutionary War, Davis would be the new nation's Cincinnatus. "He neither desired nor expected the position," Varina recalled, thinking of the moment when he had been notified of his call to serve as the Confederacy's first president.[65] Davis delivered his inaugural address at the Virginia capitol building, while standing next to an elaborate statue of the first president of the republic. In his orchestration of Confederate nationalism, Davis appealed to the only successful revolution of white slaveholders in the New World, styling himself as Washington and imagining—as many of the earliest colonists did—that the rejection of Northern empire would ensure Southern expansion. It is Washington, not Davis, who appeared on the Great Seal of the Confederate States of America, where he is depicted seated on his horse, in a classic pose, gesturing westward toward the horizon. He is surrounded by a ring of corn, sugar cane, cotton, and tobacco, a reference to the interests of "an agricultural people" caught up in war.[66] The words "Deo Vindice" ("God will vindicate") appear beneath Washington and reflect a growing sense, as Drew Gilpin Faust suggests, that the war was fought "not simply to achieve independence, but also to defend the moral right of survival for the South's peculiar civilization."[67]

The reference to the American revolution was a powerful one. In 1861, as in 1776, the will of "the people" was presumably about to be quashed by a heavy-handed "foreign" power. Then as before, there were grumblings about the need to acquire new territory, the ignored rights of supposedly peripheral states, and the "enslavement" of white men by a distant metropole. But the perpetuation of slavery—the root and branch of the "common social system" linking the South to the Caribbean—was the single most important concern in 1861. For these reasons, the Confederate revolution has long been described as an uprising rooted in parochialism, as a "rebellion without larger significance," pruned of all contemporary liberal excess and narrowly focused on the preservation of slavery.[68] "What possible ties have Virginia and

Louisiana?" asked the *New York Times,* then answering its own question: "None whatever. They have no trade except in *slaves.*"[69] Indeed, the "corner-stone" of the new government, as Confederate Vice President Stephens put it famously, was "the great truth, that the negro is not equal to the white man, that slavery—subordination to the superior race—is his natural and normal condition." "The new constitution," he continued,

> has put at rest, *forever,* all the agitating questions relating to our peculiar institution—African slavery as it exists amongst us—the proper *status* of the negro in our form of civilization. This was the immediate cause of the late rupture and the present revolution. Jefferson, in his forecast, had anticipated this, as "the rock upon which the old Union would split." He was right. . . . But whether he comprehended the great truth upon which that rock *stood* and *stands,* may be doubted. The prevailing ideas entertained by him and most of the leading statesmen at the time of the formation of the old constitution, were that the enslavement of the African was in violation of the laws of nature; that it was wrong in *principle,* socially, morally, and politically. . . . Those ideas, however, were fundamentally wrong. They rested upon the assumption of the equality of races. This was an error. It was a sandy foundation, and the government built upon it fell when "the storm came and the wind blew."

The Confederate constitution was, then, not simply a document that extended new protections to slaveholders; it was a proslavery and white supremacist compact, an agreement that slavery was not just necessary but good, and that "the Negro" was clearly inferior. "Our new government," Stephens concluded, "is the first, in the history of the world, based upon this great physical, philosophical, and moral truth."[70] Territory acquired by the Confederacy was to feature the "institution of negro slavery."[71] New states, Stephens enthused, must "adopt the fundamental principles on which our social and domestic institutions rest."[72] "Slavery," one editorialist wrote, "makes the South a blooming Eden. Its abolition (now or in the near future) would make it a Jamaica,—or even worse a St. Domingo." "Suppose," the writer continued, that the present population of slaves in the South should be "restricted to their present area. Suppose them, in addition, to be free. Imagine the misery, the crime, the poverty, the barbarism, the desolation of the country? The grass would grow in the streets of our cities, our plantations would become a wilderness of cane brakes."[73] As a reflection of this embraced dependence on slavery, the new white republic offered a most unusual symbol of friendly diplomacy to the world: "In old times, the olive branch was considered an emblem of peace," Stephens suggested. "We will send to the nations of the earth another and far more potential emblem of the same, the cotton plant."[74] Each branch of the cotton plant, carried abroad as a marker of the Confederacy's global mission, would be read as a reflection of the tropical white republic's political commitment to slavery's future in the world and as proof of the purity of its racial supremacy.

Where did the image of the master class fit in this Confederacy? One writer focused on the "isothermal laws" of human settlement as an explanation for the racial gap between the Union and the Confederacy. "Slavery has already made its exodus from the inhospitable shores of New England, *never to return;* there is no climate there, there is no soil there, there is no *master* there."[75] "The master" was a physical type manifested wherever there was slavery. But he was most perfectly produced in the South, where hardy "Norman" blood produced a base character that was then forged by heat, humidity, soil, and racial domination. These "Tropic Nordics," to borrow from Hamilton Eckenrode's formulation, were superior to their Northern brothers, with a more intuitive sense of "national citizenship" and with a profound militarism and a sense of order, discipline, and honor. They were concerned with the purification of language: with the removal of "AFRICANISMS" and the establishment of refined English. They did not match the popular abolitionist portrait of the South as a blended, miscegenated space, as something "Latin." In defining the white South, Confederate nationalists thus emphasized its contrast to the Union and to the rest of the Americas, illuminating its extraordinary whiteness, its superior civilization, its qualities of character, and its presumed racial purity. The master class was a race apart.

Not everyone was so confident. The triple threat of social equality, racial rebellion, and postemancipation racial mixing—the Southern slaveholder's jeremiad—was at the very heart of Confederate nationalism. State secession commissioners sojourned across the "border states," painting a terrible portrait of what life would be like under the rule of "Black Republicans." Andrew Calhoun, speaking in Columbia, South Carolina, noted that "the white fiends" of the abolitionist North would do to the South what had once been done to the *grand blancs* of Haiti—to raise "the fury of the beast," to transform the "poor, ignorant, and stupid nature of the negro" through the introduction of egalitarian ideals, and to cultivate the bloodlust of the enslaved African. British newspapers, fearing a massive slave uprising, critiqued the

Emancipation Proclamation as "Abe Lincoln's Last Card; or, Rouge-et-Noir."[76] Jefferson Davis, for one, hoped that "all countries [would] pass judgment on a measure by which several millions of human beings of an inferior race, peaceful and contented laborers in their sphere, are doomed to extermination, while at the same time they are encouraged to a general assassination of their masters."[77] As Davis saw it, Lincoln had attempted to kill off the white republic imagined by the leaders of the Confederacy by bringing the Haitian nightmare to life. Sentiments such as these—and especially, the repeated mention of "the horrors of San Domingo"—were invoked in a powerful argumentative shorthand, unifying white Southerners around the fear of amalgamation or racial "Armageddon." Salvation came, then, from a rejection of the heresy of egalitarianism, the establishment of a viable and independent nation-state, and an embrace of God's truth of racial slavery.[78]

Still, the South would also regularly note, as a sort of wish fulfillment, the supposed happy contentment of bound black labor. Jefferson Davis, speaking to the U.S. Senate just days before his resignation, charged that the lesson of "San Domingo" was not that the slaves would, at the onset of any war, rebel and lay waste to the plantation world of the master class, but, rather, that if they did so it would be because of the removal of "the master" and his replacement by harder, less benevolent military despots. "History," Davis opined in all sincerity, "does not chronicle a case of negro insurrection."[79] Minstrel songs and touring troupes of performers in blackface gave "Negro" voice to the defense of slavery. Popular paintings established a visual romanticism in which master and slave understood and accepted their respective and highly unequal duties in Confederate society—the former charged to educate and protect and the latter to labor until his or her hands could no longer grip a handle or pinch off a cotton boll. William Washington's 1864 portrait of *The Burial of Latane,* a visual representation of a popular broadside poem, brought slaves and planters' wives together at an impromptu burial for a young Confederate soldier. Setting the slaves in shadow, slightly in the background, and off to the left, and displacing them from both the center point and the sunlight, the painting emphasizes the whiteness of those Southern women left behind by gray-clad soldiers and includes a woman who stands in for the absent minister to deliver the funeral oration, her eyes drifting upward. The women are too finely dressed and seem—excusing the lack of men—untouched by the day-to-day concerns of a nation at war. One of the few wartime paintings to survive, and perhaps the only one to garner anything close to critical acclaim, *The Burial of Latane* reflected long-standing Southern fantasies about the slave population, represented on canvas as supportive of the Confederacy. There is no hint on the canvas of any fear of bloody slave rebellion or of violent rape, no sense at all that any one of the slaves attending to the needs of the funeral party could become another Toussaint L'Ouverture.[80]

Like William Washington's fanciful portrayal of the loyal slave standing quietly to the side at his master's burial, Confederate currency glorified slavery in the present tense, offering a soothing representation that stood in stark contrast to concerns about the possible "Haitian" future. The printing and valuation of currency was, of course, an important obligation of the nation-state, but the images on the bills, in addition to providing information about the site of manufacture and value, are generally laden with nationalist iconography. In the early nineteenth century, even as the United States wrestled with the institution of chattel bondage, Southern banks called for Northern printers to include images of "the Negro" on their currency, which at that time was issued by local banks. Sectional differences manifested themselves on the means of exchange, so that slaves might be purchased with a piece of paper that included the stylized, even fantastic representation of a slave. Smiling, contented slaves were often featured on the fronts of banknotes, where they were depicted picking or carrying cotton, working the fields, helping white planters, or holding small black children. Confederate bills continued the trend. Though no longer printed in the North and now subject to the South's paper shortages and lack of adequate printing technology, currency continued to foreground race, often on state-issued bills. They often, as one historian describes it, "returned to the realistic approach, wherein slaves worked the fields or hauled the products of the fields to market."[81] Some bills could feature more dramatic expressions of the slave power's anxiety about the future. The front of one $5 bill, produced for the Georgia Savings Bank in 1863, draws attention to Moneta, the Roman embodiment of wealth and excess, who is seated. She is a thin white woman with a slight smile, holding a branch of ripe and full cotton in one hand and an overflowing bag of gold coins in the other. Hundreds of slaves toil in the background, while a train arrives to carry away ready bales to eager world markets.[82] In a nation where "the order and security of the state" was of paramount importance and where fear of the "horrors of San Domingo" was routine, the calming certainty of slave contentment found here and in *The Burial of Latané* is notable.[83]

The image of abundant, contented, and hard-working black slaves found on locally produced Confederate currency stands in subtle, if complementary, contrast to the pastorals of itinerant Southern landscape

Detail from a Confederate $10 bill, printed in 1861. From the Prints and Photographs Division, Library of Congress.

painters, who were dependent on the patronage and ego of the great planters. Marie Adrien Persac, a watercolorist and amateur mapmaker working along the Mississippi River, often reduced the size of black slaves and set them in a corner to decrease their significance; dressed them in fuller, more humane clothing to deemphasize their brutal treatment; or simply failed to include them at all. His paintings are "meticulous renderings" of peaceful, orderly, civilized Southern life. Deliberately avoiding African subjects, painters such as Persac provided "a pleasant propaganda that covered plantation life with a sweet veneer of tranquility," a Southern landscape tradition that was almost completely stripped of black people.[84] (A proposal to include a black stripe on the Confederate flag, representing "the Negro," not surprisingly came to naught.)[85] Great planters and Confederate patriots, it seems, preferred to have the image of the docile "Negro" on currency—which, in their imaginations, was transferable, disposable capital, like slaves—and not on their prized plantation portraits, which hung on an intimate wall inside the big house. In private, planters preferred to have their plantations represented as pristine, segregated spaces. Not until after the war would African Americans, depicted generally as abstract, inferior gang labor working hard and without coercive supervision to harvest cotton, become a regular and popular feature of the Southern aesthetic. By that point, of course, the Civil War was a distant memory. So, too, was the Confederacy.[86]

The South's wartime fantasies of control and order would not last a lifetime. Indeed, in the end, as "the Confederacy" faded, Jefferson

Davis and his cabinet struggled to find a safe place for the South's supposedly contented slaves. After the publication of the Emancipation Proclamation, as greater numbers of Africans escaped bondage, fled north, or joined the Union armies, Davis theorized that the future of the Confederacy depended on its ability to free some small number of slaves and to equip them to wage war against the Union. This was a counterintuitive sort of foresight that depended on the perverse idea that slaves were enormously contented in the South, that some reasonable number would fight for "the master" and for the perpetuation of bondage even if they were, as fighting men, to be freed. "We should endeavor," Davis wrote to Virginia's governor, William Smith, "to draw into our military service that portion of the negroes which would be most apt to run away." This was hardly an antislavery position. Indeed, if Robert E. Lee, Benjamin, and Davis have long been held up as iconoclasts who, in the waning days of the Confederacy, found a way to imagine a world with slightly fewer slaves, this did not mean that any of them had given up on the peculiar institution. Instead, they had given up on the Old South. What they offered in its place was a new order of things, where the master class would retain all of the important political rights and all the land, offering only very modest "reforms," including personal liberty rights and property rights to freedmen—a kind of demi-freedom for the subhuman "Negro." Lacking land and compelled by the law, former slaves would, once the war was over and the South's independence secured, labor once again for their former masters. "Prewar southern society," historian Bruce Levine writes, "was already irrevocably lost. Davis and his allies flatly denied that arming and freeing the slaves was to abandon—indeed, was to betray—the cause of the plantation South. They did grant that the course they advocated involved large costs and real risks. They nonetheless insisted that their plan—and their plan alone—offered a way to salvage at least something of slavery from the Old South's wreckage." It is striking, as Levine notes, how neatly the scheme for Confederate emancipation anticipated the Black Codes passed immediately after the Civil War, especially in their desire to isolate some means of compulsion beyond the lash.[87]

Death of a Nation

In 1866, in the immediate aftermath of the war, Thomas Kelly, an artist from New York, produced two popular lithographs. The first, *President Lincoln and His Cabinet,* was modeled on another quite successful rendition of the initial reading of the Emancipation Proclamation. In

Kelly's group portrait, Lincoln, the largest figure, is seated slightly to the left, holding a rolled copy of the document that would, by executive fiat, free the slaves. Another copy is spread out over a large table, which the president's cabinet has encircled. Secretary of State Seward, no friend of Lincoln, stares intensely at the president. Ulysses S. Grant, at the very center of the painting, stares directly at the viewer and uses his right index finger to mark a specific passage on the unfurled proclamation. There is a massive chandelier above the table, with twisting oak leaves and glass globes, and two landscape paintings on the wall in the background. A large fireplace with elaborate scrollwork on the light stone mantle gives the room a formal, even imperial quality, establishing the nine figures in view as statesmen, as men of influence and power. Kelly's second painting, *Jefferson Davis and His Cabinet*, borrows liberally from the first. With a few notable exceptions, the posture and general comportment of every figure and background detail is precisely the same. Davis, like Lincoln, clutches a rolled-up document, and Robert E. Lee, like Grant, points to a specific passage. On a seat in the corner, a hat bears the label "CSA." The title of the lithograph, in large caps under the image, does not offer Davis the meaningful title of "President," simply referring to him by name.[88]

Davis had been captured in Georgia in early May of 1865. With a "few demoralized followers, and a train of camp followers three miles long," the beleaguered president of the Confederacy had been unable to secret himself to Florida, where he might have caught a skiff to Havana or tried to capitalize on Braxton Bragg's mythical "pontoon bridge" to Cuba.[89] Kirby-Smith waited hopefully to receive him in Mexico.[90] After his capture, Davis's hard transport by overland train and coastal steamer as a prisoner of war, a subject of public ridicule, and a presumed accomplice in the assassination of Lincoln left him despondent and grim. His jailors feared suicide. Some also feared escape. He was being held as a military prisoner under heavy guard at the old stone fortress in Virginia, named Monroe after the fourth president of the United States. He was being held for trial on the charge of treason, though it was increasingly unclear what court would hear the trial. These facts, and the startling reversal of fortune for the once great Confederacy, offered "a lesson to our nation," one newspaper report concluded, and "will furnish food for reflection to Jefferson Davis himself, as he lies in his solitary confinement," lessons about "the dangers that surround unhallowed ambition, of the perils that environ pride, or the retribution that follows crime."[91] "With the capture of the capital,"

Davis himself summarized, "the dispersion of the civil authorities, the surrender of the armies in the field, and the arrest of the President, the Confederate States of America disappeared as an independent power, and the States of which it had been composed, yielding to the force of overwhelming numbers, were forced to rejoin the Union from which, four years before, they had one by one withdrawn. Their history henceforth became a part of the history of the United States."[92] Davis would be held at Fort Monroe until February of 1869, at which time the case against him was dropped.[93] After hearing rumors of "growing despondence" and "expatriation," Davis wrote to his wife, reminding her that there was still much work to be done in the South: "All cannot go, and those who must stay will need the help of all who can go away," he instructed. *"The night may seem long, but it is the part of fidelity to watch and wait for morning."*[94]

The debate over Davis's supposed treason brought to the surface more significant concerns about the fate of the nation-state and the reputation of the United States in the world. Gerrit Smith, a former abolitionist and one of Davis's most unusual supporters, argued that "the law of war knows no treason." Convicting, imprisoning, or executing Jefferson Davis, Smith continued, would bring great "shame" to the republic, "the shame of abusing the power of success." "The holding of Juarez or some other Mexican Chief for treason," he explained, "in case we should conquer Mexico, would be a no more gross, a no more immoral, breach of faith than our holding of Jefferson Davis for it."[95] In contrast to Smith's position that "a rebellion is not a riot" or that "a civil war, conducted by armies in the field, dissolves the State, and places the contending parties in the position of contending nations," a *Harper's* editorial concluded that "no special plea, no appeal to history, no argument drawn from the fact of war, can obscure the plain fact that Davis's life is forfeit to the law."[96] Abolitionist Wendell Phillips, incensed by the release of Davis on bond, suggested that the former Confederate's sympathizers had made "treason . . . easy and respectable." "The nation which pardons criminals because it has not virtue enough to punish them," Phillips caustically noted, "is on the highway to ruin; but the nation that opens its prison-doors on the pretense that there is little difference between traitors and honest men, has accomplished more than half that journey."[97] The fate of Jefferson Davis, *The Nation* argued, was "not merely a contest for empire . . . not merely a struggle to settle a political difference, but a struggle between moral right and moral wrong." To argue otherwise, to diminish the significance of the war, or to repudiate the religious and moral significance of nationalism would render the principle of union a farce: "To Frenchmen and Englishmen the American flag, from a purely political point of view, was no more than the Brazilian or Paraguayan flag."[98] Comparing the diverse fates of Jefferson Davis and the emperor Maximilian (whose empire had ended in 1867 with his execution), one letter writer lamented the former's "escape from the hangman's noose" and enthused over the "brave death" of the latter. A response, published two days later, simply asked, "What is the Mexican nation?" and in doing so raised a very different set of questions: Was there, or had there ever been, a Southern nation?[99] Was Jefferson Davis a traitor? Or, as Gerrit Smith put it, was he something rather like a Juárez or a "Mexican Chief"? Or was he, indeed, like Maximilian, who had been installed by Napoleon, displacing Benito Juárez, and had welcomed Confederates into his Mexican empire? Was the union of states established in 1776 a special, blessed New World republic, possessed of manifest destiny and religious mission? Or was the United States about as unique as Brazil or Paraguay, which is to say, from the perspective of Europe in the mid-nineteenth century, not terribly unique at all? A trial would have raised these same questions. But Davis would not, in the end, be tried as a foreign national. He would not be treated as a head of state or as the chief executive of a defeated or conquered nation. Nor would he be treated as a lowly criminal. In the end, he would not be tried at all.

Upon being released, he left, first, for Canada, where Varina had sent their children and where he was greeted by a carefully orchestrated group of thousands. While there, he visited a small community of Confederate exiles in Niagara. He and Varina, then, headed back toward Mississippi, hoping to revisit Brierfield and to see his brother, Joseph, at Hurricane. "The Canadian winter," Varina explained, "proved too severe for Mr. Davis's enfeebled frame, and he was advised to spend it in the South." There were no masters in Canada. They traveled along the old circuits of the American Mediterranean, with stops in Key West and then in Havana. "We reached Havana just before Christmas," she continued, her prose turning florid and nostalgic. "The bright-colored houses which presented façades of green, pink, and blue, before which Moro Castle stood guard and glowed a soft rose color, seemed very strange, but we were after a little while generally in harmony with the brilliant tropical foliage and flowers that peeped out everywhere through the city." They stayed, as so many Confederate exiles did, for a week at Sarah Brewer's Hotel Cubano, a bountiful pied-à-terre for the old slaveholding South in Havana and a welcome respite from the unfamiliar Cuban diet offered elsewhere. Sarah Brewer "was a Southern woman of a respectable family," as Varina put it, "who owned and had successfully kept a hotel there for years. Her liberality and kind offices to the Confederates had been the theme of many panegyrics by them, and we found her kindness had not been exaggerated."[100] The Confederate exiles who gathered at "Ms. Brewer's"—chasing Northern travelers out of the hallways—were in search of new utopias.[101] Davis, in contrast, only stopped at the Hotel Cubano on his way home.

He returned to the ruins of his past life. There was a warm reception waiting for him in New Orleans, where Davis greeted the abundant and occasionally tearful crowds from the second-floor balcony of the St. Charles Hotel. Moving northward along the Mississippi, he stopped to visit his sister in West Feliciana, Louisiana. "The desolation which everywhere presents itself in that once prosperous country," he admitted, "fills my heart with sorrow."[102] Arriving at Brierfield, Varina remembered, "we found our old property destroyed, our friends impoverished, and our old brother very feeble but cheery." "As many of our negroes as could," she added, "came to see us." Joseph Davis, once one of the largest landowners and slaveowners in Mississippi, and the foundation of his younger brother's earliest success, had regained his land in 1866 and had leased Brierfield and Hurricane to Ben Montgomery, a former slave, in the hopes that the terms of the lease would provide a regular income. The old plantation house at Hurricane was destroyed. The flooding of the Mississippi had pinched off Davis Bend, turning it into an island. The Montgomerys, though able, were hamstrung by the crashing Southern economy and other factors beyond their control and were unable to pay for the property as quickly as the elder Davis had hoped. There would be no return, for Jefferson Davis, to the Old South, only a "cumulative sorrow over the changes wrought in his life."[103]

Judah Benjamin's route to the Caribbean was different. For him, the globally oriented, "hybrid" South might well have been the basis for his daydream of a Caribbean empire emanating from New Orleans, but it also served an important, practical purpose in the wake of the Civil War.[104] After the fall of Richmond, he rather dramatically fled the South, donning a series of elaborate disguises, including a cloak to hide his roundish frame, and several fake accents, heading always farther south toward the Caribbean, and escaping through the keys of Florida first for Bimini and then on to Nassau, Havana, St. Thomas, and, ultimately, England. Tellingly, his return to the West Indies and his departure from the conquered South relied on the very same social networks and commercial connections that he had once exploited as a planter and that he had labored to keep alive during the Civil War. He was, too, hardly alone in using these links to run away to the Americas. Jubal Early had followed a similar route, leaving the South through Galveston and stopping at Bimini, which he described as a "working settlement of negroes," as well as at the Bahama Banks and "Nassaw," and testing the waters in Maximilian's Mexico, before establishing himself in Havana. Indeed, for a brief moment after Lee's surrender, much of what remained of the Confederacy's leadership—including Early and Benjamin—was gathered at Sarah Brewer's Hotel Cubano in Havana, sipping dark Cuban coffee as the light from the hotel's massive windows fell upon them. They plotted their new lives and shared their stories, surrounded by slaves and slavery, by the sound of the *volante,* or by the *calisero,* or driver, bringing in the bags of the latest Southern exile to pass under the shadow of Castle Moro and enter the city of Havana. "The Hon. J. P. Benjamin and General Breckinridge were the first to arrive," Eliza McHatton, another such exile, remembered years later.[105] Someone walking past this hotel, looking in through the open window, and noting the torn, dirty uniforms, the quietly shared looks of fear and desperation, the more public expressions of bravado mixed with patriotism and enthusiasm for slavery, all of it staged in this second, quite familiar and more southern "South," would have seen the inner life of the planter class in its greatest moment of crisis. Perhaps the end of the Confederacy cannot be marked, as Emory Thomas once suggested, by Davis's capture and Edmund Ruffin's unrepentant suicide.[106] Perhaps the Confederacy lived on for a little while longer. "My motto," Early proclaimed in May of 1866, "is still 'war to the death.'"[107]

Were it not for the defeat of the South, Jubal Early's defiance would have been unnecessary. But perhaps he was destined to end up in Havana either way. In the years that followed Lee's surrender at the Appomattox courthouse, fantasies of Confederate triumph have been a revealing obsession of "Lost Cause" enthusiasts. In most of this self-styled "alternative history," the South looks southward, toward the Americas, soon after the war's end. In MacKinley Kantor's 1960 classic, *If the South Had Won the Civil War,* Cuba becomes "a plaything of young Confederates" in the 1880s, a staging ground for a second generation of *filibusteros,* and, in rapid succession, a territory governed by the Confederate States of America, a new Southern state, and "sugar capital of the world."[108] The more recent, wickedly satirical "mockumentary" *C.S.A.: Confederate States of America,* a faux filmic account of the Confederacy after its victory in the Civil War, begins with the exile of Abraham Lincoln and the free labor ideology to Canada and the permanent expansion of Southern slavery into Latin America.[109] Howard Means's futuristic thriller *C.S.A.* is set in a present that is rooted in the nineteenth century and Southern victory in the Civil War and begins with the rather startling premise that Jefferson Davis had long ago committed suicide through self-immolation and that the vast Caribbean is now simply known as "the territories."[110] In Harry Turtledove's novels, an early Southern victory brings with it the appropriation of Cuba and Mexico, and peace settlements with the North are modeled on Brazilian reforms of slavery.[111] Historian Roger Ransom's thoughtful exploration of the various "what if?" scenarios includes, among its many likely outcomes of a Southern victory, the acquisition of Cuba not long after the war's successful prosecution.[112] Such fictions inevitably depend on a myth of privation, defeat, and victimization. The Southern loss to the North, they suggest, was complete and total. There would be no "Caribbean empire," except in these counterfactual exercises, and no further perpetuation of the chivalric ideal, except in science fiction and fantasy. Sparta had crushed Athens. And Athens, in this telling, became a tightly held colony of Sparta.

The truth is far messier. Whatever relationship might have emerged from a more formal union of the South and the Caribbean, or might have continued as a reflection of less formal antebellum patterns and relationships, was rendered irrelevant by the certain outcome of the war. Slavery was a dead issue, forever haunting the mind of the South, but no longer a matter of flesh, leather, and iron. And if the wide and troubling sweep of Caribbean history had served as an encyclopedic guidebook of sorts for the slaveholding antebellum South, there were precious few positive lessons to be learned when the subject therein turned to emancipation. Still, some postbellum Southerners looked south again, for some approach or tactic that would enable them to control their previously bound laborers and to preserve what remained of the world of the slaveholders, from indentured servitude and the coolie trade, to European immigration for a system of apprenticeship. Others, less sanguine, perhaps, about what the short-term future in the United States might bring, simply chose to leave, imagining their often surreptitious departure or border crossing either as temporary escape from prosecution for war crimes or as a semipermanent exile. Eliza Frances

Andrews, bemoaning the slow death of "our doomed Confederacy," noted that "the men are all talking about going to Mexico and Brazil; if all emigrate who say they are going to go, we shall have a nation made up of women, negroes, and Yankees."[113] It was better to take a chance elsewhere than it was to stay behind, fearing that the South would become, in short order, a murderous charnel house or another San Domingo. These "Confederate colonies" in the Americas were, as one historian puts it, "a desperate foothold in the tropics rather than a realization of the once vibrant dream of a slave empire."[114] But they were real colonies or settlements, not just pipe dreams, and as such they revealed just how tightly connected the South had been—and still was—to the American Mediterranean, even after the war. Looking around at the conquered South, occupied by "negro troops," deserted by its slaves, controlled by the imperial idealism of abolitionists, and depopulated by death and destruction, it was better, some thought, to take flight. Some of these exiles from the new South would find themselves, like Jefferson Davis and Jubal Early, in Havana, taking tea at Sarah Brewer's Hotel Cubano and enjoying once again the gruesome comforts of slavery.

CHAPTER THREE

The Promise of Exile

So I rode away from Arlington, leaving the sugar-house
crowded to its utmost capacity with the entire crop of sugar
and molasses of the previous year for which we had been unable to find a market within "our lines," leaving cattle grazing
in the fields, sheep wandering over the levee, doors and windows flung wide open, furniture in the rooms, clothes too fine
for me to wear now hanging in the armoires, china in the
closets, pictures on the walls, beds unmade, table spread. It
was late in the afternoon of that bright, clear, bracing day,
December 18, 1862, that I bade Arlington adieu forever!

—ELIZA MCHATTON, *FROM FLAG TO FLAG* (1888)

In August of 1867, W. W. Legaré of Orangeburg, South Carolina, issued
a circular letter to his fellow Southerners, spelling out the grim circumstances that confronted the state and the region. "We cannot look upon
this country as *ours* much longer," he began. "Our best men are disen-
franchised, negroes are put into power," facts that would inevitably
erode "the chivalric spirit of the Southerner." There was, however,
cause for hope. Legaré informed the readers of his letter that certain
"gentlemen" had urged him to consider Brazil as a new home for the
South-in-exile. For a few years, former Confederate General William
Wood had been acting as an agent of possible émigrés from Mississippi,
Virginia, and New Orleans and had secured promises of land from the
Brazilian emperor, Dom Pedro II. Guidebooks for those interested in the
country were available throughout the South, and although reports on
Confederate settlements were mixed, the largest South American nation
offered, at the bare minimum, a warmer embrace than the victorious
North. Brazil, Legaré concluded, offered the better classes of South Carolina a chance at success and self-improvement away from the delete-
rious proximity of "lazy negroes and low lived whites." It offered "a delightful climate, an honorable and hospitable people, a most excellent
government, *stable* and *free* . . . [and] a fertile soil, yielding all our great
staples in profusion." It was also home to "*colonies of our Southern
people already established* in the most desirable locations—containing

hundreds of families, and growing larger every month." After collecting a total of $5 from fifty interested persons—the true purpose of the circular letter—Legaré hoped to travel to Brazil and to collect the details necessary for another permanent settlement in the Southern hemisphere.[1]

In the aftermath of the Civil War, more than a few Southerners considered relocating to Brazil, Cuba, Venezuela, or Mexico. By the thousands, they fled the place they knew best. Some simply wanted a new life in a new place, where hard labor could bring success. Some were looking for a comfortable, slaveholding alternative to the conquered Southern states. Most ignored local, Latin American distinctions that mattered—the concepts of "free wombs," self-purchase, skin color gradations that went beyond the black/white dyad, the rights to marriage and baptism enjoyed by some slaves—and focused instead on the institution of racial slavery in the abstract. Many were hoping to avoid the coming race war, foreordained by the arrival of "negro troops." Wherever they went, or wherever they dreamed of going, these Confederate expatriates often encountered strikingly similar debates about labor, land, race, and citizenship. Where and when they entered these debates, they did so as Southerners cast adrift by war, as Americans triumphant over their neighbors in the hemisphere, and as former citizens of two nations—the Confederacy and the United States. A sense of dislocation, diaspora, and exile settled across the depopulated and destroyed South. The world after slavery was much more frightening and potentially far less profitable. The twin ghouls of Haiti and Jamaica suggested that the near future of the region would likely be violent and traumatic and that the distant future would be hellish. The presence of "negro troops" made racial rebellion certain. And without slavery, the business of the South would grind to a halt. In this context, there were many different versions of W. W. Legaré, many different entrepreneurs and adventurers leaving the South to scout out suitable locations for a settlement of Confederates. For nearly all of them, the ideal site would have some form of slavery or dependent labor and a tradition of white supremacy or authority. And in nearly all cases, the new settlement would bring with it a commemoration of the Old South.[2] And yet, despite its roots in local circumstance, the establishment of these outposts was utterly dependent on older networks of exchange, older patterns of thought, and older understandings of the circum-Caribbean. Southerners engaged in this postwar expansion—a sort of extranational filibustering—drew deeply from their faith that the Old South was the superior part of a singular civilization on the edges of the "American sea," but they were also motivated by their fear that the earth had shifted under their feet.[3] In scrutinizing them, we capture the very last breath of the slaveholding Old South, exhaled, perhaps not so strangely, on safer, somewhat more solid, foreign soil.

Andrew McCollam, for one, set out in the summer of 1866 to investigate the range of options available to him. Like many others, he began with Brazil, assuming that the presence of slavery and a similar climate would allow him to easily transplant the Old South into the southern hemisphere. Perhaps, like many, he knew of the long-standing, multigenerational links to the "deeper South," connections that by 1860 had produced a "frayed idea of citizenship," pushing the planters of the South "away from allegiance to Washington and toward a firmer relationship with Brazil."[4] In the 1850s, McCollam had been the master of the old Tanner sugar plantation on Bayou Black in Terrebonne Parish, Louisiana. It had been a profitable decade for the former New York native who had turned South in the 1830s to find his future: under his direction, the plantation produced seven times more sugar in 1860 than in 1850, the number of slaves had grown from fifteen to eighty-seven, and considerable household debt had been replaced with a modest credit balance. McCollam had even ordered a new sugar engine and mill in 1860, assuming—as a Southern Whig—that the differences between North and South could be worked out peacefully. But the election of Lincoln and the provocations of South Carolina disproved this assumption, and so, like so many other Southern planter families, the McCollam's fortune on Bayou Black began to look a bit pinched. His familiar complaints included the charge that former slaves seemed bent on a redistribution of the wealth and had taken a few of his mules, and that it was increasingly difficult to grow and harvest cane at the same rate. Andrew's brother, John, ventured to New Orleans in search of pliant, docile freedmen, but with no luck.[5]

In the summer of 1866, Andrew and John traveled throughout the Caribbean and South America. Surveying across the Americas the labor problem that existed after the ban on slavery, Andrew hoped to find a suitable alternative to chattel bondage for the deteriorating American South. Like the "Confederados" who settled in Brazil after the Civil War, his exploration of Brazil was a search for a new home for a planter class considering exodus, but it was also a contemplation of the parallels between two multiracial societies with similar "problems" in the dusk of the slaveholding age. Docking at Saint Thomas in early June on his way to the east coast of the South American continent, Mc-Collam quickly noted the preponderance of "free negroes lounging on all quarters" in his diary and concluded that "the isleand [sic] is not cultivated" and that "fredom [sic] destroyed all agriculture."[6] If Saint Thomas was so troubling, perhaps the great empire of Brazil—the hemispheric counterweight to the United States—might offer some labor scheme through which the work of the newly emancipated slave could be controlled and redirected back to the needy plantations of Bayou Louisiana and the Mississippi Delta.

But from the moment McCollam arrived in Brazil, everything seemed just a bit off the mark. In Peidade, some twenty miles from Rio de Janeiro, he found soil conditions "no better in quality than those about Baton Rouge." "The country," he guessed, "has evidently once been in a better condition when slaves could be bought for $100 . . . but slaves at $700 worked on such land by such people will not pay." Indeed, it was doubtful that Brazil, with such exorbitantly expensive slaves, could support the lifestyle to which the old master class had become accustomed. The "finger of decay," he concluded sadly, "is everywhere visible." This poor opinion of Brazil would only get worse during his two-month sojourn. In mid-July, he encountered a planter from San Julien who was hopeful that white laborers could be brought from the United States and who complained that "the negroes wer [sic] passing away." McCollam divined that there were half as many slaves in Brazil as there should have been, and while this posed other obvious questions, it also answered his primary charge in visiting the empire: the search for a new home for the planter class of the South. Brazil, he concluded, wants "labor not capitolists [sic]. . . . And I think if we settle in Brazil we must look for competition and combinations against us."[7]

McCollam spent the rest of his travels investigating the quickening decline in Brazil's slave population. Still in San Julien, one planter showed him "conclusive evidence that the black rase [sic] will disappear on this continent in three or four generations," evidence pointing to the dangerously high ratio of male slaves to female slaves. In early August, a long evening stroll with another Brazilian gentleman produced a similar claim: "Mr. D. admitts [sic] that the negro will disappear from Brazil in 25 years. . . . [The] causes are the wish on the parte [sic] of the people to abolish slavery and the great preponderance of males over females. In such a condition there will be but few births." Throughout McCollam's diary, there are crude descriptions of "negroes equality," of the persistent social intermingling of black and white Brazilians on boats, in homes, and on street corners—on the River Paraiba, he saw "8 men half negroes & half white or nearly so . . . all chattering and eating together." Finally, on August 29, McCollam spent a day with fellow Louisianan John McCue in Pernambuco and was given "the most sickening picture of Brazilian society that [he had] ever heard," in which "the ludest [sic] conduct is no bar to a mans [sic] entree into society," and where there was "no distinction between the whites & negroes mixed and Indians except that produced by wealth." If Brazil succeeded in recruiting white labor from the United States and Europe, it would admit those immigrants as actors in McCollam's tragic nightmare: indiscriminate sex, race mixing, and no racially prescribed roles for anyone. "The President of Bahia," he wrote, "is anxious to see the negroes freed and their place supplied by poor white laborers from the U.S. [This] he said to McCue who told the President that he would live a damd [sic] long time before he would see that."[8] Brazil's "mulatto escape hatch," as described by Carl Degler, was, for McCollam, McCue, and others, hardly an escape hatch at all.[9] Perhaps not surprisingly, given his fears, McCollam left Brazil for New Orleans within the week, hoping for the cold comforts of the Deep South.[10]

McCollam was not interested in a solution to his problems that relied on wealth alone to determine social distinctions, but he was interested in the way that racial distinctions could determine wealth. On the voyage back to the South, McCollam continued to explore the racialization of work after slavery, participating—once again—in a personal dialogue with other planters from across the Americas. Much like he did in his interrogation of Brazilian planters, he pressed an Englishman "planting in Trinidad" for details about the "working [of] East India men," to which the Englishman replied that he "[did] not like China men." McCollam went to Cuba to further explore the issue of Chinese labor. A week later, after a bullfight, he left Havana early in the morning to meet with James McHatton and Richard Chinn, two renowned experts on the master class in exile. These two men were linked by marriage—McHatton's wife, Eliza, was Chinn's sister; she, in turn, was the true master of *Desengaño,* their substantial sugar plantation south of Matanzas, and often authored essays comparing Chinese coolies and African slaves for New Orleans newspapers. "Chinn," McCollam confided to his diary, "thinks [Cuba] a much better country to make sugar in than to live in." The "coolies," Chinn continued, "are all a set of Rascals [sic]," but "the poor white people of this country are good workers and can be hired cheap." But, McCollam asked, could the profits of sugar continue without slavery? Would white workers continue to be "cheap," or would Cuba, at that point, experience the downward spiral he had seen at Saint Thomas and, more troublingly, in Brazil? Chinn, ever the pessimist, could see only storm clouds on the horizon.[11]

Eliza McHatton's Escape

The foundation for Andrew McCollam's investigation of Brazil and the establishment of Southern "colonies" in the Empire had been laid during the Civil War, once the early optimism of Confederate victories had given way to the dreariness of a longer conflict and then, eventually, to the inevitability of defeat and prostration before the North. Flight was a certain topic of conversation, especially flight to Brazil, to Cuba, and to other similarly welcoming locations. For some, the urge to flee came in the wake of the Emancipation Proclamation, as Union armies swept into Southern states and upended the slave economy. For others, it came with the onset of Radical Reconstruction. In 1864, the port cities of Galveston, New Orleans, and Mobile were not yet the overexcited sites of Confederate exodus, as they would be in the later 1860s, but they were buzzing with rumors, and as the logical points of departure for Brazil, British Honduras, Cuba, and Mexico, they witnessed a slow trickle of the most disenchanted. Southern newspapers were beginning to advertise the possibilities of open land, easy labor, and rich soil in Central and South America. Only a few years later, the haunting specter of the former president of the Confederate States of America, Jefferson Davis, clapped in leg irons at Fort Monroe encouraged many Southern army officers and slaveholders to flee Dixie. When the time came to leave, small communities of true believers gathered in river cities along the Gulf coast and then fled the reuniting states, clinging to antebellum dreams of yeoman republics carved out of the wilderness and built on hard work, obedient labor, and racial entitlement.[12]

Of all these exiles, the few who went to Brazil and to Cuba are the most interesting—if only because they seem to have been wealthier than their comrades who went elsewhere and because they appear to have been more successful in reproducing the slaveholding society lost in the great conflict with the North. The exile stream to Brazil is more familiar to us today. A steamship line between Rio de Janeiro and New York had been established in 1865, inaugurated, ironically, by the steamer *Havana* in November of that same year. Brazil, the *New York Times* reported, was enthusiastic about the prospect of white American immigrants, but its minister of agriculture had forbidden the importation of slaves from the South; "they seem," the *Times* said of the Brazilians, "to mistake the South for the North, or to be entirely ignorant of the past of the late slaveholding and rebellious states."[13] Those Southerners who left for Brazil had no such ignorance about what had been lost in the war to free the slaves and what could be gained in emigration to the world's largest remaining slaveholding society. Still, they appear to have seriously misjudged the similarities between Brazil and the Old South, believing, perhaps, that the architectural and commercial parallels between Rio de Janeiro and New Orleans reflected nearly identical sensibilities about race and power.[14] In addition to the perils of settlement in an unfamiliar environment, the presence of a significant free African population and the comparatively playful relationship between race, skin color, and wealth—embodied in the Brazilian fantasy that "money whitens"—made it difficult to rebuild those moss-draped plantations that lived on in the imagination of the exiled South. As Andrew McCollam had learned, Brazil was, in some sense, the Old South turned upside down.[15]

Cuba was different. If British and American abolitionists saw Cuba as the most grotesquely abusive slave system in the Atlantic world, Southerners and venture capitalists from the eastern seaboard believed that the island had a certain mystique about it, an intoxicating aroma of decadence and profit, decay and slavery. In this case, Southern dreams of Cuba were largely accurate. In the 1840s and 1850s, as the growing split between North and South threatened to tear the United States in half, conspiratorial defenders of slavery and ardent celebrants of the "manifest destiny" of that country urged the purchase or even the outright annexation of Cuba from Spain. Southern slaveholders leapt to "claim" Cuba, lest Britain wrest control of the island away from Spain and surround much of the American South with "a cordon of foreign colonial governments, the population of which would be emancipated slaves."[16] Urging his fellow congressmen to consider the annexation of "this western *Eden*," Georgia's representative in the years before the Civil War, E. W. Chastain, could barely restrain his excitement over "the varied productions which spring forth spontaneously from her soil—salubrious in climate—exhaustless in her natural resources—she needs but the influence of American institutions, and the progressive spirit of American enterprise, to raise her to a condition that would challenge the admiration of the world."[17] By the mid-1850s, children of the Cuban elite were being educated in the United States, the island's sugar estates were populated with American mechanics, and a number of stateside Southerners were absentee landlords or property owners in Cuba. Goods and people regularly crossed from Mobile or New Orleans to Havana.[18] Still, the relationship between Cuba and the South was always something more than mere flirtatiousness and something less than marriage; so long as the antebellum political atmosphere had been thick with sectional conflict, the urge to annex Cuba and parts of Mexico would always come to naught.

When the North and South went to war, well-off Southerners who desired a mature slave economy with tremendous short-term potential looked to Cuba, not to Brazil or British Honduras, for their immediate salvation. One such person was Eliza McHatton.[19] Born in 1832 in Lexington and raised in New Orleans from the age of three, Eliza was a child of the American border surging westward during the nineteenth century. Her father, Richard Chinn, was "one of the first lawyers" in Kentucky, a partner of Henry Clay, and a man of tremendous personal fortune. He had a penchant for slaves and fine cigars, and he educated his daughter in French so that she might travel with him to Europe.[20] By all accounts, Eliza was a woman born into comparative affluence and was well schooled in European culture. But the New Orleans of her memories was not besotted with Victorian clutter. It was, instead, a muscular frontier synthesis of imported wallpapers and hard-worn homespun. In a conversational memoir written in the early twentieth century, Eliza persistently romanticized the spare furnishings and straightforward conventions of the frontier Gulf South in the age of Jackson. "It is hard to realize while we are surrounded by so many housekeeping conveniences what an amount of time, energy, and above all, knowledge of the craft were necessary to the giving of a reception seventy years ago," she wrote. There were, she continued, no "postmen to deliver invitations," only a "bewildered" and typically lost "darky."[21] Over the long course of her life, she would offer this tough, varicolored antebellum world as something precious and permanently lost in the wake of the Civil War; her memories of the heyday of slavery are laced with the same sensations of loss, wartime privation, and social turmoil found in the writings of many Southern slaveholding women.[22]

At the time of her departure from the South, Eliza was a young mother, thirty-two years old, with brown hair and brown eyes, a "fair" complexion, and an "Aquiline" nose.[23] She was married to James A. McHatton, a Louisiana and Mississippi planter with deep

A portrait of the young Eliza McHatton, reproduced as the frontispiece for her memoir, *Social Life in Old New Orleans,* published in 1912.

roots in Kentucky politics, whose forbears included a distinguished military man of the Revolution and a member of the House of Representatives, and who could list as onetime family friends the generals Lafayette and Jackson. If a New Orleans newspaper editor could describe Eliza as "one of the most elegant, intelligent and accomplished of her sex," James was likely just as dashing and famous, though his letters reveal imperfections of grammar absent in Eliza's voluminous correspondence.[24] He was, she remembered, a "far-seeing, cautious man," whose "disability, from the loss of an eye," meant that his heartfelt loyalty to the slaveholding South would be expressed in actions other than military service.[25] He also owned enormous plots of land and in 1857 donated two thousand acres to a plantation formed in partnership with Illinois senator Stephen Douglas in Washington County, Mississippi. (Douglas, for his part, contributed 157 slaves.) James and Eliza were, in sum, members of the elite planter class in the frontier South, a fact not lost on their children; when writing of his mother's side of the family, their son Henry would proudly note his great-grandfather's limitless wealth and his grandfather's frontier friendship with Henry Clay.[26] Eliza's marriage to James in 1852 was, therefore, a union of dynasties, and they soon settled at the handsome sugar plantation named Arlington; their attractive two-story mansion with fluted columns and alluring verandas was nestled up against the curving banks of the Mississippi just south of Baton Rouge. "We were born to [slavery]," Eliza wistfully remembered, "grew up with it, lived with it, and it was our daily life. We did it well; no people could have done better."[27]

She would leave the South ten years later, in 1862. As the Confederacy slowly collapsed, the trans-Mississippi became, as another exile put it, a "City of Refuge from which it is hoped a door of escape may be found to Mexico or Cuba."[28] Eliza's situation was no different: "We have been annoyed and harassed by the Yankees, until we begin to think the time may not be far distant when we will have to flee for our lives—We turn our thoughts to Texas—as a kind of 'Land of Canaan' to which we may have to journey, without a Moses to guide us."[29] Arlington had been a profitable plantation in 1860, but the years that followed had been disastrous. Union occupation meant brutish savagery and forced emancipation, and so the McHattons schemed to send their slaves to the Texas plantation of Eliza's "loving brother." Such a situation was hardly unique, as the *New York Herald* reported that "the rebels" had been running caravans of slaves to Texas and Mexico in the hopes, perhaps, of getting them to Cuba—one such group, captured by Union general Weitzel, was four hundred wagons large.[30] However, along the route to Texas, the McHattons' slaves elected, instead, to present themselves to the Union army and, in so doing, to escape their bondage. Concerned about freed slaves, Union armies, and social disorder, a pregnant Eliza found herself following James first to Texas and then on to Mexico in a slapdash escape from their old home.[31] In the year after their departure, the family plantation jointly owned with Stephen Douglas was sacked and looted by Union soldiers.

It would take them over a year to get to Cuba. No matter how disconcerting this vagabondage might have been, Eliza never seems to have lost her sense of the extraordinary power of race in her life. On the way to Piedras Negras and after four days of hard wagon trails, the McHattons entered "the scattering town" of Laredo, then a borderland nowhere-colony with its "numberless little, half-naked *muchachos.*" This did not mean, for Eliza, that Laredo was without a certain hideous charm. Upon entering the hamlet, the road-worn and tired McHatton entourage was greeted by small children running and clutching at the wheels of their conveyance. These happy children, Eliza presumed, conceived of her arrival as a world-changing event. "If they had ever heard of Queen Victoria," she wrote laughingly, "they might have thought she was coming to town, for I was the first *white* woman and my attendant the first *black* one the generation had ever seen."[32] The American memsahib had come to the threshold of Mexico, even if she arrived dirty and sweaty from her inglorious escape ahead of the marauding Union army.

As the sister city to Brownsville, Texas, the coastal port of Matamoros soon became the McHatton family staging area for an eventual move to Cuba. As James ran the Union blockade and sold cotton across Mexico and Texas, Eliza settled in, at least for a little while, and waited for the eventual departure for Havana. And although she was nearing the end of her pregnancy, she was a beehive of activity. She took a house, used two wagon covers as carpets, and put up some curtains and a screen to keep the mosquitoes at bay. She saw to it that Henry was sent off to a school and immersed in the Spanish language. She acted as chief financial officer for the family economy, handling the grim businesses of cotton and bondage with a skill born of several generations' experience. She did all of this, of course, with the help of a few remaining slaves. But Mexico, where slavery was already illegal, was hardly a safe haven. High-ranking Southern army officers may have shared a martial affinity to the emperor Maximilian, and in the aftermath of the war, agricultural settlements like Carlota might have sprung up overnight—but even during the war, it was clear to some that only Maximilian and the royalists in Mexico welcomed Confederate exiles and that these smallish expatriate communities could flourish only if protected by royalist troops. Tellingly, Eliza's brother, Richard, dined with one of Maximilian's adjutants in Matamoros before leaving for Cuba in 1864.[33] Maximilian, of course, was executed in 1867; Carlota was burned to the ground soon afterwards.[34]

Eliza could not have anticipated the execution of the emperor, but she had plenty of cause to worry about her future in Mexico anyway. Upon their arrival in Matamoros, Humphrey (the oldest of the three remaining McHatton slaves) had raced straight to the Mexican authorities. Fourteen-year-old Martha had already been too closely questioned by the *alcalde*, who had also tried to separate her from the McHattons.[35] The family's one other slave was Zell, a teenage Louisiana creole boy, whom Eliza described, using the vulgar vocabulary of slaveholding, as "black as ebony . . . with a big mouth, full of dazzling ivories."[36] In Mexico (and later in Cuba), Zell handled the horses, acted as a driver for Eliza and guests, and was a surrogate protector for her in the absence of her husband. He also shepherded young Henry to school and served as a critical financial agent, trading and bartering for much-needed supplies and quickly learning Spanish. Eliza clucked dismissively about his corner bodega schools where he provided English instruction for meager profit in his spare time. And she fussed over his supposedly deteriorating work habits: "We really had very little for Zell to do," she worriedly wrote to her sister-in-law, Anna. "If he had liked to cook & had been less dirty about it—it would have suited me to have made a cook of him—but Martha does better in the kitchen." To keep Zell busy, James and Eliza sent him to Havana. When they eventually joined him in Cuba, she believed, they would be "*nigger sure,*" an ominous, forbidding reference to their lust for slaves.[37] Within a few months, the family followed Zell to Havana in preparation for permanent settlement on the Caribbean's most profitable slaveholding island.

Eliza's life in Cuba was illustrative of the nineteenth century itself, when national borders were impossibly porous, when citizens of one nation or colony were very often landowners or occasional residents in another, and when the United States was just one of many white settler colonies or republics struggling to survive. And yet, this same century was also the great era of nation building, when national borders and cultures and destinies were being defined and redefined. Postslavery debates about labor, land, race, and citizenship were then as much transnational as national, as much about the fate of the master class everywhere as they were about a particular set of circumstances in one specific place. Eliza's attempts to grapple with the widening gaps between her interests as an American, her interests as a "white" person, and her interests as a slaveholder cast a bright light on those same postemancipation debates. But her story also illuminates other pressing and present-day concerns. Then as now, issues of capital mobility and the need for cheap and docile labor led Americans—and America—abroad. What we have, therefore, in this story of a Louisiana sugar plantation relocated to Cuba, is an earlier model of that process of globalization that leads modern-day companies like RCA to the *maquiladoras* region and Nike to the Philippines, or brings *domesticas* to California health care facilities and West Indian cane cutters to the sugar fields of Florida. One generation's slaves and coolies have evolved into another's H-2 workers and third world dispossessed; and Eliza's brutal chauvinisms are a crude precedent for the breezy and callous

A Havana street scene, captured in 1860 by George Barnard. Note the tall masts of ships in the background. From the Prints and Photographs Division, Library of Congress.

corporate style of the modern-day executive, relentlessly folding up factories and moving them to ever cheaper sites with little regard for the human cost.

For the true believers of the former Confederacy, the urge to flee to Cuba was strongest after Lee's surrender at the Appomattox courthouse. Once in Cuba, these angry, unforgiving enthusiasts of human bondage joined a heterogeneous ruling class of white planters, composed of native-born *criollos*, American entrepreneurs, and plucky escapees from other former slave societies, most notably rebellious Haiti or prostrate Jamaica. Like other unwilling American exiles, then, Eliza soon found herself in Havana and at the Hotel Cubano, where she and her husband were guests of the talented Mrs. Brewer, dining and gossiping with the finer class of Southern expatriates, most notably former Confederate secretary of state Judah P. Benjamin, former vice president and U.S. senator John C. Breckinridge, and Confederate generals Robert Toombs and Jubal Early.[38] Sarah Brewer, herself an expatriate American with considerable Confederate sympathies, ran the hotel on "American lines," where those who were "chafed at Cuban cooking" and were "sick of garlic and crude oil diet" could happily consume batter cakes and mince pies while proclaiming the virtues of the slave power.[39] There was a regular buzz about which famous (or infamous) Confederate had shown up, including a supposed sighting of Jefferson Davis in May of 1865; according to rumor, he had been shuttled to Matanzas from Galveston on an old Confederate blockage runner.[40] "How prosperous and rich Cuba was in those days!" Eliza remembered later. "How animated and gay! We arrived when it was at the very acme of its opulence, when fairly drunk with the excess of wealth and abundance."[41]

Coolies and Slaves

By 1866, James McHatton had purchased an impressive home from "a Cuban named Royo"—a former *cafetal* that had been converted by a Spanish slave trader into a sugar plantation.[42] Gathering up their possessions (including Zell), Eliza and her husband left for the aptly named Desengaño—in Cuba, the word means "disillusionment"—in Los Palos near Matanzas, on the northern coast of the island, some sixty miles east of Havana. The broad single-story home was whitewashed in the Spanish style, with Romanesque arches opening up a large veranda that, in turn, looked down a main entrance nearly one-third of a mile long and lined with mature palm trees, their smooth gray trunks reaching skyward in excess of one hundred feet. The house stood on an area roughly the size of a baseball diamond. In the bright sun, surrounded by the impossibly verdant green of the Cuban countryside, the McHattons' new home was a singularly impressive structure, "the most pretentious and substantial in the Matanzas district."[43] The property itself included more than one thousand acres, which demanded considerable brawn to produce profit. Within two years of the arrival of James and Eliza, there were sixty-five slaves at Desengaño (forty men and twenty-five women) and nineteen Chinese workers (all men) on temporary contracts. Those numbers would grow slowly over the decade or so that Eliza was in residence.

When visitors arrived at Desengaño on horseback or by *volante*, after taking the train from Havana to Matanzas, they passed first through a road lined on both sides with a short stone wall and then on through that grand avenue of palms. They would have seen impenetrably thick fields of cane growing up behind the stone or on the other side of the palm trees, with jumbles of shafts shooting off randomly in every direc-

Desengaño, c. 1867. The McHatton family can be seen at the end of the row of palms. From the McHatton Family Papers, Hargrett Rare Book and Manuscripts Library, University of Georgia.

tion. They would certainly have seen the mansion gleaming in the distance, bright white against a rich green backdrop. Off to the left was the tall, broad chimney and long roofline of the sugar mill itself. And there would have been slaves and coolies all around, bending and lifting, sweating and cutting cane. If the visitors came by *volante*, Zell would be seated right next to them, handling the lead horse.

Settling in, Eliza decorated her new Cuban plantation with those few remaining things brought from their old Southern home and marveled at the thickness of walls designed to stand up to the terrible weather of the hurricane season. With walls three feet thick, Eliza was safe—even during the 1870 hurricane that was rumored to have killed five hundred in Matanzas.[44] But if conjuring up furniture, tapestries, and silverware for the inside of their new home was relatively easy, populating Desengaño with the "right" sort of laborers for their *ingenio* proved much more difficult. Domestic labor, Eliza believed, was different than work in the cane fields. Remembering the "horrors of the early days," Eliza was most especially disturbed by the memory of "the black woman, in a dirty, low-necked, sleeveless, trailing dress, a cigar in her mouth, and whining child on one arm, [who] went about spreading the table, scrupulously wiping . . . plates with an exceedingly suspicious-looking ghost of a towel."[45] "Until a tidy Chinaman was installed in the kitchen," she remembered later, "I was very dainty."[46] And as for the many laborious tasks waiting in the cane fields, there simply were not enough African slaves to go cheaply around. A trusted overseer soon departed for Havana to "secure the only kind of labor available—Chinese coolies."[47]

Eliza's choice between African slaves and Chinese coolies reflected the changing economy of work in the nineteenth-century Caribbean. Before the so-called sugar revolution came to Cuba, the island had possessed only a smallish population of about 200,000, some 20 percent of whom were slaves. The lure of greater profits from sugar cultivation soon encouraged greater attention to this cash crop, and by 1828, Cuba was the largest producer of sugar in the West Indies—this despite having "only" 286,942 slaves, "a figure deemed highly inadequate for the successful pursuit of sugar cane growing."[48] For one absentee landlord from Bristol, Rhode Island, we can trace the exact moment he turned away from coffee and toward sugar to November of 1838, when he asked his overseer, Jose Seymour, if a plot of land near his "Ingeño Nuevo Esperanza" was "good sugar land."[49] By the 1850s, there were roughly half a million slaves on the island. To complicate matters, slave traders invariably tended to bring male Africans to Cuba, many of whom would be worked to death, leaving the island with a seemingly insatiable and counterproductive appetite for only male slaves. "Natural increase is disregarded," the abolitionist Joseph John Gurney noted in 1840 in a letter to Henry Clay. "The Cubans import the stronger animals, like bullocks, work them up, and then seek a fresh supply."[50] Long before the arrival of James and Eliza, then, Cuban planters had been worried about the production of sugar in the age of "the labor problem."

Wherever there was too much arable land and too little labor, the end of slavery engendered a serious "labor problem" that could be solved most easily with contract labor. After tentative experiments with freed slaves from the United States and the disastrous importation of Europeans, the British turned to another colony with a "surplus population": India.[51] In the case of Cuba, it was the end of the supply of slaves that posed the problem (rather than the end of slavery), but many of the pressures were the same. Planters there simply refused to give up slavery. Between 1800 and 1850, years that correspond roughly to the emergence of Cuban dominance of the trade in sugar, this Spanish island colony was transformed from a small, hopelessly backward outpost incapable of self-sufficiency to a magnificent entrepôt whose largest city, Havana, the most active port in the Caribbean, was often favorably compared to Paris. An illegal and highly profitable slave trade drove this rapid expansion, at least until the British (having freed their own slaves) began stricter enforcement in international waters. At that point, things began to get quite rough for Cuba. Planters and investors there could not boast of colonial ties to a land such as India, where poverty, famine, and "imperialist disruptions" drove thousands from the Raj to other British colonies suffering after emancipation, most notably Natal, Jamaica, and British Guiana.

From the vantage point of the 1860s, it must have been astounding to survey the transformation of the Cuban socioeconomic fabric. By then, Cuba had already been transformed by newer, more efficient technologies of sugar production and the massive construction of railroads that sped and cheapened the connections between coastal ports and inland plantations. A consortium of Cuban planters had invested heavily in telegraph lines and railroad developments and had imported newfangled machines that made the entire process of sugar refining more productive. Steel and iron were grafted onto abundant, uncontrollable plant life. These changes infused new lifeblood into the Spanish colony and into Cuban slavery.[52] "Progress is amazing," the *cimmaron* Esteban Montejo mused, remembering his first impressions of the new sugar mills. "When I saw those machines moving all at once, I was impressed. . . . They seemed to go of themselves. I had never before seen such progress."[53]

All this innovation, Eliza did not see. It was all right in front of her, of course, but her life—her past in the South, her disdain for those racially distinct from herself, her veneration of the United States—made it impossible for her to properly understand and appreciate the changes all around her. "The native Cubans," she wrote dismissively, "are a century behind the age in agriculture, as well as everything else." They were "a race that could not economize time, labor, or anything else." Visiting a neighboring plantation, she noted that "nobody seemed to be working, every living thing had a lazy, idle air." "Cuba," she summed up, "is a paradise for those who are too lazy to do anything but exist."[54] Here, then, were her American gifts to the island: a proper sense of time management, an acute awareness of how to better maximize profits, and the supposedly generous bestowal of technology and knowledge. In short, Eliza proposed a cold-hearted scientific management of bound labor and land in Cuba and offered it as if she alone (and certainly no Cuban) could see its virtues. She had the hubris, as well, to suggest that the harvest of guano from the local mountain caves was an idea whose value was lost on those "thriftless Cubans" all around her—though there was much contemporaneous excitement about this prospect throughout the Americas.[55] Members of the Cuban planter class who visited Desengaño, she wrote with great self-satisfaction, would gaze in spellbound adoration at the McHatton family library, as if the rows and rows of books brought from Arlington were ironbound chests washed up on a beach and the information within, pirate treasure. Such was her life as plantation mistress in supposedly backward Cuba, where she had only enlightenment to impart and nothing at all to learn herself.[56]

The emergence of the Cuban "coolie trade" was contemporaneous with the island's technological innovation in the mid-nineteenth century. If the planters could not, or would not, have any more precious African slaves—precious because, as in America, they were thought to be physically and temperamentally suited to work in tropic climates—they wanted only the "right" sort of labor as a replacement. Driven by fear of black rebellion (a fear exacerbated by census numbers from 1841 indicating that slaves outnumbered whites), Cuban businessmen and planters had vainly struggled to encourage widespread "white" immigration to Cuba, largely from Spain.[57] A slave rebellion in 1843 encouraged the *Junta de Fomento y Poblacion Blanco*, a corporation of planters and other interested parties, to authorize a contract for over five hundred white laborers.[58] The next few years witnessed the arrival of a few thousand immigrants, many of them from Ireland or the Canary Islands, who were put to work on modernization projects geared toward making the transport and processing of sugar more efficient.[59] But the Irish were too expensive, and they wilted under the oppressive heat, and the several thousand Galacians brought in—"Spanish Irishmen," as they were called—soon broke into open mutiny.[60] The shortage of workers on sugar plantations threatened to undo everything. Cuban advocates of white immigration would never convince large numbers of Europeans to head for the Greater Antilles in the age of emancipation. Unlike Brazil, where the labor "crisis" came later, they were forced to look outside of Europe for a way out of their quandary.[61] Laborers had to come from somewhere, the great planter Miguel Aldama believed, even "from Siberia, if necessary."[62]

In 1847, much like the rest of the Caribbean, the West Indies, and Latin America (most everyone except Brazil, in fact), Cuban planters began to turn to the human abundance of Asia, and more specifically to Chinese laborers tricked or coerced into boarding coffin ships, as the solution to the perennial problems of scarcity and cost. The first group of Chinese coolies arrived in June of that year. They were subsequently doled out to "the island's most prominent planters and a railroad company."[63] Champions of "Asiatic colonization" stressed the economy and efficiency of their new field hands, railroad builders, and factory workers and urged planters to consider the "in-born" intelligence of the Chinese when deciding on certain punishments. Those seeking greater numbers of Africans blamed the failures of the former slaves of Jamaica on abolitionist permissiveness, also hinting that the Chinese were pitifully weak and brought with them numerous epidemics. Strict rules and uncompromising authority, not wages, were what the emancipated slave needed. Despite the debate, the combined influx of these two unhappy peoples, the U.S. Consul reported, had at least lowered the price of slaves considerably.[64]

For transplanted Confederates in Cuba like Eliza and her husband, the need for labor thus came down to a hard choice between two very dissimilar peoples ("stupid negroes and dazed Chinese," Eliza called them), one inexpensive and the other familiar, one "tidy" and the other not.[65] The first group of Chinese coolies "bought" by James McHatton might very well have come aboard an American vessel, on a voyage quite similar to that of the New England ship *Forest Eagle,* which unloaded its unfortunate human cargo at Havana on July 4, 1861, just a few years before the arrival of the McHattons. Indeed, though the *Forest Eagle* may seem horribly unlucky, there is no reason to describe its trip—and the travails of those aboard—as anything other than typical of the trade. The charter for the coolies was issued by the firm of Koopmanschap & Bosman, well known for its expertise in this matter. Again, as usual, nearly all of the Chinese on board had given their occupation as "farmer," and they were all male and under thirty years of age.

Bound for Cuba from Macao, the *Forest Eagle* was captained by Thomas Pillsbury, a stalwart Maine sea captain with some experience hauling sugar from Cuba to London. The ship carried five hundred "Emigrants" (as the log book described them) under the control of John O. Shaw, the "Coolie Master" assigned to the voyage. The ship was cramped, and the coolies were tightly packed below decks, except for their daily "airing." The presence of the coolie master testified not only to the significant profits to be gained from the coolie trade, but also to the lessons learned from over twenty years' experience in the trafficking of Chinese bodies, for he was there, ultimately, to prevent two things: revolution and disease at sea. The handwritten set of instructions given to Pillsbury by the ship's owner described Shaw as a veteran of the Cuban coolie trade. Pillsbury was given significant—though not unusual—financial incentive to keep as many Chinese coolies alive as possible: an additional $5 a head if the mortality rate did not exceed 5 percent and $3 a head if it did not exceed 10 percent.[66]

The ship left for Havana—studiously avoiding all American and British ports along the way—on the 9th of February. Onboard and now at sea, the coolie master, Shaw, carefully chronicled the obscurant hygiene practices of the mid-nineteenth century, from the use of vinegar to clean the decks, to the use of chloride of lime below decks, to the denial of cold water, which was thought to lead to diarrhea. He also struggled to uncover various plots to take over the ship, either through the explosion of stolen gunpowder or through the poisoning of the ship's crew. A number of coolies committed suicide, and an even greater number seem to have attempted it at one time or another and were put in irons for the attempt. Opium use—and withdrawal—was another complication. And Shaw's desire to feed and hydrate the coolies and thus keep them content was often at odds with Pillsbury's interest in keeping the overhead down. On March 13, Shaw doled out over seven hundred pounds of rice, "the largest amount yet"; the very next day, Pillsbury, fearing a steady increase in the cost of food, set seven hundred pounds as the absolute daily limit.[67]

Pillsbury would not collect his bonus. By April, the passengers on the *Forest Eagle* were suffering from various dietary and venereal diseases, with symptoms ranging from rheumatism and diarrhea to an extreme swelling of the penis. The modest fatality rate of February quickly bloomed into more gruesome daily death tolls, a trend accelerated somewhat by an increasing number of successful suicides. By May 19, the day the ship arrived in Havana harbor and was immediately placed in quarantine, forty-four of the Chinese on board had perished; by July 4, the day that the quarantine was lifted and the cargo was transported to shore for sale, another sixty-nine had died. Out of five hundred coolies booked to Pillsbury and the *Forest Eagle*, only 387 arrived "safely" in Havana. There is no way to know how many survived their first month in Cuba.[68]

The arrival of Chinese contract laborers forced dramatic changes in Cuban culture, not the least of which involved radically shifting meanings of race and labor.[69] "Once the quest for agricultural laborers for the Cuban planters had shifted from Europe," historian Franklin Knight writes, "the words 'white' and 'free' underwent an interesting semantic change."[70] As non-Africans, the Chinese were sometimes legally classified as "white" and "free." Their "voluntary" labor contracts, one scholar notes, studiously avoided any mention of race, and the coolies themselves were referred to "euphemistically as 'colonos asiáticos.'"[71] Pillsbury, Shaw, and Boye repeatedly described them as "emigrants." But however "white" the Chinese were in Cuba, the reality was that they suffered under the lash much like slaves and were "bought," not "hired," by their new creole masters, often in the same open air markets where slaves were sold. By 1860, all Chinese coolies were forced either to re-sign contracts at the conclusion of their original eight-year labor term or to leave the island.[72] And more important, they found themselves suffering extreme mistreatment and familiar abuse; as one Chinese laborer in Cuba put it in 1873, "I was treated exactly like a negro slave."[73]

Their appearance also sharpened racial sensibilities by forcing some slaves away from work requiring technological skills and limiting them to work primarily as field hands and manual laborers, further solidifying the connection between blackness and backwardness. Here, Eliza McHatton's disdain for her African house woman and her eager appreciation of the Chinese cook were part of a broader racial division of labor. When Eliza advised the readers of the *New Orleans Times* (who were then thinking about getting coolies of their own to replace newly emancipated slaves in the United States), she described her erstwhile Asian cook as entirely ignorant of English or Spanish or of the virtues of the Victorian home. "It was astonishing," she wrote, "the rapidity with which he learned. At first, by dint of soap, and ashes, and rags, and signs, he was given to understand that 'cleanliness was next to godliness.' So he rapidly got 'order out of chaos' in our Cuban kitchen, over which a Creole darkie had ruled supreme." He had, she claimed, learned everything about the culinary arts and the keeping of a Caribbean kitchen in less than a week. Indeed, within just a few busy years of her arrival at Desengaño, Eliza had even come to believe that the Chinese were better in the home than the Irish— "As a house servant, John is preferable to Bridget," she wrote.[74]

Other Cuban planters were also "learning" that Chinese laborers were best suited to "household service" or "lighter work in the new and modern sugar mills."[75] A contemporary of the Cuban planters, Ramón de la Sagra, suggested that the "initial disappointment" in Chinese coolies stemmed from a deeper ignorance about how "to use or manage a more intelligent labor force."[76] Some came to believe that the Chinese were strikingly different and that "practical" grimoires written to advise sugar planters on "breaking in" new slaves were useless when it came to "the celestials."[77] U.S. Consul William H. Robertson even suggested that the African slaves were themselves almost immediately aware of this distinction and had "great confidence" in the natural wisdom of the Chinese; "Negroes," he offered, "have already been heard to remark, '*Los Chinos saben mucho*' . . . and on being questioned why they say so, the reply is again, '*The Chinese know much; they know everything.*'"[78] "The Chinese," Eliza summarized comparatively, "were intelligent."[79]

The novel diversity of Cuba's labor force was a source of great fascination for outsiders. One American visitor, who commented on the use of "Chinese masculines" in lieu of women and slaves in domestic work, described the situation as "funny," further noting "the curious and out-of-place position of everything useful and useless."[80] Others developed complicated interpretations of the Cuban racial division of labor, with some tasks perfect for the Chinese and others allotted to African slaves on the basis of attitudes and abilities unique to particular tribes. A popular travel guide opined that the Carabalí were "by nature traffickers," that the Congos made better house servants, and that the Lucimí "prefer[red] the monotonous labor of the water carrier." "The Africans," the author concluded, "retain their clanship in Cuba . . . with [their] own polity, relations, and a world of ideas and thoughts, to which the whites can rarely, and then only superficially, penetrate."[81] For those who longed for a more "traditional" in-home servant class (Richard, Eliza's brother and partner in Cuba, still preferred the Irish), things could get even more confused and disorderly. Eliza's nephew relayed complaints about the "hysterics" of one particular Irish maid who longed to return to the United States: "an old bad tempered Irish woman is the *biggest* lady in the house & has already threatened three times to leave."[82]

Just as many wondered at the whiteness of an upper crust suspended somewhere between the questionable achievements of Spain and the more troubling world of racial amalgamation in Cuba. Noting that the features of "whites" in Cuba were outwardly "opaque" and "beautiful," one unnamed author wondered whether there was any inner beauty: "I wonder," he or she asked, "where the Cuban people keep their souls?"[83] "The more we see of the Cuban character," Eliza confided to her sister, "the more we are convinced that a military government is what they need. They are totally unfit for freedom & the pusillanimous puppies will never have it unless some strong nation fights for it, for them."[84] The average Cuban, she argued elsewhere, lacked a refined awareness of social boundaries, choosing to dangerously mingle with all sorts of undesirables "at every street corner and every cross roads grocery."[85] Eliza was hardly alone in thinking this way. Indeed, many of her contemporaries saw the future of democracy in Cuba as one of American outsiders gently and slowly leading the childish *mestizaje* toward "civilization." As early as 1873, popular penny plays staged on the eastern seaboard of the United States urged either direct American intervention or individualist participation in Cuba's wars for independence. Perhaps the most telling of these was *Little Cuba*, an unflattering fictional story of how one young white woman, in "male disguise" and aided by the timely arrival of U.S. forces, "led" and inspired the dusky masses of that "Western Eden" to victory.[86] Even small and dainty white women, the lesson went, were better able to fight for freedom than Cuban men, whether Spanish, African, or Chinese. This protracted commentary about the abilities of Cubans—white, black, yellow, and everything else—to properly govern themselves socially and politically would eventually inspire the turn-of-the-century generation to satisfy its long-standing fantasies about white American stewardship of the island.[87] And to a certain extent, it continues to do so today in the age of the embargo.

Nearly every visitor to Cuba studied the Chinese, the most confusing addition, they thought, to the political economy of slavery. Consider, for instance, the travel memoir of Samuel Hazard, an aging Civil War veteran who suffered from an infernally weak constitution and who therefore took an extended holiday in the opulent surrounds of Cuba to regain his strength. Once settled into his daily routine of bacchanalian dining, flirtatious exchanges with "the sly and retreating segnorina," and luxuriously sexualized baths, Samuel could hardly restrain himself from extended discussion of the dissimilarity between the toil of Asians and Africans. Wherever he saw the Chinese, they seemed to be generally well clothed, hard working, and engaged in labor that required some manner of technological sophistication. Surveying a cigarette factory in Havana, he found much to approve of in "the facility and dexterity" of the Chinese workers, all clad in their "blue dungaree clothes" and "scrupulously neat and clean."[88] In contrast, he sketched "colored human nature" as pure, unadulterated laziness. His drawings of "the negro" in Cuba are grotesquely comical, featuring cartoonishly large breasts, the barest rudiments of technological intelligence, open mouths, doltish expressions, and a striking absence of gender differences between African men and women. "Now mark that great negro," he urged his readers, "with his ridiculous looking wheelbarrow, appearing as though it had come out of the ark, such is the simplicity of its construction; the negro himself, without head covering, with as little clothing as the law allows . . . generally ragged pants, and a portion of a shirt only."[89] "Did you ever see anything more disgusting," Hazard asked, echoing Eliza, "than that great negro wench—a large clothes basket on her head, a colossal cigar sticking out from between her two thick lips, while she walks along, majestically trailing an ill-fitting, loose dress?"[90]

On this exact comparison, Eliza McHatton gained a certain amount of well-noted expertise, publishing short essays solicited from her by popular newspapers in Louisiana, where there was some interest in reproducing the supposed successes of the coolie trade.[91] "Buying a chino," she reminded her readers, was tricky business. It began with an ethnological process of "selection," wherein a coolie with "a good face" was chosen from the lot as they left the boat after their "long hard ocaen [sic] voyage" from China, as if their physical strength and mental character could be more clearly divined when they were at their weakest.[92] After a brief period of seasoning during the first year, a carefully chosen coolie would work as "regular as an automaton."[93] The machinelike result was perfect, she believed, when paired with the tropic brute strength of the bestial African slave. "The Chinese," she advised, "when once acclimated and accustomed to the routine, were docile and industrious; they could not stand the same amount of exposure as an African, but they were intelligent and ingenious; within-doors, in the sugar factory, in the carpenter-shop, in the cooper-shop, in driving teams, they were superior to the negro."[94] But Cuban "negroes," Eliza thought, were perfect for the dreary, mindless, bloody work of cane harvesting—they were, she concluded, "more or less stupid and stolid, like 'dumb-driven' cattle."[95]

Beneath this chilling debate about the abilities of Africans and Asians lay a plantation economy that only occasionally used contracted laborers differently than it did slaves. "Many of the Chinese," one historian writes, "were not employed with machinery at all but were used as agricultural workers, performing precisely the same tasks as slaves. . . . This is not to deny that indentured laborers stood, to some extent, in an intermediate position in the labor hierarchy and were on occasion perceived as especially suited to work with machinery."[96] Indeed, it seems quite likely that, despite a popular sense that the Chinese were ideally suited for house labor and were adroit at mechanized tasks, decisions about the actual use of contract coolies were made on a planter-by-planter basis. Many, however, were clearly convinced that Chinese coolies were better at skilled labor and lacked the purportedly tropical constitution of Africans, a conviction that grew in strength as modernization of the sugar industry proceeded.[97]

The relationship between Eliza McHatton's slave Zell and the Chinese is not nearly so easy to summarize. Several times (to Eliza's chagrin) Zell served as a gentle mediator of sorts between the concerns of Asian contract laborers and those of Eliza. At other moments, Zell's liminal position worked to Eliza's advantage. In the mind of the planters, the "natural" intelligence of the Chinese for more sophisticated work could pose other problems and seemed often to lead to collective legal action. "These indentured laborers," Rebecca Scott writes, "were aware of a distinction between slave labor and free, one which they felt was not being observed."[98] One morning, Eliza remembered:

Our ears were assailed by a low, rumbling noise in the distance, which rose rapidly to shouts and unearthly yells. . . . The Chinese were in full rebellion: stripped to the middle, their swarthy bodies glistening in the hot sun, they rushed with savage impetuosity up the road, leaped the low stone fence that surrounded the cluster of plantation-buildings, of which the massive dwelling-house formed the center, brandishing their hoes in a most threatening manner, and yelling like demons, as with hastily grasped rocks from the fences they pelted the retreating overseer.[99]

After invoking the grand leitmotif of Southern race relations—the threatened rape of a white woman by a person of color—Eliza's memoir only casually mentions the ultimate cause of the uprising: a "demand for an unlimited supply of food."[100] Perhaps her own tightfistedness was to blame, as she was perennially in search of less expensive fare for her coolies and was prone to test the tender limits of their hunger.[101] But on this particular day, the truculence of the Chinese at Desengaño ended quickly once Zell fired a gun into the air. And to ensure that such wanton displays of technological mastery would not be needed in the future, Eliza had their queues, their "long pig-tail," removed. "How quickly they wilted!" she squealed, "how cowed they looked!"[102]

Zell's broader role at Desengaño was understandably unique. His arrival with the McHattons set him apart from the plantation's slaves and coolies. He was American; he was Southern; he was a creole from Louisiana. He had control of a dangerous weapon, an ancient blunderbuss, as well as a pocket watch with which to mark his duties and those of others. In public, he acted as Eliza's ceremonial *calisero,* the driver of the trace horse of the *volante,* though she also described him as a simple *mandadero,* or messenger. As the *calisero,* he would have been gaudily dressed, wearing gold-plated buckles and bracelets, a formal uniform of some sort, and feather-plumed hats of spectacular scale. Given his young age and the range of horrible possibilities in Cuba, that position would have indicated to all that he was a favorite of some kind (whether he wanted the reputation or not). I can find no reference to him cutting a single piece of cane or working a single hour in the sugar house. Still, he acted as a critical liaison between Eliza and her laboring force, teaching them English, learning their many languages even as they learned his. He appears, therefore, to have mastered the art of shuttle diplomacy, keeping the diverse and conflicting interests of the McHattons, the various African peoples, and the Chinese in reasonable focus—no easy task considering that he was the only line of communication between any two of these groups. His developing skill with numbers would have been as important to the Chinese, who were concerned about being cheated, as it was to Eliza, who was equally concerned with maximizing profit.

A *volante*, possibly driven by Zell, pulling away from Desengaño, c. 1867. From the McHatton Family Papers, Hargrett Rare Book and Manuscripts Library, University of Georgia.

If the Chinese understood that their role in Cuba was that of "free labor," or even of "free white labor," that understanding never translated into any of the real social privileges accorded to European immigrants in Cuba, in the United States, or anywhere else. The report of the Chinese Imperial Commission of 1873, which visited Cuba to investigate rumors of mistreatment and breach of contract, is replete with stories of abuse and protest, of resistance and legal argumentation. "The administrators and overseers are as wolves or tigers," Ch'ên Ku complained to an investigator of the Imperial Commission. "When they detect only a little slowness in work they chastise us until the blood drips the ground."[103] "Five months have now elapsed, during which no wages have been issued to me," Lo A-êrh complained desperately. "If I ask for wages the threat of chaining is made. I in all earnestness now meditate suicide."[104] Trapped in the barracoons at night, stuck on a hot, lonely island in the Caribbean, the Chinese worked in burned-out fields of sugar cane, and they were beaten ruthlessly until they worked "like slaves." "The Chinese didn't fly," the former slave Esteban Montejo once remembered, but "they sure did kill themselves. They did it silently. After several days passed, they appeared hanging from a tree or lying dead on the ground. Every thing they did they did silently."[105] "I have seen some 20 men commit suicide," Lin A-pang remarked sadly, "by hanging themselves and by jumping into wells and sugar cauldrons."[106] Hoping that in death they would return to their faraway homeland, half of all suicides in Cuba in 1862 (173 out of 346) were committed by Chinese contract laborers.[107]

American interpretations of the suicide of the Chinese were often ghoulishly clinical, revealing an abiding concern for rich profit margin and little else. Visitor Julia Woodruff, for one, only noticed with disdain that the Chinese seemed stuck in "a state of chronic sullenness" and took "comfort" in that "their propensity to suicide operates as some check upon the worst forms of cruelty."[108] Eliza's brother, Richard Chinn, believed that a few clever Chinese coolies had faked their deaths by suicide to escape bondage.[109] Eliza herself blithely suggested that the "nostalgia" and "melancholia" behind the self-destructive urges of the coolie in Cuba were limited to the "the lower classes" and should be understood as evidence of mental defect.[110]

Twilight of Arcadia

By the mid-1870s, the spectacle of abuse and the regularity of suicide led China to quickly foreclose any attempt at a renewed agreement with Spain and to end "the coolie trade" to Cuba. Indeed, in its report of 1876, the Chinese Imperial Mission sent to Cuba to investigate the persistent rumors of coolie abuse found much truth in the charge that the Chinese were treated poorly. There had been rumors of an end to the trade for some time, but the damning report issued by the Imperial Mission sealed the fate of *la trata amarilla* to the Spanish Caribbean. Where once African slaves had been inexcusably expensive and there were too many Chinese coolies, now there was soon to be too few of either. Of course, the Confederate exiles at Desengaño were already busy trying to protect their role as slaveholders in Cuba. Indeed, at the first rumor that the agreement with Spain would soon end, Richard Chinn rushed out to inspect six coolies newly contracted to a dissatisfied planter outside of Havana. He happily paid $700 in gold for them—roughly the cost of one very good male slave—and bragged to Eliza that it was quite a bargain, as they were already seasoned to the Caribbean climate and had "gotten through their change of blood."[111] Richard went so far as to "spoil" the Chinese, providing them with what he believed were too generous quantities of food.[112] At another point, on the verge of losing some of these priceless coolies, he and Henry McHatton, Eliza's son, raced to Matanzas and begged the intervention of a Spanish official to force these unhappy sojourners to re-sign with the transnational planter family from Desengaño. "It was," Henry wrote to his mother, "just the closest shave that I ever saw."[113]

The era of human bondage, the McHatton clan unhappily concluded, would soon pass, and with it "the *dolce far niente* of the sweet Arcadian life."[114] In the midst of competition for coolies and slaves, there were those, Richard wrote to Eliza, who "consider the time for manual labor & constant following of negroes & chinese as over. They aim to ride about, call here & there—entertain and be as popular as possible & by doing so get the whole place in their hands . . . all of this of course at the expense of the owners."[115] "The free negroes & poor whites are very scarce," he complained in another letter.[116] Looking back on the middle years of the 1870s, when competition with new European beet sugar manufacturers added further torque to the intensifying pressure for laboring bodies, Eliza could only offer her disgust with what had become of her precious tropical paradise at Desengaño. "During the latter years of our residence," she wrote bitterly, "the gradual emancipation of slaves was enforced, the importation of coolies prohibited, and, as an inevitable sequence, an untold number of valuable estates were abandoned by their impoverished owners, thereby revolutionizing the entire financial and domestic status of the island."[117] For Eliza, Richard, and many others, all of this was unthinkable. "A few years later," she remembered, "we left the island forever."[118] And by 1886, the last contract had expired and slavery had been formally abolished.[119]

In the midst of Radical Reconstruction, soon after the McHatton family fled to Texas, to Mexico, and then to the island of Cuba, letters from home seemed to emphasize the dangers of living in the conquered Southern states. "Nearly all the [legislators in the] house are Negroes," James wrote to Eliza from New Orleans in 1867, "things look gloomey here & everyone I have conversed with appear to be down harted."[120] Cuba, in contrast, seemed to have precisely what the postbellum South lacked: most particularly the human bondage that made intensive agriculture profitable and, more generally, clearly defined social roles for everybody, with the whitest folks as the top rail. But as the idealism of Reconstruction collapsed under the weight of political compromise and then quickly faded from memory, the American South and Cuba seemed to be on different paths—the former rebuilding its regional commitments to white supremacy but dependent on the North in disturbing ways, the latter engaged in a remarkable series of anticolonial struggles against the aging Spanish empire and profiting from nearly half a century of technological investment and modernization.

In 1868, an unbalanced coalition of Cuban dissenters—ranging from planters who witnessed the collapse of the American South with horror and who favored very gradual emancipation, to free people of color hoping for an immediate abolition of slavery—found common ground in distrust of Spain and launched an armed rebellion that would last ten years. Although antiracism was only occasionally (and usually rhetorically) at the forefront of this so-called Ten Years' War, the revolutionary Liberation Army was a sizeable force composed of every conceivable group of peoples in Cuba, including both former slaves and coolies. The contrast between these two places, then, would grow stronger with each passing year, for the trend in the South was toward separate development and racial hierarchy. "The escalation of racial violence, the spread of spatial segregation by race, and the dismantling of political gains made during Reconstruction in the South," historian Ada Ferrer sums up brilliantly, "occurred in the United States precisely as black and mulatto leaders gained increasing popularity and power in Cuba."[121] This world turned upside down, when coupled with the imperatives of demographic parity between "blancos" and "negros" and the gradual emancipation of the slaves, would have made balmy Cuba seem much more immediately threatening than the United States. Indeed, Eliza's reaction to all of this cannot have been much different than one unnamed Gilded Age traveler who appreciated the restorative qualities of the clear air, blue water, and lush landscape but who loathed the "crowds of African negroes black as night" with their exuberant Emancipation Day celebrations, which he ridiculed as "thoroughly nigger."[122] Cuba was no longer the lost world of the Old South—it was, instead, the New South gone mad.

"We never for a moment contemplated a return to the United States,"

Eliza McHatton explained, "until peace was restored and quiet assured."[123] However, for these American expatriates, the same revolutionary forces of freedom that had driven them abroad into the Caribbean and Latin America now encouraged another exodus back to the United States. The "Confederados," displeased with the future of slavery in Brazil, were now famously returning to their "erstwhile homeland," appearing somewhat chastened but also emboldened by the growth of Jim Crow, the "peaceful" social guidelines of the postbellum South.[124] Eliza, too, wondered whether it was time to complete the circuit. "When my family went to Cuba," Eliza wrote in 1912, "it was to escape from war troubles at home. We sought for rest and peace, but it was not long before we felt we may have 'jumped from the frying pan into the fire.'"[125] The advent of the Ten Years' War witnessed the devolution of Cuba into an unwelcome state of "lawlessness," and the now aggressive attitude of men of "diminutive size and questionable appearance" posed serious threats to the safety of Eliza, herself the flower of white Southern womanhood.[126] Soon, she and her daughter were unable to "promenade" anywhere other than on the carefully groomed, tree-lined avenue that led to their plantation home. Her husband, James, had died unexpectedly in 1872. The specter of rape and murder at the hands of smallish, swarthy brigands of "inferior" type was everywhere. But in America, regional rapprochement and the emerging architecture of Jim Crow would provide precisely the sort of "quiet" for which she and her husband had so eagerly hoped. Although she had escaped a war to free the slaves once before, to McHatton the powerful antiracist rhetoric of the Liberation Army, with its well-armed men of many colors, seemed even more dangerous. No wonder, then, that Eliza soon chose to leave Cuba altogether, leaving their trusted slave Zell—who, she remembered fondly, always signed his letters "esclavo"—in charge of Desengaño.[127]

Leaving the slaveholding lifestyle behind for the uncertainties of the postemancipation United States was cause for reflection. Henry, now in his twenties, stayed on as an occasional assistant to his uncle Richard at Desengaño. He spent most of his time there engaged in self-described "manly" pursuits—hunting and writing, brawling and smoking cigarettes, "carrying a life in your hands always"—and Eliza worried about him constantly. In 1877, he sold Desengaño for a mere 100,000 pesos, an amount far less than they desired, as the pace of robberies had increased. More than a few of Henry's closest friends had been killed by armed bandits, leaving him filled with melancholy about Cuba and the world of his childhood. "Life in the yela," Henry summarized in the concluding passages of his diary, "has been even harder this year than at any other time. Now I leave that life, perhaps forever. . . . I walk away with a lot of sadness."[128]

Like Henry, Eliza would never again find what she had at Desengaño. Arlington was lost, and the old Chinn plantation just a few miles upriver from Baton Rouge had been doomed when the Union army had cut a nearby levee. In her final years, Eliza would warm herself with memories of that homestead, recalling how each visit would commence with her running "to find mammy first thing" and how that woman would "fold me in her warm embrace." "That hospitable house," she lamented, "has long since vanished into the river, with its store of pleasant memories."[129] Cypress Hall—worth $11 million in 1852—was in ruins by the end of the war, and as it slipped into the Mississippi, so, too, did the lifestyle that best suited Eliza. When Alfred R. Waud, an artist and illustrator for the *New York Illustrated News* and *Harpers,* traveled up the Mississippi during Reconstruction, he captured the demise of the great plantation, finding only shadows and ghostly columns and a single, solitary freedman on a small skiff—poignant reminders of what had been and what could never be again.[130]

Remarried to Dwight Ripley, a lawyer from New York City, Eliza had a new baby and a young daughter from her marriage to James to worry about. The newborn occupied most of her time. "The library," she wrote with tired contentedness, "is littered with blocks and toy books." Still, she could not let Cuba go. Before the baby was born, she had regularly taken a steamer to Havana and then caught the train out to Matanzas, where Zell or some other slave would be waiting in the *volante.* When at home in Brooklyn, she kept a series of "Chinese knives," taken back from Cuba, on a display table in the library. She was hard at work (in her spare time) on her memoirs of a peripatetic life along the Caribbean and on a series of semifictional stories about Zell and Mammy, about coolies, and about sugar cane. She was biting her nails, again. And she was dreaming of the "Ever Faithful Isle." "I fell asleep last night thinking of you," she wrote to Henry. "I dreamed that I went to Havana with four trunks . . . and the vessel was ordered to land her passengers in California and go by stage to Havana and I was in great stress about my baggage."[131] Eliza missed her old life and could not get it back.

For his part, Zell stayed on in Cuba, married an Afro-Cuban woman named Maud, and started a family. When Eliza sold Desengaño, she arranged for Zell to procure U.S. citizenship and, by her recollection, deposited a small amount of money in a bank account for him. She also

The ruins of the old Chinn Plantation, from a chalk sketch by A. R. Waud, c. 1866. Courtesy of the Historic New Orleans Collection. Accession no. 1965.49.

bound him by contract to the new owners of the estate, much like the Chinese coolies he had chased away with the blunderbuss that morning. In the concluding passages of her memoirs, as her thoughts turned to those left behind in Cuba, Eliza recalled the many letters she had received from Zell. She commented on the signature line he attached to each missive: *"Serviente,"* she wrote, "was the conventional phrase used from equal to equal, and may not have appeared expressive enough to suit Zell, so it was *esclavo*."[132] Perhaps this is so. But Eliza preserved every possible shred of paper relating to her sojourn in Cuba—every passport, hundreds of letters, countless Spanish and American documents—but not much from Zell. And against the grain of her intentions, he emerges from her memoirs as a clear-eyed, politically savvy, and otherwise intelligent person, who could hardly have been unaware of the contradictory drifts of Cuban and American politics. He was still young and now multilingual and binational in ways that Eliza (always the self-styled expatriate) could never be. And by the late 1870s, it would already have been clear that, for a former slave, universal male citizenship was a hardly a panacea for what ailed the United States; an antiracist republic jointly led by people of color was likely to seem far more promising. The same forces that lured Eliza back and drove her from Cuba most likely kept Zell there.

Eliza published her memoir, *From Flag to Flag*, in 1889, only a few years after a royal decree brought an end to slavery on the island. She had been working on the book since her return from Cuba, polishing her melancholy commemoration of the Old South, and bemoaning the destruction of her beloved Arcadian paradise. The nostalgia of a younger generation of readers for the supposed chivalries of the antebellum South and the Confederacy ensured a welcoming reception, especially for the memoir of a great cosmopolitan planter, a child of the globe-trotting elite. Hailing the work as "a contribution to the new Southern literature," one reviewer noted that "she can write of all that is past without the shadow of bitterness." A professor from Tulane, offering his assessment of the work in a letter to the *Picayune*, remembered Eliza as a "handsome, sparkling" child and praised the "sweetness of temper" in the work. In the uniform praise for the book, there are echoes of the great and calamitous compromises that followed Reconstruction, reminders that the "bloody shirt" had already been buried, and a yearning to read Eliza both as a "woman of the South" and of the United States. "Her hardships are endured with the rarest pluck and good humor," one review noted, "and her shifty way of meeting difficulties seems almost to point to a Yankee strain in her blood."[133] But despite the reconsolidation of the South into the republic, the cover of *From Flag to Flag* reminded readers of a different kind of border-crossing connection and called attention to the author's onetime embodiment of part of the world that had long laid claim to multiple, overlapping identities. Three frames ran from the top to the bottom of the cover. At the top, there was an image of Arlington, Eliza's fairytale manse, surrounded by tall tress dripping with Spanish moss and hugging the east bank of the Mississippi. At the bottom, there was the white façade of Desengaño, with the avenue of giant palms and the tall chimney off to the left, peeking through the thick foliage. In between these two images, a black-bordered square showed only untamed tropical wilderness, an homage to Eliza's middle passage between the two Souths. And in the background, providing an organic architecture to the whole set of vignettes, two long stalks of sugar cane stretched for the sky, rising uncut from the ground. Eliza, the cover suggested, may have traveled to Cuba, from the domain of one flag to another, but she found it to be surprisingly familiar, a slaveholding version of the changing same.

CHAPTER FOUR

The Labor Problem

The same phenomena are following closely on the heels
of emancipation here as in Jamaica, and with even
greater rapidity.

— "LESSONS FROM EXPERIENCE," *NEW ORLEANS DAILY
CRESCENT* (DECEMBER 21, 1865)

For those who stayed behind, and who resisted the urge to flee to Cuba,
Brazil, or Mexico, the immediate reaction to emancipation was informed by the hemispheric history of slavery. In the summer of 1865,
white Southerners in the Deep South were, as they saw it, confronted
with a serious, unprecedented labor problem. They took cold comfort
in noting that this problem was fairly common in every developing
world. Almost every other slave society had confronted the end of
chattel bondage, and most—by the South's careful measure of it—had
failed to meet the challenge. There was, it seemed, a sort of iron law at
work, governing the fate of these societies. In the wake of emancipation, crops were invariably ruined, social codes were always upended,
and racial lines were uniformly transgressed. More often than not, it
was believed, only terrible bloodshed could consecrate a new postslavery society. It had been so in Haiti and in every subsequently emancipated place. Those repeated failures had been, of course, incorporated
into the proslavery argument as evidence. But these failures were also
useful signposts for the postwar era, when it became necessary to
fashion a full-scale response to what historian Ira Berlin once called
"freedom and freedmen." Planters, politicians, and ordinary white
folks had generations of local knowledge to draw on, including the
lengthy corpus of laws devoted to the control of free blacks in the antebellum slaveholding South.[1] They could draw, too, on preexisting vagrancy laws that were class inflected or on laws of apprenticeship that
were meant for orphans or wards of the state. For some, the story of

Jamaica—where slaveholders had been paid for the loss of their laborers and where slaves trained for years to work as free labor—served as a touchstone for Southern discussions about the future. But the great planters of Jamaica, as almost everyone knew, had not survived. Their world had been lost. What, Southern planters asked, could be gleaned from that great and tragic vanishing?

Apprentice

In 1837, three years after the end of slavery in the British West Indies, James Williams, a former slave, described his "total liberation from apprenticeship."[2] "I am about eighteen years old," Williams began. "I was a slave belonging to Mr. Senior and his sister." Williams had been one of some fifty or so slaves on the smallish pimento plantation "Penshurst," owned by Gilbert William Senior and his sister, Sarah Jane Keith Senior. Williams's *Narrative of Events,* published in England in the midst of other scandalous news of the West Indian penal system, was explosive enough to warrant, in a brief preface, the sworn affirmation of "two free negroes and six apprentices, all members of a Christian church in Jamaica." Those witnesses testified that the story of James Williams was, in fact, a true and honest account of life after abolition in what had once been the world's largest sugar-producing and slaveholding colony. If his opening remarks used the past tense to note what he had been—"I was a slave"—the rest of his *Narrative* focused on more recent concerns: specifically, on the evils of the apprenticeship laws that were, in theory, to have guided former slaves into a Protestant work ethic and, as importantly, to have kept the labor-dependent sugar industry afloat in the age of emancipation.[3]

Three years earlier, like many other former slaves, James Williams had been made an "apprentice"—a bound laborer, obligated by contract and by law to work a certain number of hours each day for a specific number of years. For "Mr. Senior," this narrow time frame was a license to "weaken" him, as Williams put it, which meant, in practice, that the former slaveholder limited provisions far below what had been doled out during bondage and that he increased the use of the lash. "When I was a slave, I was never flogged," Williams noted. "Since the new law begin, I have been flogged seven times and put in the house of correction four times." After an aborted escape, Williams was sentenced to nine days of detention at the St. Ann's Bay workhouse, where he received fifteen lashes upon his entrance and "danced the treadmill morning and evening," a reference to the compulsory work performed by apprentices in penal mills, where those former slaves who had been labeled idle or lazy were tightly bound to massive wooden treadwheels and forced to turn them with their legs, or "dance," as he put it, for hours.[4] As Williams and others saw it, the apprenticeship laws had become carnal and violent, more a matter of punishment than of reform. Apprenticeship itself was worse than slavery. *"Slavery has not been abolished,"* wrote his interviewer; rather, "it exists with unmitigated rigour, in its most ferocious, revolting, and loathsome aspect."[5]

Williams had escaped to London in late 1837, where he—his life, his *Narrative*—were quite quickly turned to good use by the movement to end apprenticeship, and most notably by Joseph Sturge, one of the principal figures in that struggle. The anti-apprenticeship movement, much like the antislavery movement, used the formulaic "narrative" of an "escaped slave" as a public weapon against the institution of racial slavery and then arranged for speaking tours by the most eloquent former slaves. Ends and means, however, did not always match up. Sturge's proprietary feelings about Williams—his desire for control of Williams as a useful weapon in the struggle, his concern over the former slave's supposedly "indolent" behaviors, and his sense that Williams had found interests outside of the anti-apprenticeship movement—led to a deterioration of their relationship. Four months after he arrived in London, James Williams was returned to Jamaica. In one of the great ironies of world history, the chief witness at the trial of gradual emancipation and the apprenticeship system was sent back to the site of his most famous punishments by his chief counsel, Joseph Sturge, who went so far as to ensure that Williams was apprenticed into a good trade in Kingston upon his return to the island. Even the most stalwart critic of apprenticeship, it seemed, could be convinced that labor and hard work, not life, liberty, or the pursuit of happiness, were what the newly emancipated African needed.[6]

Apprenticeship was not slavery, but neither was it freedom. The half-life in between these two poles was a consequence of the need for labor, the power of the planters, and the nearly universal sense that coercion was not just a hallmark of slavery but also a standard feature of the relationship between labor and capital. With emancipation, wrote James Phillippo, a British missionary to Jamaica, "Man now ceased to be the property of man," but the "humane and well-intentioned provisions" of apprenticeship "were evaded and neutralized by local enactments and by partial and viscous adjudication." "During the short period of two years," Phillippo summed up mathematically, "60,000 apprentices received, in the aggregate, one quarter of a million lashes, and 50,000 other punishments by the tread-wheel, the chain-gang, and other means of legalized torture."[7] Simultaneously embarrassed and outraged by revelations of abuse, the British brought the apprenticeship period to a quick and early conclusion in 1838, accelerating a downward spiral for the colony. As the labor-starved plantocracy faltered and as former slaves left for the truer freedom of the inland regions of the island, Jamaica's sugar production declined. Early efforts to secure white immigration failed.[8] "Labour," noted one visitor in 1835, "is a disgrace for a white man in all slave countries."[9] The introduction of "coolies" (or temporary contract laborers) from India or China could not stave off the stumbling fall of Jamaica and the startling rise of Cuba, where slavery was still legal and coolies were a complementary—and not a replacement—labor force. By the 1860s, popular travel accounts—like Anthony Trollope's oft-cited and thoroughly dismissive *The West Indies and the Spanish Main*—emphasized the awful consequences of emancipation and the end of apprenticeship: a population of "idle" former slaves interested only in "lying in the sun and eating yams."[10] Jamaica now stood with Haiti as an object lesson for slaveholding societies in the age of emancipation.

"I know of no country in the world," admitted former Jamaican governor William G. Sewell in 1862, "where prosperity, wealth, and a commanding position have been so strangely subverted and destroyed, as they have been in Jamaica."[11] Still, not everyone agreed that the story of Jamaica was exclusively tragic. For free African Americans and abolitionists, the celebration of the first of August as "Emancipation Day" had been a standard event since the early 1840s, featuring all manner of parades, formal "Emancipation Balls," and even steamboat cruises, and including communities as far away as Canada and Liberia. Black Americans, Frederick Douglass noted, had "no July fourth here," a bland truth that turned the "Anti-Slavery Pic-Nic" into a celebration of universal freedom in the abstract.[12] During the American Civil War, the radical abolitionist movement in the Northern states portrayed West Indian emancipation as a startling economic success. Challenging two decades of proslavery finger-pointing, Lydia Maria Child, Lewis Tappan, and others offered a different interpretation of the island's supposed collapse, noting, for instance, that the end of slavery had witnessed the breakup of larger plantations and the end of the West Indian sugar monopoly. When these factors were taken into account and when one also considered the stabilization of sugar yields in the 1850s to preemancipation levels, freedom looked less like a dangerous experiment and more like a modest success. Of course, abolitionists generally employed a fairly unique calculus when measuring that success, "plac[ing] the Negro's welfare above questions of profit and loss."[13] William G. Sewell's two most oft-cited conclusions—that free labor was a "superior economy" to slave labor and that the emergent, productive black middle class in Jamaica was hardly lazy or idle—were, of course, perfectly unsurprising consequences of the end of the "old plantocracy." Success, for Sewell, was measured against general markers of economic productivity, not by the perpetuation of the planter class, nor by the willingness of the freedmen to labor for their former masters. The moral logic of this argument would have been appealing to the merchant class of New York and Boston or to policymakers in the nation's capital, who feared that the end of slavery in the American South would ruin the national economy. But it was an argument prepared, by and large, for Northern tastes and appetites and not, conversely, for the Southern palate.[14]

For the British, the apprenticeship laws were a humanitarian disaster and their removal, no matter the result, a triumph of liberalism; for American abolitionists, the collapse of the Jamaican economy was the result not of emancipation but of other economic factors; for the U.S. South, these appraisals were completely reversed. By the middle of the nineteenth century, Jamaica had become a powerful symbol of what Thomas Holt has called "the problem of freedom" in the United States, a symbolism that was even more greatly important in the aftermath of the Civil War. The island narrative of decline and disintegration dramatized the uneasy relationship between notions of free labor, race, and coercion. Jamaica served as a sort of conceptual shorthand for the process of emancipation; it could be used to parody the soft-hearted radicals from the North, or it could be used to frighten Southern legislatures into quick action. Doubtful that freedmen might be ready for the "duty of regular, continuous, faithful, methodical labor," one newspaper noted that weak laws would only encourage former slaves to flee the plantation, as they had in Jamaica: "The humane philanthropists of Great Britain preferring to see the negro relapse into barbarism rather than subject him to . . . restraint and compulsion . . . made no provision by which the planter can be assured of the certain and faithful labor of his hands during the term of his hiring, and hence the planters and capitalists abandoned the island and have never returned to it."

"Our reformers and industrial organizers," the newspaper concluded
presciently, "must be prepared to content themselves with like results
from persistence in the same policy."[15] In short, without some version
of apprenticeship, or some form of like-minded coercive scheme designed to keep blacks at work on the plantations where they had previously labored as slaves, the South would, like Jamaica, become a
hellish, rebellious nightmare.

If some planters took refuge outside of the South, others sought to
apply the knowledge of the slaveholding American Mediterranean to
the new postbellum milieu. This was especially true in the summer and
fall of 1865, before the civil rights laws of Reconstruction were put in
place. During that summer, the state of Mississippi—the first of many
states to pass laws regulating the lives of the freedmen—showed that it
had been meditating on what to do about the freedmen and that it had
been closely watching the drama in the West Indies. In the brief window
of time between the end of the war and the onset of Radical Reconstruction, the state legislature and two successive governors acted to
preserve the tattered remnant of Southern lifestyles by passing a wide-
ranging set of laws that mimicked some of the most powerful features
of apprenticeship. To put "the Negro" back to work in good speed, to
offset the chance of a St. Domingo or of a Jamaica in the Deep South,
and to check the ill-conceived humanitarianism of "the Jacobins of the
North," the Mississippi state legislature authored the Black Codes.[16]
The codes were "race-specific"; focused exclusively on the freedmen
and, in the parlance of the day, on "mulattoes"; and included vagrancy
laws, compulsory employment, restrictions on movement and the ownership of private property, and strict moral and economic guidelines for
the control of "the Negro." The purpose of these laws, much as in Jamaica, was to shore up white supremacy and to ease the transition to
free labor by restricting as many of the privileges of freedom as
possible—especially those related to work and social liberty. Both the
Black Codes and the Jamaican laws sought to replace physical compulsion with legal and penal compulsion, holding physical violence, flog-
ging, and the biblical thirty-nine lashes in reserve for the laziest, least
capable freedmen. Both relied on new and extraordinary judicial improvements, from stipendiary magistrates in Jamaica to county courts in
Mississippi. And both mandated that former slaves should and must
work and relied on emerging postslavery links between the achievement
of civilization, the cultivation of good work habits, and the accumulation
of profit, along with the equally powerful association of laziness with

savagery. The Black Codes were short-lived, imposed by the state governments of the American South on former slaves in the months right after the Civil War, and were quickly undone by the passage of the Fourteenth Amendment by an increasingly radical Congress, which understood the codes to be nothing more than a new form of slavery; apprenticeship was installed by Parliament at great cost to the British public and was meant to mitigate the immediate effects of abolition in the British West Indies, though it quickly devolved, in the public eye, into another form of "SLAVERY in its darkest shades."[17] Both the codes and the Jamaican laws established state control over the movement of freedmen, over the conditions of their labor, and over their right to free speech and assembly.[18]

Desiring safe labor and fearing rebellion, apprenticeship was one frame of reference for the South, but there were others, too. Indeed, in sorting through the tangled issues of citizenship, labor regulation, and the meaning of freedom in a war-torn, multiracial postemancipation society, the debate over "the future of the Negro" in the American South drew on several wildly different, if sometimes overlapping, traditions of historical and legal interpretation. Locally, there were the immediate precedents offered by the Freedmen's Bureau, alongside the history of poor laws and slave courts in the South. There were also the state and federal constitutions, which were in drastic need of realignment after the end of slavery and which, even at the federal level, offered no singular guidance on the competing and color-coded citizenship claims of the postwar South. Then, more broadly, there was the enormous body of law and custom—national and international—on the uneven relationship between masters and apprentices, ships and sailors, labor and capital. "There are certain classes," one editorial concluded, as it weighed the merits of binding blacks to the land, "such as sailors and apprentices, clerks, overseers, and others, whose faithful execution of their engagement involves so seriously the rights and interests of others, that the law provides stringent and rigorous measures to compel them to perform their contracts."[19] Third, there were the immediately relevant and unhappy precedents of Haiti, routinely described as hell in miniature, and the West Indies, where the attempt to provide planters with compensation and temporary labor had been, at best, a mixed bag. Finally, and most powerfully, there was what some in the planter class might have called "natural law," a philosophy of historical racism that drew from the same wellsprings as Darwinism: "No two races," the *Daily Clarion* professed, on the first day of the Mississippi state convention in August of 1865, "so unequal as the Caucasian and the African can exist together in the same space upon the terms laid down in the abolition platform. One must inevitably give way to the other, and it is not difficult to tell which one must give way."[20]

The vocabulary of this discussion can be confusing. "Let the untrained and incapable African be placed under the indentures of apprenticeship to his former master," pleaded the former Confederate secretary of the treasury, Christopher G. Memminger, to President Andrew Johnson.[21] As a reflection of the postwar South, Memminger's request exposes the multivalent and interlocking meanings of the words "apprentice," "freedom," and "labor." "Freedom," for instance, could mean the right to run away, as James Williams did, and also the right to fairly negotiate over the terms of a contract to buy or sell. It could also, conversely, capture the sense of danger in the air, specifically the racial threat posed by unfettered and presumably embittered Africans in the South. "Apprentice" was, likewise, a word with a long history but no singular meaning. It could refer to a state of legal paternal guardianship or to a period of craft training, or it could be shorthand for "former slave," as uttered by former "masters"—an expression, therefore, of the hope that one could take those "untrained and incapable" freedmen and reduce them, as "Mr. Senior" did, to some poor measure of their previous existence. The word "labor," at last, could allude to organized labor, to labor republicanism, or to the dignity of hard work, but much of the time it was described as a commodity, for sale or for purchase, and as such was often a signifier of "the Negro," who had only recently been just that. The significance and meaning of "wage labor" in the North was, even then, just as confused, overburdened with metaphors of slavery and sex, so it should not be surprising that the very terms of "the Labor Question" in the South should be so completely confounded.[22]

"The Labor Question" could, of course, also be about land. The problem in Jamaica, most planters understood, was that former slaves had been eager to become individual proprietors, to own land or work land on their own. In the South—where the traditional Jeffersonian love of the yeoman farmer was still strong—the presence of free blacks was doubly dangerous. Although it was not always framed in this fashion, a certain kind of algebra was at work in most Southern fears. If "the Negroes" were not working for whites, they might be independent or working for themselves. And if they were working for themselves, they might desire to own property, to buy some small parcel of land. And if they were small farmers or owned their own property, they could use that Jeffersonian archetype to make a powerful point about their role in the postbellum South and about their full citizenship. Southerners talked about "labor" because, in the end, it was a safer word than "land." When, in late 1865, freedmen decided to hold "back on any commitment of their labor until the question of land had been resolved," their actions revealed the dialectic between these two concerns. And when parallel rumors circulated among both blacks and whites that the federal government might "take away the planters' lands" at Christmas and "give it to the colored people," the fears of a conquered population were revealed.[23]

"Compulsion" was another vitally important keyword. In the weeks after the end of the war, the issue for Mississippians and other Southerners was ultimately one of practical control—more specifically, how to best encourage black bodies to labor. Variants of the word "compel" appear in every newspaper, legislative forum, or diary, though the word and the concept certainly meant very different things to different people. The drive to closely manage newly emancipated African Americans and to spur them back to work was a reaction, in large part, to the local travels and labor relocations of the freedmen across the South, suggesting that the freedom of movement was the most powerful and dangerous freedom of all. To correct the impulse for self-improvement shown by African Americans, much of the South chose the proverbial stick over the carrot. Traveling through Mississippi on a fact-finding mission, Union army officer and Republican raconteur Carl Schurz noted that "those who like to whip a negro but do not like to pay him wages" universally believed that freed Africans could only be made to work with "physical compulsion."[24] "Wages," here, were reflections of the freedmen's humanity, of their emerging status as individual actors, capable of bargaining for the worth of their crops or, indeed, the worth of their labor. Most, however, chose to see it differently. Only through draconian jurisprudence and hair-trigger violence, white Southerners argued, could the degeneration of "the Negro"—manifested in thousands of "documented" cases of rootlessness, immorality, and laziness—be slowed or halted.[25] "When the work becomes oppressive and severe," the *Daily Picayune* commented, "the negroes will dodge outright, take to the woods and the swamps, and live on fish and game, and let the plantation go to the bad."[26] For the planter class, any movement at all was simply too much. Writing in 1864, James Lusk Alcorn of Mississippi predicted disaster: "Our negroes will soon be ashes in our hands," he wept angrily, "our lands valueless without them."[27] "Unless the

Southern fields can be successfully worked by the white man," one newspaper editorialized, "our prosperity will never return. Our land will never be valuable. We should . . . use all the negro labor possible . . . [but how] can this kind of labor be made available?"[28] This great fear throughout the South—a fear, in some sense, of abandonment—was strengthened by a strong global and comparative perspective. The inland farms and great alluvial valley of the Mississippi River, the agricultural lifeblood of the state, would follow Jamaica into the abyss if the newly freed labor force of "Negroes" were not disciplined, controlled, and protected from their own proclivity toward uselessness and transport in freedom. "The free negroes of Georgia," one planter averred somewhat nervously, "will not deteriorate so fast as those of Jamaica, because they are more in the presence and competition of white men, and the country is not so insular."[29] What might have been seen as the actions of a self-interested body of laborers was, instead, reduced to a simple but awfully useful racial stereotype.

The need to reestablish control over former slaves was also consistent with the broader reaction of the planter class to the end of slavery throughout the Americas. "With the exception of Haiti," historian Pete Daniel reminds us, "the old planter classes continued as the exploiters; their attitude changed little from slavery days. Nearly all plantation areas emerged from slavery with parallel ideas and laws that perpetuated forced labor. To foster labor discipline, vagrancy laws appeared. To guarantee steady work from planting to harvest, contracts bound workers to the soil. Supply merchants or planters encouraged workers to become indebted to them and bound them tighter to the land with peonage. Throughout the plantation areas of the world, involuntary servitude continued after slavery was legally abolished."[30] The "labor problem" in the South was, then, just one chapter of the bigger story, the hemispheric "problem of reconciling force with freedom, and liberty with necessity" in postemancipation societies.[31] But this would hardly have been a novel idea in the nineteenth-century South. The collapse of Jamaica was meaningful to the planter class precisely because of these parallels and because Jamaica had once been the crowning jewel of the slaveholding world, and the Deep South had never been more than a hardscrabble knock-off of its wealthier, more prosperous Caribbean cousins. The pull of history—the link to the Americas and the shared circumstances of emancipation—was precisely what concerned the master class of Mississippi, South Carolina, and everywhere in between. Memminger's plaintive cry for "the bonds of apprenticeship" had a certain explosive contemporary meaning and was a reference not only to the formal contract between skilled artisan and his pupil, or to a ward of the state, but also to the disastrous and brief legal relationship that had existed between former slaveholders and former slaves in the British West Indies in the first few years after slavery. Likewise, when Judge Evans of Vicksburg, a candidate for Congress, reminded his fellow Mississippians that "we do not want the scenes of St. Domingo and Hayti repeated in our midst," he was speaking literally or, if you will, analogically.[32] Unless the circumstances of the South changed, unless "the Negro" was removed or hammered by brute force into compliance, the past was an iron precedent: a repeat of the collapse of Jamaica or the racial rebellion of Haiti would be foreordained. When, in 1865, rumors of unrest in Jamaica were transformed into reality, when word of the Morant Bay rebellion spread to the United States, these two dreadful concerns—Haiti and the West Indies—collapsed at precisely the moment when the state of Mississippi was debating the passage of the Black Codes.

The General Strike

It was the summer of 1865, and Union general Carl Schurz was anxious. Schurz was a first-generation German American with an extraordinary political mind. W. E. B. Du Bois would later say of Schurz: "One the finest type of immigrant Americans, he had fought for liberal thought and government in his country, and when driven out by the failure of the revolution of 1848, had come to the United States, where he fought for freedom."[33] A deeply committed liberal, Schurz had actively wooed his countrymen in the new world to the Republican cause in the election of 1860 and had been a wartime appointee of Lincoln to the Union army, despite a military pedigree that was limited to book reading and research in the library during his brief term as minister to Spain. He was a confident, assertive radical presence in Republican circles, consistently offering advice to Lincoln and firmly planted on the far left edge of the political spectrum when it came to "the Negro question." Lincoln's assassination in April, as the war came to a close, had cut Schurz to the bone. Lincoln, he wrote to Fredrick Althaus, "was the living embodiment of the popular will." As Schurz saw it, the destructive Civil War had come to a close as a result of Lincoln's determination and intelligence, and the country would miss the Great Emancipator's intuitive understanding of the need for a proper and patient governance of the reconciliation of North and South.[34]

Carl Schurz, c. 1875. From the Prints and Photographs Division, Library of Congress.

Schurz's greatest anxiety stemmed, however, not from Lincoln's death but from the actions of Andrew Johnson, Lincoln's successor, in the early stages of what is known as Presidential Reconstruction. Johnson, he wrote, comparing him to Lincoln, "is a narrower mind."[35] To the great surprise of the general, Johnson had decided to hold the trial of Jefferson Davis in secret (against the advice of Schurz) and had also called for the white folk of North Carolina to reform their government (also against the advice of Schurz). The closed trial of Davis, Schurz advised Johnson, would only raise suspicions that the United States had something to hide, and the encouragement of North Carolinians, he feared, would soon put the South "in the hands of the pro-slavery element" again.[36] Under Johnson's plan, locally elected delegates would form a convention, revise their state constitution to bring it in line with the Thirteenth Amendment's prohibition of slavery, and then, once that state was readmitted, hold an election for a new legislature. Misjudging his powers of persuasion, Schurz consistently pestered the new president to change his course. Johnson, seeking relief from the assault, promptly commissioned Schurz to perform what the Tennessean president hoped would be a fool's errand: a tour of the Deep South during the hottest months of June, July, and August. Johnson promised him, as Schurz later put it in the opening remarks of his report, that the Tennessean's version of Reconstruction was "merely experimental" and that the president's mind "would change if the experiment did not lead to satisfactory results."[37] Schurz thus took up the idea of a Southern tour in good faith; with the help of radical Charles Sumner, he upped his life insurance and headed down South, hoping to find proof of his suspicions—proof that could be used to convince Johnson to change course.[38]

Schurz's radical tour of the postwar South commenced in Charleston, South Carolina, and took him across the Gulf Coast, ending in Mississippi. Along the way, he detected a growing animus toward African Americans, a certain hardening of the mind of the South, and a persistence of the liminal status of the region in the New World. "There is," Schurz summed up, "as yet, among the Southern people, an *utter absence of national feeling.*"[39] The most troubling aspect of the South, as Schurz saw it, was the concern of the planter class for maintaining controls over "the Negro." "Reasonable" ideas—which Schurz idealistically defined as an acceptance of the general economic and civil rights of freedmen—were "confined to a small minority." In South Carolina, Schurz divined, some planters had written new contracts for the freedmen that would instantly incur a perpetual indebtedness, thereby tightening a "permanent hold" on black labor.[40] "Aside from the assumption that the negro will not work without physical compulsion," Schurz argued, "there appears to be another popular notion prevalent in the south. . . . It is that the negro exists for the special object of raising cotton, rice, and sugar *for the whites* and that it is illegitimate for him to indulge, like other people, in the pursuit of happiness in his own way."[41] Unable or unwilling to tolerate African Americans as equals or as free labor, Schurz continued, the South first looked south at the Caribbean, with the idea that they might extract and export the black population to some island remove, obtain a "supply of coolies," or install "something like the system of peonage that existed in Mexico."[42] As Schurz saw it, all aspects of Southern life had turned toward the most severe methods of control, using the experiences of the entire Americas—from mills at Lowell, Massachusetts, to the guano deposits on the Chincha Islands—as a textbook for handling the "general confusion" of emancipation.

The former Union general found little evidence to support the widespread suggestion that repatriation, exile, and peonage were the best and only solutions to the complexities of emancipation. "The transition of the southern negro," he wrote, "from slavery to freedom was untarnished by any deeds of blood, and the apprehension so extensively entertained and so pathetically declaimed upon by many, that the sudden and general emancipation of the slaves would at once result in 'all the horrors of St. Domingo,' proved utterly groundless." The twinned charges of laziness and criminality were equally powerful in the South. However, after crisscrossing the region in the hottest months of summer, Schurz dismissed this indictment of "the Negro" as well, noting, with little humor, that "idleness seems to be rather strongly developed in the south generally." Indeed, given the circumstances—the evolving chaos of the region, the lack of education available to former slaves, the fear and loathing of the master class—Schurz was quite happily and assuredly optimistic about the future of African Americans as potential citizens in the body politic. "The emancipated slaves of the south," he concluded, "can challenge comparison with any race long held in servitude and suddenly set free." Fair treatment, uniform laws, and universal education across racial lines would ensure the profits and the civilization of the region. Instead, as one historian put it, "anxious whites were feverishly attempting to reassert the race and labor controls they had lost with emancipation, and they were increasingly willing to sanction any means necessary."[43] The "labor problem" in the South, Schurz concluded, was nothing more than an illusion created by the planter class to justify its urge to pay out bloodshed and mayhem instead of wages to the freedmen.[44]

The very worst of it, Schurz soon learned, could be found in Mississippi, where a callous disregard for human life—and especially for African American life—had taken hold. Like much of the South, the state had been left desolate by the war. Of those Mississippians who had fought in the war, 30 percent had died, and many others were either permanently disabled or temporarily and severely wounded. Most of the state's industrial capacity had been lost, along with considerable capital. The scorched-earth policies of Grant and Sherman had reduced the Southern Railroad line to a pathetic twelve-mile stretch between Vicksburg and the Big Black River.[45] "Fire has done its work," one visitor commented, "and most of the way stations are but mementoes of what they once were. At Canton we counted the wreck of twenty-two locomotives—grim and now helpless monsters, as it were."[46] Southern agriculture had fared no better. Wounded from the war, angry about the occupation, concerned for their livelihood, and fearful of black rebellion, white Mississippians used violence preemptively, alternately hoping to kill off, scare away, or intimidate "the Negro." "This is the most shiftless, most demoralized people I have ever seen," Schurz wrote to his wife from Jackson. "The influence of slavery has confused their moral conceptions, their childish, morbid self-complacency has not allowed them to approach, even in the slightest degree, a correct realization of their situation. . . . Since the negro is no longer a slave and no longer costs a thousand dollars, his life is not deemed worth a wisp of straw."[47]

If the life of a freedman was worth little, his or her labor was worth considerably more attention. There was no precedent, as the South understood it, for the emancipation of slaves without strict martial law or the use of force to compel the continuation of work. Across the West Indies, militiamen routinely forced former slaves back to work in the days and weeks to follow the Slavery Abolition Act, putting an end to small-scale resistance and work stoppages. As early as 1863, the U.S. federal government had considered—and rejected—apprenticeship as an option in the South, though the Freedmen's Inquiry Commission had also "strongly recommended a very similar 'guided' transition from slavery to free labor, during which the federal government would act as the temporary guardian, protector, and educator of the freedmen."[48] After the war, Freedmen's Bureau agents scattered across the American South instructed former slaves to stay at work in the rural South and discouraged them from "idleness" even as they protected them from the forces of racism. This was especially true once Presidential Reconstruction began and the issue of "homesteading"—the distribution of former plantation land to independent black farmers—had been settled, once and for all, in the favor of white planters. From 1865 to 1867, then, the bureau became an increasingly schizophrenic labor agent, mediating the irreconcilable economic needs of the region, the nation, and the former slaves. In some cases, this meant simultaneously challenging planters to offer reasonable contracts and badgering freedmen to sign contracts or face punishment. Local agents had considerable discretion to post ominous-sounding circulars, soliciting reports on "every inhuman and brutal act perpetrated by bad men on the bodies of laborers" and threatening "forced work on colony lands" for those who refused "to work when able to do so." "All freedmen," one such circular indicated, "are required to secure places of employment without delay or they will be taken and put to work at forced labor. . . . It is to their own interest to work faithfully like other laborers in any part of the world."[49] "The sum of army and Freedmen's Bureau policies," one historian wrote, was to "protect the Negroes from violence and actual enslavement, but keep as many as possible on the plantations and *compel* them to work. . . . They, too, wanted stability and a cotton crop."[50] With "free negro labor being the only thing in immediate prospect," Carl Schurz suggested, "many ingenious heads set about to solve the problem, how to make free labor compulsory by permanent regulations."[51]

The dynamic relationship between "self interest" and "compulsion" was a hallmark of debates over "the Negro" in the United States, the West Indies, and elsewhere. All of the major parties involved in the reconstruction of the American South—evangelical missionaries, Freedmen's Bureau agents, federal troops, and Southern planters—were united in their distrust of a free, independent, black landowning class. Their shared preference was for Southern agriculture to continue as one of the engines of the nation's economy, which was, in turn, dependent on a compliant, rooted labor force. But if there was a uniformly desired end—a self-interested black working class, content to labor in the fields for a reasonably low wage—there was no consensus about the means through which it might be achieved. Nor, as historian Thomas Holt has demonstrated, was there any common faith that former slaves might be quickly turned into full-scale, working class laborers; under the best of circumstances, the development of sustained commitment to hard labor several days a week and the desire for a life better than that which was most easily available would, most assumed, take some time. The question before the South—whether one was a unionist or a secessionist, planter or carpetbagger—was ultimately about the shortest route to those good habits of the mind.

In this context, most of the parties involved agreed to the importance of a labor contract to bind planter and freedmen to common terms, a fairly standard practice. Missionary societies, war department agents, and radicals in Congress advocated labor contracts just as strongly as they pushed for the marriage contract or the extension of the social contract, if not more so. It was just as clear, though, that the freedmen themselves disagreed and sometimes viewed the labor contract not as an unambiguous step forward from chattel bondage but, rather, as a device to bind them to the land and to ameliorate the effects of abolition on the planter class—much as apprenticeship had been improvised to stave off the "problem of freedom." Freedmen, to be sure, were quite apt to use the language of contract to assert their rights and to lobby for redress from the Freedmen's Bureau, but they were just as quick to reject the notion that the signing of a contract was an obligation of emancipation and that the absence of a contract was evidence of vagrancy or idleness. "In the imperfect world of the South after emancipation," writes Amy Dru Stanley, "the forms and language of contract validated social relations that in certain ways resembled slavery, but they also inhibited the dominion of former masters over freed slaves."[52]

In some sense, liberals in the United States were struggling to understand the relationship between physical coercion, or forced labor, and "moral" or "rational" compulsion. The infamous treadmill in the West Indies—on which James Williams had been whipped and nearly broken—was, in this context, one failed shortcut put into use. There, the interior of the country was underdeveloped, offering an escape from hard labor, and slaves had been allowed to cultivate provisional grounds capable of supporting them with very little effort. "It was necessary," Thomas Holt writes, "that industrious habits be inculcated in some manner; work discipline must be internalized by the freedmen without the normal spur of necessity or desire."[53] The treadmill, at the level of conception, was meant to do just this, though in practice it also seems to have served some deeper, crueler purpose. In Jamaica and in Port Royal, Holt concludes, other more sensible policymakers, missionaries, and colonial officials turned to the philosophers of political economy, and specifically to those who—like penal expert Jeremy Bentham—described a certain kind of soft compulsion not dependent on physical violence or the lash. To foster a "moral compulsion arising from the presence of felt wants," they reasoned, freedmen should be offered reasonable inexpensive consumer goods (thoughtfully imported from London or New York), ranging from common household items to more expensive luxury goods. Ambition, the logic went, would emerge from the desire for these glittering baubles, producing, in a very short time, a Protestant work ethic.[54]

This same approach to the schooling of blacks was put into place in Port Royal, South Carolina, in 1862, upon the arrival of the *Atlantic*, with its cargo of missionaries bearing the gift of "civilization." A deep water port and wealthy cotton community, Port Royal had been captured early in the Civil War, forcing Union army officials to wrestle

Timothy O'Sullivan's 1862 portrait of African Americans working with cotton on a plantation on Port Royal Island, South Carolina, a site of Union "free labor" innovation and experimentation. From the Prints and Photographs Division, Library of Congress.

with the "problem of freedom" long before the end of the war. For some, the island's significant slave population—and its progress after emancipation—offered the best chance to test the effect of abolition on "the Negro." At the urging of a few radical army officials, the American Missionary Association—now well seasoned after thirty years' work in Jamaica—sent a handful of its best and brightest to the Southern latitudes, hoping to demonstrate the power of the Gospel to inspire hard work and clean living.[55] Susan Walker, who a decade earlier had nursed the radical Charles Sumner back to health after his rude and public caning on the Senate floor at the hands of Preston Brooks, was one of the first to arrive. A busy little angel of both cleanliness and godliness, she sold clothing to the needy freedmen of Port Royal, a worthy task, as she saw it, given that their wardrobe at her Sunday

Bible study consisted of "table cloths for shawls, showy gowns left by Sesesh ladies, and trousers, coats and vests made of carpeting taken from the floors." But if one could stimulate consumer demand by increasing consumer desire (a very popular idea in American culture), the pace of change might increase dramatically. Soon enough, she noted, a fledgling consumer economy made her Saturdays—"a day of leisure"—very busy: "Men and women come by twenties and thirties to buy clothing. Men buy gowns and chemises for their wives when they can buy nothing for themselves. They want very long dresses and ask often for white skirts. . . . It is hard to turn them away for want to such articles as they greatly need."[56] It was this "great need," she believed, that would produce—in very short order—a remarkable transformation in the freedmen.

In the long summer of 1865, in the Deep South, as the cotton sat and swelled quietly in the fields, there was precious little room for "the Negro" to emerge as a protoconsumer, let alone as a citizen or an equal. If missionaries and Freedmen's Bureau agents hoped, at times, to gently and slowly lead African Americans from the shadow of slavery and backwardness to the light of freedom and civilization, it was, in part, because they had some small kernel of faith or some other suspicion that "the Negro" could permanently change for the better, as they understood it. Few in the South shared this faith. Even fewer wished for a world where African Americans could participate in the emerging consumer culture, where one's citizenship and racial status were contingent on the purchase of goods. It was this same faith in the white citizen-as-consumer that lay beneath the fear of the Chinese, who were thought to ship their wages "home" and not to spend them in the United States. One hears echoes of it in Governor Benjamin Humphrey's lament that "our fields have been deserted for the filthy garrets and sickly cellars of our towns and cities [by the freedmen]. . . . From producers they are converted into consumers, and as the winter approaches, their only salvation from starvation and want, is Federal rations—plunder and pillage."[57] Labor, he assumed, not accumulation and display, was the proper destiny of the freedmen. Although Humphreys was most directly concerned with the absence of able hands in the fields, it was also true that the right to purchase and the appropriation of middle-class desires and ambitions could be profoundly empowering for those on the lower rungs of the social ladder.[58]

What emerged from Benjamin Humphrey's "desolated and ruined land" was a sort of color-coded society fixated on compulsion, set up at every level to keep the freedmen at work in the fields of the South. Every action of the region related to "the labor question"—the lust for coolies or immigrants, the cry for apprenticeship laws, the calling out of the militia, the numbing, day-to-day violence—was meant to demonstrate the right "place" for "the Negro." One hears echoes of the treadmill in the disparagement of the Freedmen's Bureau's decision to allow "laborers to wander from the plantation without a permit," a critique that expands into a call for "regulations and restraints that are essential to preserve [the freedmen's] morals and health."[59] Immigration from Germany, one newspaper argued, would "operate on the negro by showing him that the work is to be done, either with him or without him. . . . The planters of Louisiana [may] find it best to rely on the moral effect of the competition of white labor, rather than the dangerous expedients of provost marshals or provost guards, or the expensive ones of vagrant laws, workhouses, and almhouses." "Imported" white labor, the *Daily Picayune* concluded, "will compel the negro element to work or starve."[60] One Mobile businessman, hoping to rid himself of "loafing freedmen who loiter around his premises," suggested a "loafer-fuge," which was not so much an "invention" as the daily application of coal tar to the most popular sitting sills, prompting the freedmen to get up, move away, and presumably return to their forgotten labors.[61]

The search for the proper tools of coercion was a reflection of the challenge posed by freed African Americans to their traditional role in Southern society. In Louisiana, planters noted that the freedmen in the state's interior region were uninterested in signing contracts with "the whites, especially their former owners," electing instead to consolidate their holdings, working cooperatively on the land or working for "some freedmen better off than themselves."[62] "Our freedmen will leave us," Alabaman J. B. Moore wrote in his diary. "They will not agree to work and be controlled by me, hence, I told them I would not hire them."[63] A Tennessee woman was confronted by the freedmen who worked on her cotton plantation with a demand for greater "remuneration" (specifically, thirty-three bales, the sum total of the plantation's cotton production). Seeking support, she called upon the local Freedmen's Bureau agent, who eventually dispatched "sufficient force" to her aid and "restored order."[64] "There is," the *Planters' Banner* noted with wonderment, "an infernal influence at work upon the negroes somewhere that is urging them on to their ultimate ruin. Where do they get their ideas about donations of land houses, mules, etc? Why this sudden refusal to work at any price or to make contracts to work? Why this increased hatred to the landholder and the white man? . . . Why these combinations among negroes, and these pledges not to work for Southern men, even for wages?"[65] It could not have been plainer that the freedmen were just asking the planter class to live up to the moral code of laissez-faire capitalism, to keep, in other words, their "hands off," and yet the planter class routinely described these same actions not as powerful evidence of emergent self- and group interest but, instead, as frightening indicators of creeping lawlessness and laziness in the black population of the South.

This "General Strike" of the freedmen—a rebellion "on a wide basis against the conditions of work"—began in the midst of the wartime campaigns across the South. As the Union armies advanced into Confederate territory, they were repeatedly slowed by a rising tide of escaped slaves who had emancipated themselves in the chaos of war, forsaking their bound labors for the abstract concept of freedom and the tangible reality of land and opportunity. "This was not merely the desire to stop work," W. E. B. Du Bois wrote. "It was a general strike that involved directly in the end perhaps a half a million people. They wanted to stop the economy of the plantation system, and to do that they left the plantations."[66] It was broader, too, than the struggle over the conditions of labor. Freedom in this context might mean service on behalf of the Union army; a chance to claim a plot of land in a region occupied by federal troops; or the opportunity to find a loved one, a child, wife, or husband, who had earlier been borne away by the slave trade. Most often, freedom just meant that one could say "no"—"no" to cruel workloads, "no" to prescribed limits on one's life, and "no" to the meanness of the planter class—with the assumption that the hiss of the lash would not follow this simple refusal. Former slaves, historian Leon Litwack once noted, rarely moved very far at all, but the planter class always acted as if they had journeyed to the other end of the universe.[67] "The country," Schurz concluded, "found itself thrown into that confusion which is naturally inseparable from a change so great and so sudden. The white people were afraid of the negroes, and the negroes did not trust the white people."[68] "The negroes," former Confederate general Josiah Gorgas wrote, "cannot be prevailed to work. . . . The life of a planter is just now no sinecure."[69]

As the planter class struggled to maintain its equilibrium in the face of this "General Strike," Southern newspapers routinely drew on the parallel narrative of the West Indies. One editorial, titled "How to

Make Free Labor Profitable," offered the opinions of one especially insightful Southerner—self-exiled to the West Indies during the Civil War—on the failures of Jamaica and the chance for profit in the South. "Think of nothing," wrote the expatriate, "but how you can make your old slaves contented and available laborers. . . . Settle them on your land as permanent tenants, with good provision grounds on easy terms, and you will find that you have labor at command." This, the writer continued, was the opposite of what had transpired in the West Indies, where planters either had been too heavy-handed or had simply fled. "To scatter the negroes around in little detached holdings," he argued, "is equally adverse to the true interests of both races. I have seen the evil results in more than one of the West India Islands. The negro manages to exist, and no more than exist, on such a place. . . . Scattered and unreliable labor was for years the bane of Jamaica, and is one of the chief drawbacks to sugar-raising in the still richer island of St. Domingo." Black labor, the argument went, should be quietly (and not forcefully) consolidated and controlled, its duties carefully prescribed, compelled to labor with great gentleness, "so that they bring up their children to be willing and ready laborers at low wages." "If some are led off," this self-appointed expert concluded, "under temptation of higher wages, they will find they lose a home, in which all could help to make the family comfortable."[70] Here, in a nutshell, was a solution that substituted paternalist bedazzlement for violent, naked power.

In the end, though, the near immediate release of raw power was, perhaps, inevitable. This, at least, would have been Carl Schurz's conclusion. The August constitutional convention in Jackson, Mississippi, had reserved for the state the right to secure order, by force if necessary. Thus enabled, the provisional governor, William Sharkey, sought to bring order out of chaos not through the even-handed distribution of justice across the color line but, rather, by calling out the state militia to more effectively police "the Negro" back into submissive productivity on the labor-starved delta. Not surprisingly, Provisional Governor Sharkey's call to reestablish the state militia left some Union military officials "puzzled" or even downright dismissive. Schurz arrived in Vicksburg only two days after Union general Henry Slocum (his former superior) publicly countermanded Sharkey's proclamation. Sharkey's call to the militia, as Schurz, Slocum, and others saw it, was a poorly timed move to once again take up arms, coming "at a time when the Union men were still heartily hated and the reversal of emancipation ardently desired by the very class of men thus to be armed and organized."[71]

Andrew Johnson's reaction—to support Sharkey over Slocum, to reprimand Schurz for his meddling, and to encourage the white South to form local militias—was the straw that broke the camel's back. Determined to change the course of the administration, Schurz authored one of the most damning, politically explosive reports in the nation's history, and his allies in Congress turned it into "an important weapon of radical propaganda" in the first stages of the war against Andrew Johnson's too tame and needlessly forgiving program of Reconstruction.[72]

All of this came to a climax in Mississippi, in the summer and fall of 1865. Two weeks after giving carte blanche to the state of North Carolina, and one month before Carl Schurz arrived in South Carolina on his investigative tour, President Johnson met a small delegation of Mississippians and offered them the same terms: amnesty for all but the highest-ranking leaders of the Confederacy, restoration of all private property excepting slaves, and the appointment of a provisional governor with the power to assemble a convention that would be charged with the task of amending the state's constitution. Conservative unionist William Sharkey, an advocate of law and order above all else, was thereafter appointed as provisional governor, and he quickly called for a statewide election of representatives to such a convention, which opened its deliberations in the state capital, Jackson, on August 14, 1865. "Crime must be suppressed," Sharkey's opening statement read, and to enable its suppression the convention established the death penalty for a wide range of serious offenses and then turned its attention to the revision of the state's constitution. Two days after the opening of the convention, Andrew Johnson sent a lengthy memorandum to Sharkey, urging him to grant the franchise to all literate freedmen and, in so doing, to "disarm the adversary . . . the Radicals who are wild upon Negro franchise."[73] The members of the convention chose, instead, to skip right over this issue and to charge the state legislature with "the protection and security of the person and property of the freedmen of the State" and the protection of that same group—and of the state itself—"against any evils that may arise from their sudden emancipation."[74] "This language," Schurz wrote, "is not without significance; not the blessings of a full development of free labor, but only the dangers of emancipation are spoken of."[75]

As for the abolition of slavery, the convention's final statement on that issue rendered emancipation an aggressive act of the federal government, unhappily inflicted upon Mississippi, an approach that left a great deal of flexibility for the legislature that was soon to be elected. "The institution of slavery having been destroyed in the State of Mississippi," the amendment read, "neither slavery nor involuntary servitude, otherwise than in the punishment of crimes, whereof the parties have been duly convicted, shall hereafter exist in the state."[76] For those who hoped for some restoration of something like slavery, all that remained was to write the laws that would automatically trigger an easy conviction and the sanction of forced labor. Few had faith that the North could or would write these laws. "I am not willing," the representative from Adams admitted,

> to trust to men who know nothing of slavery, the power to frame a code for the freedmen of the state of Mississippi. I am not willing to trust these men, who have been educated from youth upward, taught in their schools, taught from the pulpit, taught by their public speakers, and taught by their writers that the white population of the South is a degraded race, as compared with our more favored Northern brethren, who live in a Northern climate, who have been taught also that slavery is odious, that the master is not restrained by feelings of humanity.[77]

To craft laws for the freedmen, one needed direct experience with slavery and an awareness of past attempts to manage the freed population after emancipation. "New modes of social control had to be developed," writes one historian, a task that required "perhaps more imagination and intellectual originality than the pre-war defense of slavery."[78] When a newly elected legislature took office in October of 1865, the composition of these new laws was the most pressing issue before them.

Black Codes

In his inaugural address, Governor Benjamin G. Humphreys lectured the state congressional delegates that "To work is the law of God."[79] Such reminders were unnecessary. When the legislators arrived in Jackson in October, they would have passed through fields of cotton, swollen with potential profit. The cotton plant is a low-slung, shrubby, tropical bush that prospers in the Deep South. The seed of the plant is contained in a small boll, or pod, and the soft, pillowlike stuff— sometimes bright white and sometimes cream-colored—that surrounds the seed in the pod is what we know as cotton. In the past, when it was ready, this fibrous material was collected by hand, through the tedious, labor-intensive process of cotton-picking, a process that required the picker to bend down, stooping for the soft fibers. Once the cotton has been picked, weighed, graded, and baled, it is taken to a mill to be carded, combed, and spun into yarn, which can then be woven into cotton cloth. In Mississippi, cotton is planted in late April and May, a bit later than in the cotton-growing regions of Texas. It is planted in long rows, which are neatened and cleaned in the late spring, a process that seems to stretch the rows out even longer. In August, when the state convention was held, the bolls would still have been green, the seeds inside surrounded not yet by soft cotton but instead by something closer to moist tissue paper. Along the Mississippi River, once home to the great delta plantations of the Old South, cotton-picking begins, then as now, not in August but in the middle of September and continues for some time after that. By the end of that month, then, the bolls would have fully opened, no longer able to contain the eye-catching whiteness of the fiber. In a few weeks, the cotton would begin to rot. The parallel situation in Texas was increasingly dire. "There is," one account of that state read, "much cotton now suffering to be picked, which is certain to be wasted for the want of a hand to pick it."[80] Thus, in the fall of 1865, with the crop ready or nearly so and "the Negro" either scarce, rebellious, or pursuing economic independence, the state representatives who gathered in Jackson decided to ensure that the cotton got picked.

There was, though, more than high cotton to think about. An unrestrained impulse in "the Negro" toward criminality, idleness, and arrogance was, many assumed, a consequence of emancipation, but it was also, it was thought, an initial symptom of a disease that would eventually advance to outright racial rebellion, pitting "the sable *sans culottes*" of the South against whites, whether poor or wealthy.[81] Soon after the beginning of the Civil War, rumors had circulated of a plotted "negro insurrection," rumors that would continue for the war's duration.[82] During and after the war, the possibility of rebellion at Christmastime—when African Americans hoped that a just God would righteously grant them their freedom or reshuffle the titles to land— weighed heavily on the entire South, bringing to mind an earlier rebellion in Jamaica in late December 1831.[83] In August, the *Daily Picayune* concluded that "unless attention is directed at once to the conduct of the freedmen, the bloodshed and massacre of St. Domingo will be reenacted in our midst before the close of the year."[84] When the Mississippi state legislature met in October and November, there were swirling third-hand accounts of a coming revolution of the African in America.

The fear of black rebellion had long been a feature of Southern life—during the war, Confederate troops routinely stayed behind the lines in case of such an event—but by the fall of 1865, such ideas were unusually rampant and excited. One senator, noting that African Americans "not in the employ of the United States" were "known to be purchasing considerable and unusual quantities of ammunition," urged the legislature to instruct the state militia to forcibly disarm the freedmen and to thereafter prevent them from the purchase of weapons that might be used against white people.[85] South Carolina's governor had been forced to veto an overly aggressive militia bill written with the nightmare of an impending Christmas uprising in mind.[86] Like the lure of profit from bulging cotton, these growing fears demanded an immediate response from the state of Mississippi.

When the uprising finally came, it was not in Mississippi, nor in South Carolina, nor anywhere else in the United States. Nor did it come on Christmas Day. It began, instead, on Saturday, October 7, 1865, in the town of Morant Bay, located in the parish of St. Thomas, on the southeastern side of the island of Jamaica. Black residents of the area arrived at the local courthouse, prepared to protest the arrest of a tenant embroiled in a dispute with his landlord. The crowd and the local officials fought, two black constables were severely beaten, and a local preacher, Paul Bogle, was singled out by the authorities as the root cause of the violence. An arrest warrant was issued for Bogle, and subsequent rumors of his apprehension sparked growing Afro-Jamaican anger and organization. This, tragically, encouraged the local authorities to request troops from the governor of the island, Edward John Eyre, who has been charitably described by one historian as a "hostile, incompetent administrator of limited intelligence."[87] Late the next day, several hundred Afro-Jamaicans clashed with a small handful of militiamen and, in the protracted battle that followed, killed seven of them, wounding many others, burning buildings, and attacking various symbols of authority in the town. For the rebels in Morant Bay, the uprising in early October was a minor skirmish in the long war against the powerful interests of the landed class. In the days that followed, before the inevitable countermove, their rebellion grew to encompass several thousand people. For Governor Eyre, though, the trouble in St. Thomas and Morant Bay was an unacceptable affront to the British Empire. Hoping to squash the rebellion completely, he unleashed the military, leaving hundreds dead, just as many flogged, and general devastation in the region. Bogle was summarily and rather quickly hanged, as was

George William Gordon, a "mulatto" member of the Jamaican House of Assembly and a presumed ringleader.[88]

Word of the Morant Bay rebellion reached England a few weeks later, "in the bundles of Kingston newspapers which had come aboard the West-Indian mail packet." Accounts of the original upheaval were followed by accounts of the vengeful response. Stories of black savagery may have contained scandalous and frightening reminders of the Haitian revolution and the so-called Sepoy Mutiny of 1857, but the accounts of atrocities perpetrated by British marines and sailors were, in some sense, equally powerful and disturbing. Much of the colonial elite feared that the rebellious Afro-Jamaicans hoped to turn the island into another Haiti. The image of soulless, dead-eyed black Jamaicans, butchering and burning British soldiers, was soon matched, then, by strangely enthusiastic portraits of mass executions, floggings, and tortures, all cheerfully perpetrated by British soldiers and depicted in the Kingston press. It was difficult, one historian writes, "to believe that thirty years after emancipation, Jamaica's black men, so often charged with indolent apathy, would erupt in so terrifying a manner."[89] It was harder still to make sense of the cruelties inflicted in the name of Britain on other God-fearing Protestants, though race surely helped when it came time to write an interpretation of the event. One writer attributed the worst acts of the "reign of terror"—the suppression of the rebellion—to the use of Maroon troops, "semi-civilized negroes" who were, he wrote, unchecked by the guiding hand of civilized white authority.[90] For many in Britain, Morant Bay was further proof that all blacks were savage, that Jamaica was lost, and that "EIGHT MILES OF DEAD BODIES"—the headline in the *New York Herald*—was the sad consequence of three decades' worth of misguided humanitarianism. "Just as Americans began their own confrontation with the consequences of emancipation," Eric Foner notes, "respectable British opinion concluded that blacks were incapable of self-government."[91]

News of the Morant Bay rebellion raced across the South, where the emphasis was on "the heart-sickening and brutal atrocities perpetrated by the fiendish blacks upon the white population."[92] "The barbarities practiced in St. Thomas and Jamaica are confirmed," one breathless telegraph dispatch read. "The authorities hanged about sixty culprits."[93] The newspaper accounts that circulated drew attention to the role of taxation and specifically to the idea that Afro-Jamaicans had fallen well behind in their payments to the state and that efforts to enforce payment (and the refusal to comply) were the root causes of the trouble in Morant Bay.[94] Tales such as these dramatized the concerns of the planter class, which had long doubted that taxation would perform a subtler kind of compulsion on "the Negro." But they also played on the worst suspicions of the South—the sharp, driving fear that any rebellion anywhere in the Atlantic world would spark another Haitian revolution, another bloodbath pitting the black masses against whites everywhere. When in late October of 1865 an "armed negro soldier, with bayonet fixed, and cap on his head," appeared in the hall of the House of Representatives in Jackson, standing silently for some minutes until he was forced to leave, the act of defiance was read through transnational lenses and understood as both a local act and an international one.[95]

In considering the lessons learned from Jamaica in the wake of the rebellion, one newspaper scoffed at the idea "that the negro could be a planter, that he could be a legislator, that he could be a judge with a gown—that he could preach and pray infinitely and pay taxes infinitesimally." Any visitor to "this negro Atlantis" would have seen "that the people were vicious, intractable, insolent, that their Christianity was only modified fetishism, and their civilization only a backward path to barbarism."[96] The *Daily Picayune,* choosing to accentuate the positive, praised General James S. Fullerton, the assistant commissioner of the Freedmen's Bureau in Louisiana, for his "determin[ation] that we shall profit by the example of British administration in the West Indies, and avoid the errors, follies, and absurd plan, by which emancipation was made a curse to negroes and a ruin to whites, and a great loss and damage to the civilized world." "Is there no hope in the future?" another newspaper asked. "The public press in England begins to show signs of sanity when it speaks of the deplorable condition of Jamaica; and the whole civilized world stands amazed at the state of affairs in St. Domingo, but it is left to the radicals of the United States of America to hug with zealous, if not affectionate embrace, the false humanitarian notions of . . . the Old World, and to cherish with fantastical earnestness the fatal errors of a past age."[97] The "Negro Insurrection" at Morant Bay served as a chilling and cautionary tale for the postemancipation South, as an excuse to beat up on "Exeter Hall fanaticism"—a phrase which, in this case, conflates British idealism with Radical Reconstruction—and, through that abuse, to critique the most radical features of New England liberalism.[98]

Jamaica, Anthony Trollope argued, lacked the very basic laws that had worked wonders in England, putting those with little chance and luck to work in "the poorhouse"; "It is not perhaps very easy," he admitted, to change "the devil's work" of slavery into the "heavenly work" of wage labor "at once." This, though, was what the state of Mississippi had set out to do. The "Act to Confer Civil Rights on Freedmen" granted blacks the right to marry but forbade interracial unions; forbade them the ownership of property in the rural countryside; ensured their right to testify in only those trials where "negroes or mulattoes" were either plaintiffs or defendants; mandated that all "freedmen, free negro, or mulatto" should have a job and should carry evidence of that job with them at all times; and gave the state the power to arrest and return "deserting" laborers and to fine those who sought to "persuade" or "entice" laborers to leave one place of work for another. In amending the vagrant laws of the state, the legislature prescribed fines and imprisonment for the blacks of Mississippi if they should have "no lawful employment or business" or if they should be found "unlawfully assembling themselves together either in the day or night time." In anticipation of Jim Crow, another law forbade first-class railroad accommodations to "the Negro." To handle the increased volume of criminal proceedings that would inevitably result from these laws, the Mississippi legislature also created a new county court system, with a far broader mandate than the old slave courts, and dictated that any freedman or woman who could not pay his or her fine could be hired out by the sheriff. The most damning, controversial bit of law concerned the relationship between "masters" and "apprentices," the latter defined as the children of indigent or morally suspect parents, who could—the law posited, confusing all meanings of the word "apprentice"—be removed from their parents' homes and be put to work. There was no room here for idleness, nor for wanderlust—only for hard work and harder, more "heavenly" work, with the "responsibility" for "discipline and regulation" now safely "transferred from the plantation to public authorities."[99]

At the most fundamental level, the methods of compulsion found in the Black Codes represented a significant improvement—an "improvement," that is, from the perspective of political economy—over the treadmill and the lash of apprenticeship. The institutionalization of the treadmill, historian Diana Paton reminds us, was originally a "progressive" penal reform, replacing the punishment of the whip, distributing its workload fairly and equally, and producing, at the end, "willing plantation workers."[100] But despite its philosophical place in penal reform, the treadmill was also a physical thing, a jumble of wood and metal with a permanent location and thus a perfect target for humanitarians and antislavery advocates and a symbol of the inability of the state to "correct" the backward slide of "the Negro" into barbarism. The Black Codes—when seen as a single system of control—presented a more elusive target. One law might make it impossible for freedmen to own property, another might forbid the hunting of game on someone else's property, and still another might mandate that anyone who was tainted by "Negro" blood must be employed or upstanding or, as a consequence of not meeting these criteria, be imprisoned and, if poor, sold off to work following a conviction—the last a practice that foreshadowed the uniquely Southern institution of convict leasing. There was no treadmill in Mississippi—only the law, the hunger for food and survival, and the necessity of work.[101]

Few white Mississippians, though, had faith in the legal system, no matter how carefully devised and controlled on a local level. On the thorny issue of testimony against white Mississippians in court, one senator offered an amendment that would punish perjury with "thirty-nine lashes well laid on the bare back." The amendment was tabled and passed over by the scant margin of a single vote.[102] "They thought," one historian writes, "that the nature of the Black beast required extralegal, not legal, control."[103] Before the Civil War, Mississippi had relied on a less formal slave court system and the infamous slave patrols to deny African Americans access to the more genteel trappings of the courthouse, with its precious and official jurisprudence. It was just a short step, some worried, from the shared and unequal access to one system of justice to the principle of equality before the law. The county court system proposed by the state legislature would, in theory, give the freedmen a greater chance at that sacred principle, giving credence to the growing belief that the courts were the least trustworthy "control mechanism" for the postwar South. Still, over the course of their short lifespan, the county courts were increasingly effective in targeting a specific population—"the Negro"—for greater surveillance and restraint, by legal and extralegal means. These "inferior" courts opened for business in January of 1866, and they benefited from the increasingly organized bands of night riders, the occasional frothing mobs, and spectacular midnight murders that made the state a very dangerous place to be both black and accused, or even just to be black. In Vicksburg, seat of the Warren County court and headquarters of the army of occupation, the opening sessions featured a largely white population of "citizens" and criminals; by April and May, the court was hearing cases that were usually about "the Negro," and there were far more of these cases than any court in Mississippi had ever heard before, and defendants were arraigned on a greater variety of charges—a trend that might have increased if those "sans-culottes" in Congress had not passed the Civil Rights Act in April of that same year.[104]

Labor Problem Redux

The response to the codes came quickly. One week after their passage, newspapers in the North began to "wave the bloody shirt," drawing attention to the restoration of order proposed by the legislators of Mississippi and threatening to turn the state into a "frog pond."[105] The Union army swiftly countermanded some of the more troubling features of the codes. Radical and moderate Republicans in Congress denied seats to those Southerners elected under President Johnson's forgiving terms and established a closed committee to handle all matters related to the South. At the end of December, as word began to spread of the codes themselves and as other Southern states began to pass similar restrictions on the lives of the freedmen, Carl Schurz's report was sent to Congress, revealing—for the true believers—that little had changed in the South and that racially specific penal codes and the denial of black citizenship could easily have been avoided, if only Johnson had not been so lenient, so sympathetic to the former slaveholding region. "Do you not think," Carl Schurz had once asked William King of Savannah, that "vagrancy laws and police regulations might be enacted, equally applicable to whites and blacks, which might obviate most of the difficulties you suggest as arising from the unwillingness of the negro to work?" "Perhaps they might," King responded, "but the whites would not agree to that."[106] This sort of punitive color-consciousness was, the radicals believed, just plain wrong, and for the next few years, as liberalism reigned triumphant in Congress, they set out to ensure the demise of the black codes and to extend civil liberties to the freedmen. Carl Schurz, not surprisingly, was celebrated above the Mason-Dixon line and demonized below it. "We now learn from Mr. Schurz," wrote the *New Orleans Daily Crescent,* with dripping sarcasm, "that the existence of the freedmen in the South is a perpetual flight from a blazing fagot and an uplifted knife." "Negroes," the paper continued, summarizing Schurz's supposed conclusion, "ought to be allowed to vote—indeed ought to be forced to vote; else they stand in imminent danger of being made to work."[107] Much of the South framed this issue just this way—as an "either/or" question, as if one could have either an extended social contract that included the freedmen or a ready supply of workers, but not both.

The passage of the Civil Rights Act, then, granted full citizenship to "the Negro" and swept away the Black Codes, but it also raised new questions about the future of a region that was, most believed, inescapably dependent on a single body of laborers. Indeed, that extension of the rights of citizenship, more than any other factor, distinguished Mississippi and the South from Jamaica and the West Indies. In the wake of the Morant Bay rebellion, the Jamaican constitution had been rewritten, further restricting the franchise, more closely guarding the interests of the planter class, and reducing Afro-Jamaican representation to a minute fraction of its former size. Jamaica itself had quickly been turned into a crown colony, making it even more dependent on London for guidance on all things related to former slaves and apprentices.[108] Jamaica and Mississippi were, in the end, very different places: the former a once-prized sugar colony, linked to the metropole by the Colonial Office and global economic interest, and the latter a vanquished, recalcitrant state in a constitutional democracy. The enshrinement of egalitarianism in the Constitution and the universal application of what would, sometime later, be called "the American Creed" would change the course of American racism, forcing it to appear in local venues, small towns, counties, and state law, but not in national law, limiting its expression in "race-specific" federal legislation. This divergence, as historian George Fredrickson once noted, did not make the United States less racist or less committed to white supremacy, but it did shape racism and racial advantage in that country in unusual ways.[109] For better or worse, Mississippi was a small part of the larger United States and could not be cut loose or left to wither and die; the same could now be said of "the Negro."

There were, though, other paths and other parallels. Citing Anthony Trollope's recently published West Indian travelogue, the *Daily Picayune* directed its readership to a consideration of neighboring Trinidad, where "ten or twelve thousand Coolies" had trebled the exports of the island: "it produced three hogsheads of sugar where, before, it had produced one." Coolies, the essay proclaimed, were wonderfully temporary noncitizens—returning, after a few years of labor, "to their own country with what, to them, is wealth." "The same thing has taken place in Guiana," the newspaper noted, "but in Jamaica, where there has been or had then been no successful effort to organize a labor system, agriculture was still in the pitiable condition to which it was reduced by the emancipation act." In addition to increasing the overall production of Trinidad, the arrival of coolies seemed to produce a remarkable change in the freedmen. Trollope, the essay continued, was no fan of "the unmixed African negro," who "will never work unless he is compelled to do so," but he also suggested that if one were to "place the Coolie or Chinaman alongside of him . . . the negro must work or starve." In sum, "after thirty years experience, free negro labor in the British West Indies had been found a flat failure; or rather it had been found to be no labor at all; and that Coolie labor, under the indenture system, promises a resuscitation of agricultural industry and a restoration of prosperity."[110]

Was it possible, some wondered, that the inclusion of "the Negro" into the United States—no matter how half-hearted or incomplete—would push the South toward a new class of anticitizens? Or could a better class of citizens be brought down South? In the years that followed, as the labor concerns of the summer of 1865 repeated themselves, this "Coolie Question"—and its flip side, the importation of white European labor—was a source of regular debate and also of routine comparison to the West Indies and, of course, to Cuba. "This subject," one newspaper noted, "is arousing much inquiry and discussion among our planters and land-holders, especially those who have attempted to work their plantations during the last four years, and are immovable in their conviction that the labor of the freedmen cannot be depended on in the cultivation of staples on a large scale, without the introduction of some competing industry." "The Coolies," it was assumed, "would supply that demand."[111] This growing excitement did not escape the notice of those same forces determined to forestall the implementation of the Black Codes. Carl Schurz, for one, had once noted the prevalence of "wild speculations" about "how to obtain a sufficient supply of coolies" as early as the summer of 1865.[112] Such interest swelled even as the codes were dismantled, as Presidential Reconstruction came to an end, and as Radical Reconstruction began. Desperate to regain its profit margin, to keep the cotton and sugar economies afloat, and to avoid the disaster visited on the planter class in Jamaica, many in the South set out to turn "wild speculation" into practical success.

CHAPTER FIVE

Latitudes and Longitudes

To escape the ills which they now suffer the white population anxiously desire to invite immigration. They want coolies and they want white immigrants. My own opinion is that they will get neither to such an extent as to render them independent of black labor for at least many years to come.

— "WHAT NORTHERN TRAVELLERS SEE IN 'RECONSTRUCTED' SOUTH CAROLINA," *CHARLESTON DAILY COURIER* (JULY 22, 1869)

Touring Missouri in 1865, newspaperman Whitelaw Reid noted a growing fear among the former slaves of the Deep South. Whenever planters or employers sought to relocate their newly emancipated laborers to a different site, more than a few African Americans seemed concerned that the real intention was "to run them over to Cuba and sell them." "Several asked him whether Cuba wasn't just across the Mississippi River," Reid reported.[1] This fear of forced relocation or sale back into slavery and the related sense that reenslavement was a proximal threat were understandable. It confirmed what had been heard in the Civil War, when both Northern troops and Southern slaveholders used the rumor of the Cuban exile to pacify "the Negro."[2] It reminded some of the antebellum efforts of Matthew Maury, who had sought to ship off the demographic excess of Southern slaves to Brazil, cementing "trade" with that country, opening the door for potential conquest, and releasing the dangerous social pressures that were thought to attend a certain concentration of Africans.[3] It may well also have reflected an awareness of the Lincoln administration's wartime plans to detropicalize the labor of the South, to relocate free blacks to British Guiana, the Dominican Republic, or Haiti, where they might find "a climate suited to their highest physical, intellectual, and moral development."[4] In any case, the prospect of laboring on some *ingenio* in the Caribbean—cutting cane for the master class once again—was certainly a reasonable fear, given the extraordinary postemancipation adjustment underway. In a short chronological window, the planter class attempted to realign race and place, importing new, less bothersome labor to the South as a substitution for "the Negro." Reid, an intrepid, slightly negrophobic observer of human conflict, might have appreciated the merits of any one of these schemes. He remarked that one of his interviewees even relished the fortune that might be made as a "negro smuggler." And then, in his very next paragraph, Reid turned to discuss the replacement labor force, focusing on the arrival of "white" German labor in "one of the northern parishes of Louisiana."[5]

The postwar labor problem forced the planter class to draw from an international network of migrating laborers, who might relieve the South of its insufferable dependence on freedmen. It also enrolled the South in a very different global competition against other "free labor" societies, who also desired those new working bodies. The course of labor movement could run north to south, east to west, backward and forward. Certainly, by any measurement of distance and time, British Guiana—where Abraham Lincoln had once hoped to export "the Negro"—was about as far from Louisiana as any place could be in the Caribbean. The place had once belonged to the enterprising Dutch, who followed the Essequibo and Demerara rivers into the interior of the continent and built an elaborate system of dykes and canals to drain the flat, alluvial coastlands. Through war and conquest, it became a British possession in the early nineteenth century and quite soon thereafter shifted its attentions to the nearly exclusive production of sugar along the Caribbean coast. Despite a transient planter class, without any sense of permanent white settlement, and in the face of massive slave rebellions, the overwhelming health hazards of the equatorial tropics, and the abolition of slavery in 1834, the colony continued as a favorite West Indies jewel, supplanting Jamaica by mid-century if only because of its unlimited potential for sugar. "A million hogsheads can be made," Anthony Trollope bubbled enthusiastically of his favorite West Indian colony, "if we only had the Coolies."[6] On the eve of the American Civil War, British Guiana had imported tens of thousands of contract coolies from China and India, "temporary" laborers tightly bound by indenture to work for a few years in exchange for land or money. Some would return to their homelands, while others would stay in the New World and seek a new place for themselves.[7]

From this distant hemispheric viewpoint, with all of the American Mediterranean in front of us, we can observe the remarkable travels of O'Tye Kim, also known as Wu Tai Kam or, elsewhere, as Tye Kim Orr. O'Tye Kim was educated at the London Missionary School in Singapore and, after a short while in London, was sent to British Guiana in 1864, where he quickly established a reputation for his deep faith and Christian propriety. After successfully preaching to the Chinese in Georgetown and on the sugar estates, he petitioned the colony's governor for the right to establish a community of free Chinese Christians up the Demerara, in what he intended to be a congregation of true believers and former coolies living together in productive harmony in a place called Hopetown, far from the plantations clustered along the Essequibo and Demerara coastlines. But by 1866, the lure of profits from charcoal production had displaced the desire for plain living, and Hopetown had become a bustling entrepôt along Kamuni Creek with forty newfangled charcoal ovens. Rumors swirled that O'Tye Kim had been swindling his flock, surcharging and taxing them to line his own pockets, or that he had been caught in an affair with an African woman who was pregnant with his unborn child. O'Tye Kim, presciently sensing an end to his role in Hopetown, escaped by boat for Trinidad.[8]

Kim made his way, somehow, to Cuba, the world's most productive slaveholding sugar colony, where, as one historian notes cautiously, "he might have worked briefly as an overseer on a plantation."[9] Whatever his role in Cuba, he must have noted the cruel and parallel subjugations of Chinese coolies and African slaves. The British, having emancipated their own slaves in the West Indies in 1834, had grown increasingly ambitious in their efforts to stamp out the transatlantic slave trade, driving the cost of slaves upward and forcing Cuban planters, who refused to free their slaves, to gamble on Chinese contract laborers as a supplemental (rather than a replacement) labor force. In short, O'Tye Kim arrived in Havana—the literal and economic center of the Caribbean universe—at just the moment when the African slave trade had been largely suppressed by the British and when Chinese contract workers were "the cheapest labor source in Cuba."[10] He would have seen the coolie ships arriving regularly in Havana's harbor, many of them quarantined to allow for the dying out of whatever pestilence had thinned the numbers of Chinese captives on board. He would have noted that the Chinese, much like African slaves, were subject to physical exams once they arrived—a checking of the mouth, the eyes, and the limbs for any signs of opium sickness or disease. He would also have noticed the easy abuse of the coolies at the hands of labor-starved sugar planters and the draconian regulations that forbade permanent settlement after the terms of the indenture were satisfied and that forced many Chinese to work in the boiler houses of the *ingenios*, or sugar plantations, long after they should have been free. He surely would have heard of the desperate suicides of many Chinese on the island and would have heard of their fantasies of a return to China. He would have seen all of this and thought, we can be sure, of some way to turn a profit for himself.

In November of 1867, in search of that better future, he—now known as Tye Kim Orr, a "priest"—found his way to New Orleans aboard the *Star of the Union,* which carried from Cuba the third cargo of Chinese to be brought to Louisiana. New Orleans was then a sister city of sorts to Havana, its fortunes bound to the price of sugar and to the plantations—like Judah P. Benjamin's Bellechase—that lined the Mississippi River up to and beyond Baton Rouge. But New Orleans no longer had slaves to cut cane, haul boxes, or load ships; it had only freedmen, who could not, the planter class reasoned, be trusted to work without physical compulsion. Like British Guiana and Cuba, the Crescent City needed labor—cheap, dependable, trustworthy bound labor, labor that would not run away or renege on a contract or protest if worked hard and long in the fields. (Benjamin himself had fled the South through Cuba, had reclaimed his British citizenship by 1866, and had become a barrister.) For O'Tye Kim, necessity was the mother of opportunity, and within two years he was a featured speaker across the South. Brought to Memphis in 1869 to complement the work of renowned trader in Chinese flesh Cornelius Koopmanschap, O'Tye Kim spoke of the supposed laziness of emancipated Africans and of the supposed thrift and efficiency of the Chinese and preached the hiring of the latter at the expense of the former. Later, he ventured to China with the Louisiana planter John Williams, who had heard him speak in Memphis and who had managed to bring the only successful coolie ship from the Far East straight to New Orleans. In a final irony, O'Tye Kim's hemispheric arc comes to a stop in Donaldsonville, Louisiana, where he came to direct the first ever Freedmen's Bureau school for African Americans, tutoring the children of those he had once called lazy, schooling them in the virtues of hard work and clean character, and scheming for a Chinese settlement in that new version of Hopetown.[11]

This seems an unusually mobile and enticing story, but the central point of this book is that it was not, in the end, so unusual at all. Within the United States, O'Tye Kim's story strengthens the important claim that, as historian Moon-Ho Jung puts it, the coolie was a "pivotal" concept in the "reconstruction of racial and national hierarchies" and that debate over that concept "enabled and justified a series of historical transitions—from slave trade laws to racially coded immigration laws, from a slaveholding nation to a 'nation of immigrants.' "[12] Setting the triangulation of white, black, and yellow labor within the context of "imperial labor reallocation," we can also remind ourselves that Southern memories of an imperial past did not vanish at Appomattox.[13] The richly provocative image of the Chinese contract laborer, quietly tilling the soil, reflected the exploitative expansiveness of the Southern imagination and highlighted the region's indebtedness to the labor switch points and cultural networks of the New World. Moreover, Chinese contract laborers moved around the American Mediterranean alongside, across, and in competition with other racialized bodies, other ideas and stereotypes, and other fantasies. "The coolie" was just one solution to the labor problem, offered at one moment in time by one aspect of the planter class and as a complement or alternative to other possible solutions. It is the full matrix of possibilities that needs to be explored, I believe, and it needs to be seen in just the right manner—from up high, where national borders fade, though not completely disappear, and where shipping routes, longitude, and latitude serve as equally stable markers of location. Seen from that angle, the debate over coolie labor in the postemancipation South reveals the evolving place of the defeated slaveholders in the world. It defies the limits of national history and challenges us to avoid giving the nation-state too much explanatory power. It reveals the global designs of the master class and allows us, in turn, to subject those designs to even brighter, clearer illumination.

Middle Passages

As spring turned to summer and the harvest approached in 1869, rumors swirled about in Charleston—rumors of laborers who were rough and ready to work hard for a decent wage. To pick the long-stapled cotton of the coast or clear the rice fields of the low country, South Carolina needed lean, muscled arms and strong backs. Sixty Swiss, one such rumor went, had arrived in eastern North Carolina; Tennessee, one heard it said elsewhere, would soon receive thousands of Chinese, thanks to a timely contract made in San Francisco.[14] For frustrated South Carolinians, these third-hand accounts were always about Europeans or Asians brought somewhere else—to Georgia, Mississippi, or Louisiana—and were often written with the hope that the next group of stalwart Finns or curious Chinese might arrive on the empty docks of Charleston. In late August, word reached the city that a ship, the *Betsy Ames,* had left Hong Kong for Charleston "some time ago." "Coolies for Charleston," read the headline, limp with relief. But was it true? There was no other information—no dates of departure or arrival, indeed no specifics of any kind. One week later, the New York *Journal of Commerce* put an end to the speculation: "No such vessel as the *Betsey Ames* is borne in the American Lloyd's Register, and no such departure from Hong Kong has been otherwise reported."[15] Still, dreams of ships running low in the water, filled with machinelike coolies or German immigrants, died hard in Charleston in 1869.

Two years later, William Lawton, a native of South Carolina, would devote a good deal of his essay on "rice and its culture," read to the Agricultural Congress in Selma, Alabama, to this same topic. Here, too, the Chinese were spoken of in the optimistic future tense—not as laborers in hand but as idealized workers yet to arrive. Describing the rice mills, Lawton enthused over the latest advances in technology. What better people to manage the milling of rice, he asked the audience, than the Chinese, who "owe[d] their early civilization" to the grain and whose labors in Cuban sugar mills had earned them a reputation for "agricultural knowledge and science"? "It is manifestly clear," Lawton opined, "that they are destined to occupy an important bearing on the industrial future of this continent, as laborers and artisans." As their arrival was inevitable, it was "the duty of every Southern man" to bring them to "the fields and factories" of the region, for it was the "only hope or prospect" for the "restoration" of Southern enterprise and profit margins. "They are coming," he assured the audience, "and will migrate in vast numbers to our shores."[16]

Those fantasies of immigrant labor, whether Chinese or European, were at least partly the consequence of the war. South Carolina had been especially devastated by Sherman's brutal march through the state to Columbia. The economic side effects of this destruction were, from the standpoint of the planters, horrific. In 1860, Charleston had been a bustling, deep-water port, one of the most important in the South, with substantial shipping connections to New York, Philadelphia, Boston, Havana, and other ports. Smaller steamship lines had regularly carried cargo and people up and down the Atlantic coast, linking the city to smaller ports and river towns to Charleston. A network of railroads had shuffled exportable goods from inland plantations to the coast and from there to the world. In 1865, at the end of the war, all of that was gone, as the various sailing ships and steamers had been confiscated by one side or the other and the railroads had been largely destroyed. It

The ruins of the North Eastern Railroad Depot, Charleston, South Carolina, in 1865. From the Prints and Photographs Division, Library of Congress.

would take years to completely rebuild the shipping lines and even longer for their absence to be less keenly felt. A yearning for coolies or for European immigrants was, therefore, an expression of loss, reflecting the phantom sensations of the global economy that had once been a vital part of the life of Charleston and that was, as a consequence of war, no longer so.[17]

The desperate thirst for workers could not be quenched by the vast sea of black people in the state. Letters, official reports, and editorials drawn from Charleston, Columbia, and smaller towns and rural communities throughout the state shrilly noted the supposed degeneration of the black population—its disappearance from the state or from the rural farming communities, its presumed postemancipation proclivity for crime and violence, or its assumed disinclination to labor for the former masters of the South. "The negro population," one editorial fumed, "is large, unruly, and ignorant."[18] "We did so badly the last season," rice planter William Johnstone wrote, "I am afraid our planters *(generally)* will [fare] no better in the coming season if the negroes do not get to work more earnestly soon. *My* business as a rice planter is *plaid* [*sic*] *out.*"[19] To explain the rapid degeneration of black Africans in America, advocates of the status quo antebellum—including South Carolina's governor, Benjamin Perry—resurrected the idea that "the Negro" had been a separate creation of God and was therefore not man. Others noted a decline in the black population and argued that "the Negro" was dying out, no longer protected from the iron laws of competition by the paternal protections of slavery. Still others hoped to hasten that extinction. Surrounded by the ruins of the slaveholding South, the master class of South Carolina offered the mobility and selfishness of black Americans—embodied in their unwillingness to line up happily and take whatever job might be offered at whatever wage—as proof positive that it was time to cultivate a new crop of workingmen. And if that new "alien" labor force should speed up the inevitable decline of African America, it would be all the better.[20]

This story was hardly unique to South Carolina. Set affright by the experience of emancipation in the Americas, the Deep South seemed incapable of understanding the freedom of movement as anything other than a precondition for economic disaster and racial ruin. Planters, politicians, and advocates of a new industrialized South traced the emerging pattern of transhumance, lawlessness, and "rioting" from New Orleans to Charleston as if it were a mathematical proof of what they knew—with terrible certainty—would soon come to pass. With teeth-chattering trepidation, they looked to the experiences of the Atlantic world—to Haiti, to British Guiana, to Jamaica, and later to Cuba and Brazil—much as sixteenth-century explorers had looked to dusty, ancient tomes for information about anthropophagi and sea monsters. The book review editor of the *Charleston Daily Courier* suggested that South Carolinians should pick up a copy of Anthony Trollope's *West Indies* to learn what had become of Jamaica after the "fatal experiment" of emancipation: "It will be curious, in the perusal, to note how true the negro is to his own nature, once left to its nomadic indulgence; and how consistent were his developments of freedom in the West

Indies, with what we see of him here, in the same novel and unnatural condition."[21] Somehow, J. C. Delavigne suggested (echoing the Cuban planter Miguel Aldama), the "void which has been caused in our labor system by the emancipation of the blacks" had to be filled, whether by the immigration of Asians or Europeans, by technological improvements, or by the greater importation of former slaves from the upper South.[22] "I feel," one planter wrote, "like I suppose a mariner would at sea without a compass and a storm in view."[23]

In the midst of this dizzying tempest, the prospect of white or Asian immigration was a veritable North Star, offering the Southern planter class and those in search of a modern industrial South a chance at one of two options: a new white citizenry of yeoman farmers and dependable laborers capable of self-government or a body of bound laborers with a reputation for docility and hard work. The image of "the Negro" as "indolent" and "devoid of ambition," as an ideal wherein "the animal largely predominates over the intellectual," would be recast in the postwar years to fit the call for some new body of laborers across the Deep South.[24] When, in November of 1865, the *Natchez Democrat* lobbied Southern planters to extend to the freedmen "kind treatment, a fair recompense for faithful labor, and a disposition to make negroes happy and comfortable" in exchange for "labor as permanent and as reliable as it was when it was compulsory," William Battaile of Mobile, Alabama, wrote to the editor to label this approach a mistake.[25] Confessing "surprise" at the *Democrat's* faith in "the Negro," Battaile admitted that "his labor, as far as it can be controlled, will be necessary and useful." "But," Battaile continued, "he must not stand in the way of the more intelligent *white* labor. . . . This is, and must be, a white man's country, here forth and forever." To that end, Battaile suggested that "foreign white labor" might be easily "adapted to the culture of our Southern staples" and admitted that he was "order[ing] them daily."[26] "[The Negro] is among us and cannot be removed except by death," a later editorial argued, in seeming response to Battaile. "He belongs to an inferior race, he is subject to our laws and ever must be. . . . Our country will need his labor, until at last his place can be supplied."[27]

For some, this simple act of substitution was all about the bottom line; for others it was equally a matter of social prophylactics: "We can," another planter put it in 1866, "drive the niggers out and import coolies that will work better, at less expense, and relieve us from this cursed nigger impudence."[28] Three radically different imagined creations thus circulated in the debates over the labor problem: Asian "coolies" and European "immigrants, both envisioned as alternatives to "the Negro." Advocates of any one of these groups would often triangulate the relative virtues and faults of yellow, white, and black quite differently. "Each race," a Louisiana planter told John T. Trowbridge, "has its own peculiarities."[29] The trick, to paraphrase Trowbridge, was finding the right "race" for the right job and the right place. Looking to break up a large plantation and encourage smaller settlements? European immigrants were perfect. Looking to maintain large plantations but not willing to pay emancipated Africans a wage? Perhaps Chinese coolies would fit the bill. Looking for a familiar body of workers and afraid of importing foreigners? Cast down your buckets amongst the freedmen. As Reconstruction waxed and waned, those three discordant peoples—Africans, Asians, and Europeans—were drawn together in the American South, just as they had been pulled together in Cuba, in Latin America, and throughout the Caribbean.

The dynamics of that brief convergence—that triangulation of peoples between the end of the Civil War and the end of Reconstruction—illuminate the final stages in the slaveholding South's relationship with the Caribbean. There are loud echoes here, especially when the conversation turns to the Chinese, of what had transpired in Cuba, Jamaica, and California. Across the broader Americas, Chinese immigrants were a "model minority" of sorts; they were hard workers; they labored, many supposed, for longer hours and for far less money and food than either whites or blacks. Thus, white modeled ideal behavior for yellow, just as yellow modeled ideal behavior for black, with black, as the tortured logic went, modeling to no one at all. Still others, from Brazil to Massachusetts, believed that the Chinese were a near lethal threat to the republic. But the arguments for and against European immigrants were different, far more a matter of mimicking the success of the midwestern and western reaches of the Union and far less a matter of borrowing from similar (and failed) attempts throughout Latin America to court workers from within the pale. The passage of this confusing triracial moment suggests something critically important about the evolving relationship of the South, the Caribbean, and the United States. The considerable debate over the strengths and weaknesses of European, Asian, and African laborers reveals a continued redirection of the idea of the labor problem in the South, the last stages of a sloppy and imprecise but still detectable shift from an antebellum mindset that ran, by and large, from north to south in the Americas and eastward to Africa, in which the slaveholding South was bound to the American Mediterranean, to a postbellum fixation on the Northern states that could sometimes cut across the Atlantic to Europe. It was as if a conversation among four parties—Europe, Africa, the United States, and Latin America—was, quite suddenly and abruptly, to exclude half of its participants. In all such conversations, where both the subject and participants have changed, silences and occlusions can tell as much as all the noise.

In the summer of 1869, William Lawton, chairman of the newly minted Committee on Chinese Immigrants for the South Carolina Agricultural and Mechanical Society, penned a letter to the influential New York *Journal of Commerce.* Before turning to his real interest, Lawton devoted considerable space to a discussion of "negro labor," hoping to convince a presumably Northern audience that former slaves were "gradually dwindling away *dying out.* And becoming year by year less efficient & reliable." The "future prosperity of the Country and general good," he continued, depended on the introduction of "a kind of labor suited to Southern latitudes." Could the *Journal,* he asked, recommend a reputable shipping firm with experience in the China trade, a firm that would be willing to bring "the proper description of Asiatic field laborers to the port of Charleston"?[30] Two days later, a restless, energized Lawton gave further thought to the Chinese in a letter to Robert Mure, president of Charleston's Chamber of Commerce. The two men had previously discussed a British ship owner—a friend of Mure—who had regularly transported "coolies from China to the Islands of the West Indies." Lawton hoped to repeat this successful enterprise and wanted Mure to help him find Asian labor that had originated in the agricultural regions of China, where he presumed there would be "scientific" knowledge of cotton, rice, and sugar cultivation. This, Lawton knew, would be difficult, so he offered, as a complementary suggestion, the example of Colombia and Venezuela, where "the emancipated African race" was "in the same condition that we now find them with us. Idle & dissolute," and where imported Canary Islanders had proved themselves to be "useful and manageable and superior." Lawton would be satisfied, it seemed, with either coolies or Canary Islanders, so long as Mure was able to secure about at least 100,000, a number that "would double the production of South Carolina . . . in two years."[31]

Lawton's labor-starved home state of South Carolina was at the far fringes of a movement that began, in earnest, in New Orleans, the so-called Queen of the South, with its history of slave trading, its port connections to the Caribbean, and its pronounced West Indian texture. Like its sister city, Havana, the fate of New Orleans was bound to global economic enterprise and most tightly to the sugar revolution. But with the war over, New Orleans found itself quarantined from any business with a number of Caribbean ports of call, including Havana. "Havana is healthy," one front page catch-all concluded: "They are getting 'free laborers' from China."[32] Encouraging a certain culture of anticipation, reports in the early months after the war emphasized both the habits of the coolies and their ability, through competition and hard work, to compel labor from even the most difficult former slaves. "In Cuba," another editorial ran, "the exportable production has been doubled in seven years. . . . In other islands, where the negroes have been emancipated, the introduction of Asiatic laborers has arrested the tendency of the *emancipados* to idleness and worthlessness, and has stimulated them to faithful work."[33]

The proximity of New Orleans to the Caribbean, when coupled with the needs of the local sugar planters in southern Louisiana, ensured that some Chinese workers would arrive in the South by way of the Crescent City. The first hundred or so Chinese arrived in Natchidoches, Louisiana, in 1867, having been brought there by a small group of cotton and sugar planters, as historian Lucy Cohen describes it, to "supplement the work of emancipated Negroes."[34] Many of these early arrivals came directly from Havana and Matanzas in Cuba upon the completion of their original eight-year contract. And some came to the United States at the request of former masters in Cuba. One of the architects of this move to "import" Chinese laborers was Jules H. Normand. The son of a Louisiana planter, Norman had been a former expatriate planter and hospital manager in Cuba during the 1850s and early 1860s. These first Chinese peoples brought to the American South were Spanish-speaking "voluntary" immigrants; as "free" laborers not part of the illegal "coolie trade," they were quickly hired off to fellow planters in southern Louisiana and along the Mississippi River. Soon, greater numbers (though never more than a few hundred here and there) would arrive from China, California, and New York, brought into Arkansas, Alabama, Mississippi, South Carolina, and Louisiana by a widespread international network of bankers, Chinese and American "agents," planters, local employers, and self-styled prophets of the virtues of Asian labor.[35]

Because these immigrant Chinese were supposed to be "first class" laborers, they were likely to find themselves hired out to railroad construction companies, factories, or mills. As in Cuba and throughout the Caribbean, the general, if self-contradictory, sense of things was that the Chinese were better at some work than at others—good at cutting cane but not cotton, excellent in the factory or as domestic labor but not in the field. When the Louisiana state legislature handed control of the cotton mill at the state penitentiary over to Samuel L. James and Company in 1870, James brought in Chinese laborers, and the mill was soon "operating round the clock."[36] Three hundred Chinese men worked on the ill-fated Alabama and Chattanooga Railroad, at least until the seizure of the railroad by the U.S. Marshal's office in a bankruptcy proceeding. After rioting with black and white workers against the seizure of the railroad and the subsequent loss of their wages, the Chinese settled near Tuscaloosa, earning wages as domestic labor and eventually being recruited for a Louisiana plantation. The 150 Chinese who settled at the Milloudon plantation near New Orleans worked alongside emancipated slaves and caused quite a stir with their "blue blouses and drawers . . . shaven crowns, beardless faces, and plaited pigtails sweeping the ground."[37]

The South came late to the table for Chinese labor, and its notion of what Asian labor could offer was rooted in the varied experiences of other former and current slaveholding societies in the Caribbean. Those very few Chinese who came or were brought to the antebellum South— for instance, the twenty coolies who came in 1854 to the Eddyville Iron Works in Kentucky—were viewed as cultural oddities or "experiments" and not as sustainable sources of labor.[38] By that time, the West Indies had almost thirty years of widespread experience with indentured labor from Asia, even if most of it came from India and not from China. Beginning in 1838, British officials offered contract labor from the Far East as a supposedly liberal reform meant to mitigate the damage done to the sugar-growing regions of Jamaica, British Guiana, Antigua, and elsewhere. A decade later, the Spanish Caribbean and Latin America— from Mexico to Peru to Cuba—leapt to claim its own Asian labor force, putting its primarily Chinese coolies to work in guano harvesting, mining, and sugar cane cultivation. By 1860, there were more Chinese in Latin America than there were in North America. Nearly every Latin American and Caribbean nation or colony had some considerable experience with the Chinese as "substitute" or "temporary" labor. With the slave trade now closed and the number of slaveholding societies dwindling, there were sizable populations of Chinese in many New World republics or colonies.

Although this longer experience had not produced any meaningful consensus about the Chinese, there were two very rough schools of thought across the Caribbean. For those who approved of coolie labor, the Chinese were perfect laboring machines and the exact opposite of "the Negro." The Chinese worked where former African slaves might have worked, had there been enough former slaves to go around and had the rumors of degeneration not circulated so wildly. The Chinese worked where the white working class might have worked, if the latter group had not gained a reputation for their expense, their unwillingness to settle in tropical climes, and their troublesome propensity for strife and strikes. In short, the Chinese worked everywhere. And, moreover, they worked hard. For those who loathed the Chinese, the association of the coolie with disease, unsatisfied sexual desires, bestiality, treachery and cunning, and hard bargaining surely outweighed their skills as a working people. These positions were typically irreconcilable—either one was a proponent of Chinese labor, or one was not. The end result, as far as the planter class of the South might have been concerned, was a profoundly mixed message: one Demerara planter described the Chinese on the Windsor Forest estate as "equal to the Africans" in their endurance and strength, as "happy, contented, and cheerful," and as versatile, contented labor; in contrast, Trinidadian Immigration Agent-General Henry Mitchell described the Chinese as a massive headache, prone to nitpick over every aspect of their contract and quick to show their considerable temper.[39]

Southern interest and disinterest in Chinese labor was also shaped by the veritable avalanche of caustic criticism from California, where anti-Chinese sentiments were more heated and more violent than anywhere else in the Western hemisphere. In the decades leading up to the Civil War, Chinese immigrants had arrived in the Northeast and in the West, where there was a need for labor in the mills, in the construction of railroads, and in mining, and where there was a dearth of white settlers. By 1860, at the advent of the Civil War, the Chinese were no longer isolated in a few scattered and smallish communities hidden in big cities, where they were primarily cultural curiosities, small businessmen, or sailors, but were, instead, a national presence and a subject of intense debate. Immigrants from China raised fears of a "Yellow Peril" among white immigrants in the far West and urbanizing North, where the average Chinese worker was, once again, presumed to be preternaturally efficient and economical and thus threatened to the livelihood of the "white" citizen. The hodgepodge of immigrant and native-born peoples in California who comprised the white working class worried, shouted, and argued that the sexualized strangeness of the Chinese—their queues, their "pajamas," their inscrutable gaze, their lack of women—would soon wash away the racial bedrock of the republic.[40] This complaint, of course, touched the raw nerves of the postwar South where they were most sensitive.

To complement anxieties about "amalgamation" and the racial bedrock, there were more calculated fears of the Chinese as "criminally cheap labor," fears fed by the abundant pro-Chinese literature, which, in contrast to earlier assertions of physiological weakness, enthused about the supposed ability of the Chinese to labor eternally for fewer wages and smaller meals.[41] Labor leaders and economists painted a profoundly ambivalent portrait of the Chinese, using broad brushstrokes to emphasize their qualities as, in the words of historian Rosanne Currarino, "the physical embodiment of emasculating wage work, as the prototypical wage worker, stricken with poverty, and as the very machines of industrial production, devoid of human desire."[42] The Chinese, whose thriftiness and work ethic was a source of perennial frustration and rage for the white working class of the western states, were targeted there precisely because of their "superior" labor abilities, because of their secretive nature, and because they "underconsumed," choosing to save money or ship it home rather than spend it in the United States.

Complaints about the Chinese as perennial sojourners and tame laborers would have made them even more appealing in the South, where they would be temporarily replacing or supplementing emancipated slaves deemed dangerously unreliable as free labor and where their labor would be welcomed as less costly and demanding than that of white workers—where they would be "coolies" first and foremost.[43] However, for the same reason, their arrival in the South would arouse the suspicion of the North, where the importation of the Chinese was widely viewed as an attempt to steer clear, whenever possible, of "the Negro." There were, moreover, powerful international legal questions to be resolved. Although Congress had banned contract labor in the 1850s and the Chinese coolie trade in 1862, West Coast railroad and mining interests brought in tens of thousands of Chinese men in that decade under the "credit-ticket" system, in which the debt of the Chinese émigré and the control over his or her labor was owned by one of several Chinese American companies in California. Concentrated in the far West, the Chinese competed with the impoverished Irish along the edge of what South Carolinian James Henry Hammond once called "the mudsill," the line between free and slave, white and black, citizen and noncitizen.[44] Laborers were hardly free, but if they were not coolies, it was not clear yet what else they might be. Nor was it clear that the South intended to bring the Chinese to the region under some version of the credit-ticket.

To get the Chinese from the Caribbean to the South, the planter class also had to navigate some rather murky legal waters. Participation by U.S. shipping firms in the coolie trade had been ended by a bill passed in 1862, though that same piece of legislation had failed to make a distinction between the general use of the term "coolie" to describe all Asian labor, the specific use of the term to denote those who were forced or tricked into hard labor in the Americas, and everything in between. In August of 1867, for example, concerned that a few Louisiana cane planters were ferrying contracted Chinese from Cuba to New Orleans, the city's district attorney impounded the *William Robertson,* a brig reputed to have some two dozen Chinese aboard, and arrested the ship's captain. The labor contractor in charge of these migrant workers had provided each of them with legal passports, but he had also illegally "bought" these Asians and had brought them to New Orleans with the fullest intention of using them as if they were in Cuba, which is to say using them as hard labor. The ensuing debate revolved around some important questions: Were these coolies? Or were they simply Chinese laborers under contracts? What, after all, was the difference? In this one case, the Chinese on board were soon reclassified by the U.S. vice consul in Havana as "passengers," meaning that at the time of their travels they had no longer technically been "coolies."

The two dozen or so Chinese on board the *William Robertson* were, then, simply contract laborers, no more and no less illegal than the Chinese in California. Newly arrived Chinese in New Orleans could be released, but only after they were shown to be free immigrants and not coolies sold to Southern planters under Spanish contract.[45] A few Louisiana planters worked to procure, through illicit means, a few hundred or so Chinese from Cuba, but before a regular smuggling trade in Chinese bodies could be established—running from Havana and Matanzas to New Orleans—the Cuban planter class moved to claim and to keep as much of their dwindling supply of coolies as possible. The search for coolie automatons then turned to California and to China, two far less likely and far longer pipelines to the labor-starved South.[46]

Those planters who managed to bring Chinese laborers to Louisiana could hardly have described the diversification of their working force as a complete success. By the late 1860s, several plantations had brought large numbers of Chinese either directly from China, from California, or from Cuba, but these pipelines were unreliable, and the laborers themselves were much more independent minded than their reputations would have suggested.[47]

Consider, for instance, the experiences of Edward Gay, a former coffee broker with substantial business and personal connections in Cuba and the owner of the St. Louis plantation in Iberville Parish. Gay was familiar with the difficulties associated with the employment of freedmen and with the use of coolies in the Caribbean. In mid-August of 1870, his son, Andrew, concluded that the arrival of "several lots of hands" on the plantation was meaningless, as "those City negroes they do not stay any length of time," and suggested the pursuit of "cheaper" Chinese labor in San Francisco. The Chinese, Andrew continued, could be gotten in just six short weeks, at "$70 pr head," a rate that was "cheaper than sending to VA for negroes as they are so uncertain after you get them."[48] Rumors of Gay's interest in the Chinese spread quickly. Three weeks later, Edward's business partner, Samuel Cranwill, urged him to set aside "the *pigtail* question," noting that "planters who have tried Chinese labor have had a surfeit of it."[49] It would be better, Cranwill advised, to bring "one hundred hands" from Virginia. The dream of cheap, easy labor—docile yellow labor and not truculent black labor—was not so easily set aside. In late October of 1870, Edward and his brother, William, received roughly fifty Chinese from California, all of them with three-year contracts, the result of a month-long negotiation with various agents, including Cornelius Koopmanschap. The Gay brothers divided the immigrants between their two plantations, and although initial reactions were positive, none of the workers would stay even a single full year. Edward's workers fled for higher wages in St. Louis, and his efforts to recover their labors through a breach of contract were unsuccessful; William's contract laborers proved to be less obedient than advertised, and they left for New Orleans.[50]

Outside of the general orbit of New Orleans and the lower Mississippi, the unrealized image of the coolie cutting cane or building railroads continued to haunt the South. By early July of 1869, the critical lack of laboring hands in the fields and factories of the region had become even more notable, and the need for replacement workers was even more desperate. In that same month, several hundred planters and businessmen attended the first ever Chinese Labor Convention in Memphis, Tennessee, chaired by Isham Harris, the secessionist ex-governor of the state and a former Confederate exile to Mexico. Given the political climate—the imposition of federal authority and troops in the South and the self-righteous idealism of the radicals in Congress—the convention delegates were largely careful to describe their desire for Chinese coolies as a matter of profit margins and not as a matter of disdain for the freedmen. With a few exceptions, they were generally disposed to repeat the usual certainties uttered by all those who favored the Chinese as laborers: that they were easy to control, that amalgamation was no real threat, that they were cheap and reliable. Former Confederate general Nathan Bedford Forrest, hoping for more dependable labor for his railroad-building project, urged the immediate importation of Chinese workers and read aloud a letter from Walter H. Gibson, a South Carolinian and booster for the coolie trade who was presently the commissioner of Chinese immigration in Hawaii. Perhaps more persuasively, Tye Kim Orr, the Chinese evangelical who left British Guiana for Lafourche Parish, Louisiana, offered to the convention attendees a portrait of the "heathen" Chinese as both ideal workers and willing converts to "the Word" and dramatized the usefulness of the coolie to the planter class by complaining at length about the "degeneration" of "the Negro" in the British West Indies after slavery. The event came to a fitting climax with the arrival of Cornelius Koopmanschap, the famous Dutch immigrant and California coolie broker, and the series of practical "how-to" workshops that followed. One year later, Edward Gay "contracted" a group of Scandinavian workers.

At South Carolina's own labor convention, held in 1870, the pro-Chinese rhetoric was even more florid. Although the bulk of the convention focused on bringing white European immigrants to Charleston and its surrounding counties, some hoped that the Chinese could complement the Europeans: "In the lower part of the state and on the islands, where rice and long cotton is cultivated, and where it is supposed white labor cannot be permanently or profitably employed, it would seem a great acquisition."[51] The Chinese laborer," argued J. K. Vance, chairman of the Special Committee on Chinese Immigration,

has shown himself industrious, frugal, obedient and attentive to the interest of his employer. He is by nature mild and pacific. His shrewdness and wonderful imitative powers enable him readily to acquire the necessary information and to perform with facility every kind of farm labor. . . . The Chinaman cannot be surpassed, either as a servant or a laborer, by any other, whether you place him in the house, the garden, the field, the workshop, or on the railroad. . . . They work from sunrise until sunset, allowing one hour for dinner, and agree to obey, unquestioned, all orders from the owner or manager.[52]

Here the figure of "John Chinaman" is a fantastic, extraordinarily obe-dient automaton, willing to work where white folks cannot and black folks will not. In light of events in the early twenty-first century, this is a familiar image, anticipating current debates over immigration from Mexico and Latin America—and it reflects a long-held sense that an unhealthy environment and harsh labor conditions cannot be reformed and that rather than creating new laws that regulate work, a new type of worker should be brought in to satisfy the needs of the rich and the powerful. "The Chinese laborers," one newspaper noted, "are said to be as agile as monkeys."[53]

Still, despite all the fanfare and the union of New South and Old South interests, the region could not agree about the Chinese. The de-sire for Asian labor was shaped by the general representation of Asians as cheap and capable workers who were, for the most part, able hands in any climate. But in the Gulf South, as in the far West, for each posi-tion piece enthusing over the virtues of the thrifty, efficient, and dex-terous "John Chinaman," there was another citing his expense, his re-calcitrance, and his troubling social diseases. When popular illustrator Alfred J. Waud set out to capture the "Chinese Cheap Labor" at the Milloudon plantation, he did so by emphasizing work—every Chinese laborer in his image is holding a tool and either bending or stooping. He also set their faces in shadow, with as little detail and as little hu-manity as possible. Another image, set in a dark, closely packed space, reveals the facial expressions of three Chinese as they take opium in the proverbial den of iniquity, but their features are frozen in an angry mask.[54] "We do not only want reliable laborers," wrote former Con-federate general and popular hero Robert E. Lee to the president of the Virginia Immigration Society, which was then considering the Chinese as potential laborers, "but good citizens, whose interests and feelings would be in unison with our own."[55] However troublesome "the Negro" might be, another argument went, he or she was at least a God-fearing Christian; the Chinese, in contrast, were a dangerous "pagan" people, "barbarous" to the end.[56] More important, many Southerners soon concluded that despite their reputation for efficiency and cheap-ness, the Chinese were every bit as expensive and insistent as their Eu-ropean counterparts. Much like contract laborers in Cuba, they knew their rights under the law, they seemed acutely aware of the value of their labor, and they expressed a confounding familiarity with both or-ganized and disorganized resistance.[57] The South wanted easy replace-ments for slaves, not yet another lesson in the labor problem and certainly not "yellow" laborers who demanded the same treatment as "white" immigrant workers from Germany and Ireland. J. W. Alvord, in his report to Major General O. O. Howard, found only contempt for the Chinese in the Sea Islands and Savannah; "these people are used to our work," one planter told him, pointing toward the homes of the freedmen, "and we are used to them."[58] The editors of *De Bow's Review* made up their mind a little faster than most; by 1870, the *San Francisco Dispatch* was praising the New Orleans monthly for its principled discouragement of "the insane movement" to bring the Chinese to the sugar and cotton plantations of Louisiana and Mississippi.[59]

Of course, even if there had been a regional consensus about Chinese migrant laborers, it is unlikely that the increasingly powerful Radical Republicans in Congress would have allowed a contract labor trade to flourish. Indeed, the fascination with the Chinese was, in some ways, a very deliberate act of subterfuge perpetrated by those who hoped to continue large-scale plantation agriculture, with all of the social and

A. R. Waud's portrait of Chinese laborers on the Milloudon Plantation in Louisiana. Courtesy of the Historic New Orleans Collection. Accession no. 1953.73.

cultural trappings of the Old South, and who loathed the imposition of "Negro rule." Writing to James Sparkman, the secretary of the Georgetown Agricultural and Mechanical Club, William Lawton urged avoidance of the term "coolie," lest it raise the suspicions of radicals and free blacks in South Carolina. Lawton laid out a talking-points memo for Sparkman, sharing the contents of a conversation with William Memminger, who firmly believed that "the introduction of Chinese labor is the true course & hope for us of the South, but very wisely suggests that we ought to act *quietly* & *promptly*, bring them before the *Negro, Carpetbag, Scalawag,* and State Legislature pass adverse laws as they likely will do."[60] The moral impulses of immigration efforts and Radical Reconstruction pushed, by and large, in different directions.

For many reasons, then, the Chinese were rarely much more than an abstract or theoretical proposition in the South. In early January of 1870, some three hundred Chinese arrived in St. Louis, Missouri, on the way to work on the Houston Texas Central railroad line between Calvert and Richmond, Virginia. In this case, a California man, Chew Ah Heaung, served as the agent for the Chinese, bargaining on their behalf for wages and for the general terms of their contracts. As was typical, a small crowd gathered at the railroad station to meet them, and like everyone else present, the writer assigned to cover the event for the local newspaper paid special attention to their skin, which he described as "olive-colored . . . a whitish hue tinged with orange and vermillion." Just shy of midnight, some 247 of the Chinese boarded the steamer Mississippi, bound for New Orleans. They boarded by torchlight, and in this near darkness they looked, as the local reporter put it, like a "cross between the Indian and the Mexican." He hoped—as many in the South hoped— that this brief, ephemeral encounter with the Chinese was a harbinger of a longer relationship. "All in all," he summarized, "they are a queer-looking set of people—queer for their ways, queer in their habits, queer in their language, and may work a queer revolution in the labor of this country." Here, as elsewhere, the Chinese were never more than "curiosities," their bodies always the source of idle speculation, always in movement, the benefits of their presence always discussed in the future tense.[61]

The search for "good help" was often a search without end. "Is Mamie's new *servant* . . . white or black?" asked Harriet Elliot of her mother in 1867. "Help," she continued, "is a northern word—which has helped to bring about the present state of affairs. I am more aristocratic now than I ever was—the poorer I am, the more proud I am of my good blood. Perhaps in *heaven* two classes might live hospitably together on the same footing, *religion* making ladies and gentlemen of all—but on earth certainly not."[62] The entire Elliot family was, at this point, in the midst of a kaleidoscopic comparative assessment of the available racial options. "The Chinaman," one family member stressed, "may make you in the future an excellent servant of all work. . . . They are so capable that they learn in a short while to be cooks, carpenters, or anything else."[63] William, however, disagreed. Writing from Oak Lawn, one of the family plantations, he confessed to his mother that "the Chinaman" he had hired was "such a disappointment." "The individual," he explained, "makes an *excuse* about not understanding—he has come to get away from negroes apparently—'is too hot & too much negroes in Matanzas' he says—he may be first rate but for us & our purposes he's a humbug."[64] Mamie, contributing to the debate, preferred to hire only "white" domestic servants with "red hair," but Hattie found the Irish to be nothing but trouble.[65] They were so much trouble, in fact, that she had dispatched her Cuban husband, Ambrosio, to Charleston, where she hoped he would "get a [pair of] fine germans'—or scotch."[66] (Johnnie Elliot, for his part, offered that a neighbor was "employing Irishmen as ditchers only.")[67] At the very least, one Elliot suggested, everyone could agree that "the freedmen work better than the crackers."[68] But despite this backhanded compliment, "the Negro" was no viable solution either. "The coast negro will not work," Ralph concluded, noting the infectious spirit of social equality that was present throughout the Reconstruction South.[69] For Harriet and Ambrosio, all this uncertainty about what was "best" and what was "available" could prompt fantasies of flight to someplace far away. "Well," Harriet sighed, writing to her mother, "if we fail here entirely we can still find a home and something to do in Cuba." Still, she worried that slavery might not last forever, even in Cuba. "A freedman," she offered, continuing her letter, "told Margaret a few days ago that 'they were soon going to Cuba to set the negroes free.'"[70] Two years later, Harriet was settled in Havana and loving it. She had gambled on the perpetuation of Cuban slavery, rather than juggle the various white, black, and yellow laboring peoples of the postwar South. "I have engaged an excellent nurse," she wrote proudly, "black, a slave & one who speaks English perfectly."[71] Five months later, Harriet was dead, a victim of Havana's annual yellow fever epidemic.[72]

Whitening the South

For many Southerners, white immigration was a better solution to the innumerable problems of freedom, for it avoided the new complications associated with Chinese labor and the tired frustrations of dealing with "the Negro." There was, of course, a fairly simple political calculus in play here: every African American "lost" and every European immigrant "gained" shifted the balance of power away from the "scalawag" governments and "Negro rule." Still, the drive to secure European immigrant settlers and laborers was only slightly less contentious than the push for Chinese coolies. No real consensus emerged around this issue. These were not, after all, English or Scotch-Irish settlers, second sons of landed gentry, or well-bred Anglo-Saxons; these were generally poor, working class, non-English-speaking peoples, coming from politically troubled regions of Europe like Ireland and Germany. As settlers or immigrants, these new arrivals were hardly "white" in the usual ways. And it remained an open question whether these immigrants should come to settle smaller plots of land made available by state or private agencies or whether they should labor in the service of the planter class as replacements for the freedmen. Still, debates over European immigrants also revealed a South that was more and more engaged in a dialogue with the free-labor Northern states.

This competition with the North for the white immigrant abundance of Europe did not, however, mean that the South was any less indebted to the traditions of the slaveholding Atlantic world. Indeed, nearly every other slaveholding society in the Americas had envisioned white immigration as a curative for the declining returns of the slave trade and the low birth rate of the enslaved African population and, later, as a form of postemancipation social engineering. In the British West Indies, the earliest efforts to encourage European immigrants after abolition were catastrophic failures. Subsequent policies brought far larger numbers of off-white Portuguese, who suffered terribly from a wide variety of tropical diseases and who served, primarily, as the foundation for an emerging merchant class that could be positioned between planters and workers, offering only an "indirect contribution to the plantation system." In Cuba, Rebecca Scott writes, "free immigrants were unlikely to want to labor in sugar," especially alongside slaves. Still, there were numerous efforts to bring Europeans to the island, many of those driven by "avowed white supremacists" who hoped to permanently alter, or lighten, the complexion of Cuban society. In Brazil, the southern twin of the United States, the enforcement of a ban on slave trading and the earliest gradual emancipation laws forced a public debate over immigration, ending in a rejection of Chinese labor and the pursuit—in competition with the American South—of European labor. In many cases, the quest for whiter labor as an alternative or

supplemental laboring force was invested with extraordinary significance, as if national progress at the warmer latitudes was contingent on
an acquisition of whiteness or white peoples or on a certain detropical-
ization of the population. The more successful the effort, the less "tropical" the place, the greater its chance for "civilization" after slavery.[73]

There was a practical dimension as well, of course. The more adven-
turous Southern planters, noting a "Negro exodus" and desperate for
field hands and manual laborers, eagerly encouraged the emigration of
Germans, Scandinavians, and the Irish, shamelessly advertising to foreign travelers that "the road to affluence is open to the immigrant who
arrives with adequate means."[74] The erasure of the Black Codes under
the Reconstruction governments and the refusal to allow coolies in the
Deep South forced more than a few Southern states to sponsor early efforts to encourage white immigration.[75] And so, even as they bemoaned
the labor problem that emancipation had wrought, some Southerners
aggressively—even frantically—tried to tap the pool of available
human capital in Europe. Their descriptions of the South—its resources, its culture, its climate—defy reality, but their hard work extended beyond mere advertisement. South Carolinians hoped for the
passage of local laws protecting immigrants and sent agents to Germany and Scandinavia to spark emigration to the labor-hungry South,
acts that incurred the wrath of the newly enfranchised African American legislators in that state.[76] Mississippi, much like its neighbors, established its own immigration efforts in the 1870s. *De Bow's Review*
carried lengthy articles on the immigration efforts of the South for
much of the late 1860s and early 1870s. "We desire, earnestly desire,"
one such editorial went, "the immigration of honest, industrious *white*
men."[77]

For much of the nineteenth century, there had been significant, if
sporadic, European immigration to the United States. Beginning in
the 1830s, millions of immigrants had arrived each decade. Driven by
the awful potato famines of the 1840s and lured by fantasies of life in
the New World's most famous postcolonial republic, millions of poor,
hardscrabble Irish had come to the United States (and also to South
America), where they were put to work at the dirtiest, most dangerous
tasks. Although the Irish were the epitome of the "alien menace" of the
prewar decades, there were also immigrants from Germany and Scandinavia, many of whom settled in the Midwest. Of course, the South was
never truly isolated from this history of nineteenth-century European immigration. Southerners had, since the 1840s, used Europeans—especially

the increasingly abundant "famine Irish"—in place of slaves. Long Island farmer Frederick Law Olmsted, sojourning along the Southern coast, had been told by one Virginia tobacco farmer that the Irish were used to drain fields because "a negro's life is too valuable to be risked at it. If a negro dies, it's a considerable loss, you know."[78] Olmsted's report on the Irish in the South has been often repeated, but it was hardly an accurate depiction of an immigrant's life in the world the slaveholders made. Port cities like New Orleans, Savannah, and Charleston were, to a certain extent, smaller versions of the great immigrant cities of the North, with significant Irish, German, and Jewish populations. Immigrants from Europe made for themselves a vibrant home in these Southern port cities, with discrete ethnic neighborhoods.[79]

Early experiments with white immigrants in the rural South were hardly successful enough to inspire confidence in the future of this approach to the labor problem. Twenty-three-year-old John Floyd King (later to be a congressman from Louisiana) spent the end of 1865 and the early months of 1866 wrestling with a few truculent German farmers. He had been forced to leave New York—and his beloved, Lin—rather abruptly and now found himself aboard the *Pauline Carroll* headed upstream from New Orleans to the Indian Village plantation, in Concordia, Louisiana, just nineteen miles from Natchez. "I have had quite a trying time with my Emigrants," he complained, "who . . . did everything in their power to desert me for the big wages paid daily white laborers in the city of N.O." He "foiled" their plans and "sent them up the river" a few days later. Writing to Lin aboard the steamboat traveling up the Mississippi, he took the time to describe what he saw "on the banks of the great river . . . deserted plantations, desolated & destroyed residences."[80]

The significance of those troublesome Germans became clearer once King arrived at Indian Village. "Yankees," he wrote to Lin, "have come down to this country, which they have desolated, and rented plantations . . . and they all expect to make large fortunes." "They will be disappointed," he concluded, and their disappointment would be rooted in what King saw as a most remarkable circumstance: the near complete disappearance of "the Negro" from the region. "Several years ago there were hundreds of negroes," he noted, "but few are to be seen, and in many instances, they are deserted entirely. Almost all the negro men and strong women have gone north or to the cities." Slavery, it seemed, had schooled blacks in the most elementary aspect of freedom: the chance to leave. Indeed, following emancipation, former slaves routinely fled the meanest and lowest places for better lives, showing a particular interest in education, religion, and land ownership. This, of course, posed only greater problems for both "emancipators" and planters, neither of whom (for different reasons) desired a small landowning class composed of the newly emancipated. Recently freed slaves moved from old plantations to the now booming Mississippi delta or to cities big and small, where they were drawn by comparatively higher wages and the lure of family or kinship ties in the South.[81] No wonder, then, that King was so keen on congratulating himself for securing white labor. "At present," he concluded, "our German Emigrants are doing remarkably well—they seem perfectly contented & I believe will far outwork the negroes."[82]

That contentment did not last very long. Two weeks later, King confided to Lin that he was spending most of his time "occupied with the white emigrant labor" and that he had "little confidence" in them "under the present laws."[83] Writing to his brother Mallery, he complained that his German immigrants would not work without a planter first offering "a supply of food" and that he could not rely on them for labor—even after giving them food—"on account of their deserting and their [sic] being no laws to bind them in person to their contract." Anticipating that he might someday need to bring more white immigrants to work in the fields, John spelled out two preliminary considerations born out of his experience: the careful selection of "German, Danish, or Dutch *Farmers*" (and not just any body of immigrants), and a binding contract for no less than one year, which would require new state legislation for its legitimation and which would almost certainly violate the constitutional ban on involuntary servitude that had been formalized in the Thirteenth Amendment. Over the brief two-week span between January 1 and January 18, King had lost a significant number of his immigrant farmers, but he had also managed to retrieve a few of these escapees through Louisiana's harsh debtor laws, which allowed for temporary imprisonment.[84] One month later, he had lost thirty of one hundred "Emigrants," though he described those lost as "the waifs of the gang."[85] And he had learned—much as the coolie masters aboard the transatlantic voyages from China had learned—the easiest way to transfer these white laborers from the docks of New Orleans, where they were prone to run away, to the plantations up north in the alluvial valley of the Mississippi; "they are," he wrote to his sister, Georgia, "considerably more trouble to provide for than the negro."[86] Indeed, the one bright spot in Mississippi, it seemed, was that the dwindling population of freedmen, "their numbers fearfully reduced by death," was working hard and for a reasonable wage—in stark contrast to the situation in Georgia, where the "influence of the Freedmen's Bureau" had instilled in the former slaves a "state of hostility to the whites."[87]

King's troubles were not unique. White immigration was the fool's gold of the postwar South. While many in the planter class hoped for cheapness or docility, they just as certainly got neither. Other regions— the Northeast, the Midwest, and California—regularly siphoned off new labor. Within the South, factory mill competed against planter, pitting members of the master class against one another and "luring" white, black, or yellow to leave one place to work in another. During his trip to the rural South, British traveler Robert Somers routinely heard complaints from the planters about an acute labor shortage due largely to the migration of labor—white, black, or otherwise—to other Southern towns and cities.[88] One South Carolina planter brought in a group of German emigrants and "treated them better than his other hands," even giving them "coffee and sourkrout [sic]—when, what would they do but demand butter for bread and milk for their coffee, and the next thing the whole crowd left."[89] A Natchez overseer, interviewed by John Trowbridge on a Mississippi levee, wondered sadly whether "the Negro" would soon be replaced by Germans. "The Germans," he remarked, "want twenty dollars a month, and we can hire the niggers for ten and fifteen. The Germans will die in the swamps. Then as soon as they get enough money to buy a cart and a mule, and an acre of land somwhar, whar they can plant a grapevine, they'll go in for themselves."[90] "Southerners," E. Merton Coulter wrote, "had a mistaken impression of what a European immigrant was looking for. They wanted him to take the place of a Negro workman, live in Negro cabins, and eat Negro foods—cornbread and bacon."[91] Carl Schurz, who universally detested the entire region, put it even more succinctly: European émigrés and Northerners, he wrote, "will not come to the South to serve as hired hands on plantations, but to acquire property for themselves."[92]

The gentle trickle of European arrivals could not offset the steady flow of African departures within the South in search of higher wages, safer lives, or new beginnings. One newspaper noted in 1866 the coming of "170 German immigrants" to Charleston on the very same day that "sixteen hundred freedmen" boarded the *Golconda,* a ship belonging to the African Colonization Society, bound for Liberia.[93] Two years later, that same ship would carry another 451 newly emancipated emigrants across the Atlantic, some sixty-five of whom came from the small city of Ridgeville, South Carolina.[94] Optimists assumed that German immigration would fill the void in the inland regions of the state, pushing "the negro . . . nearer and nearer to the coast, where on account of the malaria, the whites will be slower to go."[95] But most pragmatic planters were neither overly optimistic nor entirely negro-phobic; with an eye toward their empty fields and declining profits, they saw only disaster. State newspapers reported the loss of a million freedmen since 1860, the result, it was assumed, of low birth rates, disease epidemics, and flight.[96] "At this rate," William Lawton summarized, "in less than 44 years the entire colored population of South Carolina will have disappeared."[97] And if blacks were leaving the fields of the South, their lost labors needed to be recovered by other means—and quickly, too.

It was not easy, however, to get European immigrants to come to the South. At first, it appeared that postwar state governments in the South would be able to help. For rural planters in the sugar- and cotton-growing regions of the deepest South—in Louisiana, Alabama, Georgia, Mississippi, and South Carolina—it was especially difficult to pry immigrants away from the comparatively high wages of Southern cities like New Orleans, Charleston, and Mobile, let alone compete with the vision of California. Louisiana, like many other Southern states, created its own Bureau of Immigration in 1866, with the hope that seductive propaganda written in English, French, and German and distributed in Europe might lure hardy farmers and settlers to the Mississippi delta region.[98] Alabama's advertisement boldly laid out all of the natural resources available to anyone with the proper amount of resolve: "If the immigrant desires to raise fruits or vegetables," the commercial read, "or to make wine, to rear cattle or to manufacture timber or naval stores, let him select the southern division of the State, the timber regions bordering on the Gulf of Mexico and the State of Florida."[99]

In much of this literature, African Americans are notably absent. Certainly, there is no mention at all of the Chinese, even though most of the labor conventions discussed "white" and "yellow" labor as if they were alternatives to each other. South Carolina's contribution to the body of literature was a long, lavishly descriptive pamphlet: *South Carolina: A Home for the Industrious Immigrant*, the title read, just above a teasing image that included all of the implements for labor—hammer and anvil, scythe, and plow alongside miscellaneous gears, pipes, boxes, and barrels—that looked as if they had been hastily cast aside by those who had once used them, as if they were waiting for strong hands to grasp their worn wooden handles once again. In the background, there is no evidence of those who once labored there, only rows of corn, a single white farmer with a horse-drawn plow, and, off to the left, a tall sailing ship.[100] This image of the South as another version of the Midwest or as the home to white farming families and European settler communities stands in quiet contrast to much of the lustful rhetoric about the Chinese, which relied on the sense that the tropical South could never be home to white settlers.

South Carolina's postwar governors, Benjamin Perry and James Orr, both urged an end to nativism and the beginning of a new approach to immigration, one that was driven by Southern hospitality—and not by fear of the German or "the Celt." In late 1866, the South Carolina legislature sponsored a new office—a commissioner of immigration—and awarded that office the sum of $10,000, which was to be used to advertise in Europe the availability of small parcels of land that, in many cases, would be broken off from larger plantations. John A. Wagener, a former Confederate general, prominent Charlestonian, and founder of the German American settlement Walhalla, was appointed as the new commissioner. An immigrant, a Southerner, and a South Carolinian, Wagener brought the support of Charleston's foreign-born population to the postwar search for immigrants. With a modest budget, Wagener sent agents to Europe and spent the better part of the next two years traversing the state, registering new properties with which to lure immigrants to South Carolina, and pulling together an odd coalition of planters, shipping and railroad interests, and immigrant Southerners to support his efforts. He was moderately successful at first: after just a year in office, in the late fall of 1867, Wagener and the city of Charleston welcomed the *Gauss,* a German ship carrying well over one hundred new arrivals from Europe.[101]

But by late 1867, Wagener's efforts to get South Carolina's planter class to sell unproductive fields to European immigrants at a low price had come to naught—the planters, it seemed, wanted either cheap labor or high profits from land sale. More than half of the immigrants who arrived in the state during Wagener's tenure chose to stay in Charleston, a ratio that would hardly solve the labor problem. White South Carolinians, moreover, continued to be distrustful of suspicious foreign peoples, with their harsh-sounding languages, strange tastes, and peculiar ways. If the few months that followed offered some small hope—registered lands were up, prices for land plots had dropped, a

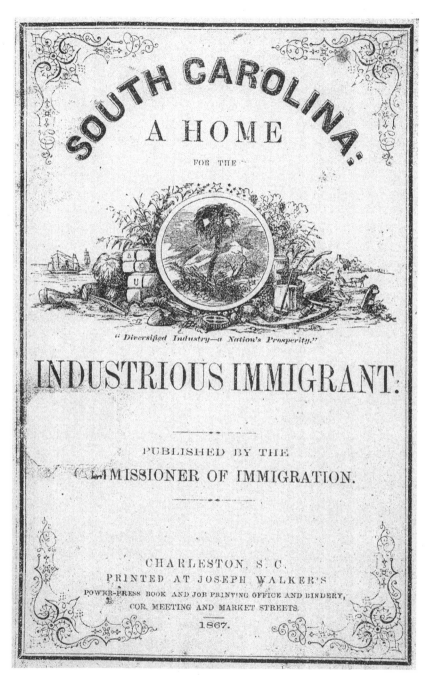

The cover of *South Carolina: A Home for the Industrious Immigrant,* published in 1867.

few railroads had reduced fares, and a steamship line was promising to connect Charleston to Europe—the chance of success soon dwindled into nothingness. The Radical Reconstruction government that swept into power in late 1868 had no stomach for Wagener's efforts, which were at cross-purposes with the working interests of the freedmen. South Carolina's commissioner of immigration soon found himself out of a job, and the Bureau of Immigration was soon shut down.[102]

The end of state-sponsored immigration efforts was not, however, the end of this story. By 1870, the planters of the state of South Carolina had grown so desperate for labor that they and their allies gathered in Charleston at the Academy of Music to discuss other possible solutions as private citizens. The three-day convention—just one of many held in the South on this subject—was almost exclusively concerned with European, not Asian, labor. "We have no faith in any other kind of labor," read the editorial in the *Daily Courier*, "than that which is free, intelligent, and which can add to the capacity, the wealth, and the self-government of the state."[103] Delegates from across the state—and from Georgia, North Carolina, and elsewhere—urged the South to copy the North, to better encourage the permanent settlement of white farming families from Germany, returning the region to the Jeffersonian ideal that Jefferson, hopelessly in debt and committed to slavery, was never able to realize. To accomplish this, delegates lobbied for reduced rail fares, for the establishment of German societies, and for an economic partnership between Charleston and one of several European ports. They called for Charleston to be the next New York or Baltimore, the next doorway to the United States for the hungry, hopeful masses of Europe. And they relentlessly called for a multifront offensive against the propaganda war being waged in Europe, in which the South's efforts to attract white immigrants was repeatedly described as an effort to find new slaves.

There was much debate, as well, about the climate of the South. In the immediate aftermath of Appomattox, J.D.B. De Bow had approached a noted German American author about the necessity of good press; Charles Fleishman, in response, urged De Bow to "publish a detailed and full account . . . of the weather and its influence on the constitutions of men coming from northern latitudes."[104] This discussion was picked up at the convention in Charleston, just as it was throughout the South wherever some hoped to bring the immigrant. Captain M.F. Maury of the Virginia Military Institute was prevented by ill health from attending the Charleston convention, but he wrote (by another's steadier hand) to stress this point above all others. "There is," he noted, echoing De Bow,

> a strong prejudice in the minds of European immigrants, generally against the South, owing to their educated ignorance with regard to us. They think that we have always despised labor; that we hate the laborer, and look down upon him with contempt. They are still taught to believe, and many of them do believe, that if they were to come to the South they would be made slaves of instantly. There is another large class of them who believe that the Southern people are a lawless and semi-barbarous set; that the Southern climate is deadly to the white laborer; and that the negro is among us only because the negro, and he alone, could endure our climate as a laborer. One of the tasks before us is to enlighten this ignorance and remove these prejudices.[105]

The notion that there was a distinct Southern climate that had a significant impact on the hierarchical order of races had long encouraged European immigrants, as historian E. Merton Coulter put it, to follow "latitude and not longitude when they moved in great numbers to a new land."[106] For much of the nineteenth century, Europe had been sold on the idea that "America" was as much an idea as a place: a sort of Shangri-La for the working man, where hard work, luck, and an upright character could bring immediate fortune to the immigrant generation. This romanticized image of the United States was put to use by state immigration bureaus, shipping lines, and railroad companies, especially during the Civil War, when the decimated Union troop lines were in need of replenishment. But Europe's "America" was hardly undifferentiated: if the gritty West was "the Eldorado that often cheers the poor man's hopes," the South was its hellish opposite.[107] For thirty years, abolitionist literature on both sides of the Atlantic had painted the region as the home to medieval cruelties, as devoid of all sexual controls, as a land where all white men and women were hopelessly corrupted by their proximity to pornographic whippings of naked black bodies and, even more disturbingly, by the irrefutable fact of interracial sex. The compulsory enfranchisement of former slaves and the occupation of the region by federal troops added only greater uncertainty to this image. Moreover, the South was widely reputed to be tropical—hot and humid, like the Caribbean—and therefore not a proper home to white European settlers, for whom such a place promised only a physiological deterioration to parallel the moral breakdown that would inevitably result from the region's history of chattel slavery. When seen in this light, the West was, indeed, a magical place.[108]

With the sense that much of Europe was bypassing the region for the fair promise of California, the proceedings of the Immigration Convention at Charleston read as if South Carolina contained the better halves of Minnesota and Florida. In his brief pamphlet submitted to the convention, A. Y. Lee of Columbia advertised the state as "midway between the frozen regions of the north and the burning heat of the tropics," which was true, so long as your points of reference were the extremes of the Arctic Circle and equatorial Brazil. "So remarkable," he continued, "is the topographical condition of the State, that wheat and sugar-cane grow profitably side by side, and the olive and the orange ripen under the same family of cultivation."[109] The convention's Committee on the Hygiene of South Carolina issued a lengthy rebuke to the widely held belief that the state was disease-ridden, violent, and tropical and concluded with a sweeping invitation to all those "seeking a new genial, happy home, cheered by bright skies and unclouded sunshine, by a mild, balmy climate, a productive soil capable of making an abundant return for labor, illimitable water power, to drive the machinery brought into existence by the restless genius of man . . . [and] where will be found an intelligent, refined and chivalrous people, ready to receive all such with cordial welcome."[110] To check the widely reported folktale in which a German immigrant to the South deteriorated quickly from red-cheeked and strong to sallow and weak, P. J. Berckmans, an associate member of the Committee on the Flora of the State, urged new arrivals to eat German foods, to steer clear of the native unhygienic curiosities of fried bacon and hot bread, and to avoid the "immoderate" use of tobacco and coffee.[111]

Immigration efforts that had failed with minimal state support could hardly succeed in the face of federal resistance, and few Southerners seemed willing or able to commit themselves financially to the grand schemes of Wagener and others. By 1870, the South actually had fewer foreign-born residents than it did in 1860.[112] The whole region's labor force seemed less stable, in fact, than it had in 1865. African Americans had begun to bring long-lost family members together and to search for better, kinder work. European or Chinese brawn and muscle vanished almost as quickly as it arrived. After the debacle with the Alabama and Chattanooga Railroad, where bankruptcy had denied several hundred Chinese workers their wages, one agent complained that he could no longer get the Chinese to "go South."[113] The Chinese, who were brought in to do the same work as emancipated slaves, promptly deserted; "those who wanted high-wage work could do much better in

California."[114] European immigrants likewise showed the same frustrating desire for betterment. Emancipated slaves and Asian and European immigrants, despite considerable competitive friction and radically different circumstances, thus repeatedly demonstrated a desire for an improved life, which was most likely to be found outside of the South or, at least, in port cities like New Orleans. Agricultural regions, poorer than Southern cities and poorer still than anywhere else, were doubly damned. In the end, the postwar South was so completely crushed that its comparatively weaker wage scale could not keep the Chinese or the European immigrant happy there for long. And even had there been a consensus about Asians—and there most surely was not—the battered and increasingly dependent South could never have managed to hold on to the Chinese, not without a formal system of indenture, a written contract, or some other Gilded Age version of the H-2 program. The same was even truer of Europeans.

Turning the fantasy of the Chinese automaton or the Teutonic protocitizen into a reality was no easy task, as many Southerners quickly learned. In its struggles to shape the postslavery world to satisfy its own interests first, the planter class revealed much about the new relationship between the regions of the United States and about the place of the South in the newly reconstituted nation. Indeed, the sad tones and angry hues of planter desperation had lasting consequences for "the race problem" in the United States. The South's inability to bind free labor of any sort—white, yellow, or black—to a specific place and its struggles to garner enough investment to tap its own remarkable abundance of natural resources would leave it vulnerable to dependence on Northern capital and would eventually force Southerners to couch their veneration of "the Lost Cause" in anticolonial tones and to tighten their hold on the only available labor force—"the Negro"—with a viciousness born of absolute desperation. If immigration and investment were not forthcoming, only racial separation and authoritarian control would solve the labor problem. Hence, the former Confederate general Nathan Bedford Forrest encouraged railroad development in his home state of Tennessee, volunteered $5,000 to secure Chinese "coolies," and, even as these efforts failed, became the head of the Ku Klux Klan.[115] If a democracy of white planters and suitably hard-working European immigrants was not possible, a coercive *herrenvolk* republicanism would take its place, seducing the white working class with its veneration of white womanhood and white civic privilege, its heavy-handed punishment of black men for supposed sexual advances toward

Southern womanhood, and its tacit approval of the power of white men over all women in the South.

There was also the place of the South itself in the rapidly evolving American economy. Compared with Cuba, where countless miles of railroad tracks and new machines had revolutionized the entire sugar industry, most Southern states looked quite underdeveloped. The slave-holding South had invested in only those kinds of infrastructural development that exploited the natural advantages of slavery rather than those advantages enjoyed by the South. It invested, to paraphrase Gavin Wright, in human bondage and not in the land. "Now that the planter has to hire his labor," argued one editorial, "it is important to render it as productive as possible by machinery."[116] But in the postbellum age, as investment shifted away from slaves and toward land, the South emerged as the low-wage region in a high-wage country, as the increasingly backward agricultural part of a technologically sophisticated nation. Additionally, the Civil War had destroyed much of what made slavery so profitable—most notably, its railroads and its bonded labor. Just when the South needed modernization the most, it was least able to bring venture capital to bear on the growing technological gap. In 1870, the Deep South—still recovering from the disastrous Civil War—was thus wrestling with developmental questions that Cuba, with its new railroads and modern sugar boilers, had resolved long before.[117] "Again and again," Wright concludes, "major initiatives by governments, planters, employers, or transport companies generated nothing by an evanescent pass-through."[118] Indeed, even as planters in Cuba continued to defy myths about slavery by modernizing sugar production and laying down "more miles of railroad than any other country in Latin America," the regional disparities in economic strength and investment in the United States diverted technological advances away from the deepest South, making economic adjustments to life after slavery extremely difficult.[119]

The politics of Reconstruction came into play as well. If Southerners had at first preached the virtues of the Chinese as factory labor and skilled farmhands, Northern politicians and their African American allies had never been fooled. Reconstruction governments and the freedmen had always suspected that the search for immigrants was nothing less than an attempt to withhold from emancipated slaves the wages, lands, and privileges of citizenship they deserved. "There is room for the Chinese and Coolie here," wrote the mayor of Charleston to J. W. Alvord of the Freedmen's Bureau, "but there is no need of them, if we will do simple justice to the laborers at our door."[120] The quest for democracy for blacks had thus long been deemed antithetical to the search for Asian and European immigrant labor in the South, and the advent of Radical Reconstruction meant that "all governmental efforts in the South to bring in laborers were immediately abandoned."[121] The postbellum federal government was a champion of free wage labor and was generally "indifferent," if not outright hostile, to the interests of the planter class and the emerging New South for some form of labor controls.[122] Thus, the members of the anxious American planter class found their worst nightmare of the nineteenth century realized: they were unable, for a wide variety of reasons, to secure immigrant labor of any color and were faced with an exodus of "the Negro" that would ruin their plantations and destroy their civilization. Having been drawn into a closer economic embrace with the North, the relationship between race and work in the South would henceforth be determined, by and large, by national concerns and by the long argument between two regions previously at war and then in an uneasy peace.

In the end, Southerners rallied around the idea that physical force could accomplish what the national economy could not and what the nation itself would not. The architects of Radical Reconstruction refused to allow Chinese labor on the scale of postemancipation societies in the West Indies and South America, and Southerners were no longer certain they wanted coolies anyway. The increased use of convict labor provided one alternative to the problems of "racial" diversity in a world of free labor; "convicts," David Oshinsky writes, "worked at jobs that free labor did not like to do, in places where free labor sometimes feared to go. Employers preferred them over Asians ('too fragile'), Irish ('too belligerent'), and local blacks ('too slow')."[123] Jim Crow was another, even grimmer solution. As Reconstruction governments were abandoned, as federal troops departed in the wake of the disastrous election of 1876, the resilient planter class—still much in control—resurrected the old plan of apprenticeship for "the Negro." To complement the evolving system of sharecropping and debt peonage, ingenious Southern legislators cobbled together one of the most disturbing and intrusive systems of labor control ever invented. When it was complete, each and every aspect of Southern life would be organized around the control and discipline of the least fortunate members of the republic. Soon, Southerners had convinced enough of their Northern fellows that "the Negro" was an "anticitizen" who would never diligently work for wages alone and that morality—a virtuous work ethic, an end to crime, the barest rudiments of a civilized lifestyle—could, indeed, be legislated, if only on a local level. If after this tentative experiment with alternative work forces European and Asian immigrants were now understood by all to be too weak, too smart, too expensive, or too prone to leave for better things elsewhere, there remained "the Negro," who needed only "compassionate" laws—or strictest governance—to curb a supposed instinct for crime and thriftlessness.

Tropical Echoes

The story of "masters without slaves" was a pan-American story. "Le maître," as Mr. Médouze, echoing Frederick Douglass, put it in *La Rue Case Nègre*, "était devenu le patron."[124] Everywhere, the master had become the boss, in a narrative that was framed differently in each location. In the South, the transformation of "the big house" into "simply the biggest house," as historian James Roark once said, had uniquely profound psychological and social consequences for the members of the planter class of the South: their prewar circumstances made widespread white flight or abandonment unlikely, and the lack of absentee landlordism, the attractions of place and tradition, and the chance of some profit, however slim, held the attention of many, despite the wrenching pace of change. "Almost overnight," Roark summarizes, "Southern planters crossed from the world of slave labor to that of compensated labor, from substantial wealth and ease to relative poverty and drudgery, from political dominance to crippled influence." This "leap across time," as he describes it, was made possible only by the reformation of the "practice of racism and rural exploitation" and by an emerging fantasy of the way things were or were thought to have been. Across the South, the memory of the Confederate dead was revered, and recently emancipated African Americans were increasingly bound to the land as unfree labor or as sharecroppers, at an immediate and insurmountable disadvantage in the local economy. The African Americans' past as slaves—standing in contrast to their present as freedmen—was redrawn to emphasize their supposed docility, their patience, their loyalty, and their gratitude.[125]

"At first," Frederick Douglass recalled, "the land-owners drove us out of our old quarters and told us they did not want us in their fields, that they meant to import German, Irish, and Chinese laborers. But as the passions of the war generally subsided we were taken back to our old places; but plainly enough this change of front was not from choice but necessity. Feeling themselves somehow or other entitled to our labor without the payment of wages, it was not strange that they should make the hardest bargains for our labor and get it for as little as possible. For them the contest was easy; their tremendous power and our weakness gave them the victory."[126] It would be a terrible mistake to think that this story ends with the fall of Reconstruction. As Douglass knew well, the various Southern solutions to the global problems attending emancipation were never limited to the South alone, nor even to the United States. The hubris of the nation may well have made it impossible to regularly acknowledge the South's willing role in a larger, extranational narrative, but the master class had no exclusive international license to cosmopolitanism or to the sorts of *bricolage* described here. Just as Southern planters and their allies had borrowed, studied, and sometimes rejected the histories, strategies, and symbols of other slaveholding and postemancipation societies in the hemisphere, so, too, did others do the same to those of the Southerners, to their awful story. The "local" struggle over white, black, and yellow labor—so deeply intertwined with earlier struggles elsewhere—clanged loudly and then redounded across the Caribbean, across the Atlantic and Pacific, and around the world. It shaped other efforts to dominate; it guided other attempts to synchronize hard power and soft power; and, for a very long time, it defined the meaning of "tremendous power" and narrowed the meaning of "weakness" in a sort of Southern vernacular. It echoed down through the centuries. If you listen closely, you can still hear it, an angry rumble from the past, with lingering influence in the present.

Epilogue

If I am not what I've been told I am, then it means that *you're* not what *you* thought you were *either!*

—JAMES BALDWIN, "A TALK TO TEACHERS" (1963)

The imagination of Southern slaveholders was not constrained by the borders of the Old South, nor was its wanderlust completely destroyed by the Civil War. In the age of slavery, a ceaseless dialectic joined the South to the innumerable islands and encircling landmasses of the American Mediterranean; in the aftermath of emancipation, it was interrupted, transformed, and somewhat weakened. When we focus on that dialectic, it raises seductively obscure figures out of the darkness and into the light. It drags our attention away from the strict geographies of nation and forces us to look more closely at the newly revealed passages, sight lines, and dialogues that tempted fantasy and shaped reality on all fronts. Gaining higher ground and a different vantage point, we can make out larger, more subtle, and previously obscured points of connection in the slope and rise of the nineteenth-century landscape. From an otherwise disconnected cluster of local stories, we can discern patterns that were once difficult to make out, patterns reminiscent of our own age of globalization and labor and capital movement, and of the soft compulsion to labor long hours for little. There, we say, is the master class of the Old South, looking, from a distance, a little bit like our own border-crossing, cosmopolitan CEOs, shifting production and manufacturing to whichever town, country, or continent can offer the least expensive—though often most abusive—system of labor. We should adjust our image of the master class, taking note of its global perspective, its drawing of labor from the deep wells of the world to the fields and factories of the Old South, and its survey of new territories for possible relocation once the rules had changed, once the ownership of slaves had been freed and the procurement of coolies had been prohibited. If we do, maybe we can understand the most powerful people in our own world just a little better. "The new elites," Christopher Lasch once wrote, describing the transnationalists of the present, "are far more cosmopolitan, or at least more restless and migratory, than their predecessors."[1] What does it mean for our world, I wonder, if Lasch was wrong?

Slaveholders and slaves, masters and laborers of all sorts, journeyed across the American Mediterranean, each imagining a New World that still shared a great deal across national borders or that was bound together by wide-open circuits, trade routes, and intellectual connections. In some strange way, the same is true today in the "Nuevo New South."[2] Capital movement and labor movement, along with human desire and changing legal and geopolitical realities, have further reshuffled the human population. In the United States, this process has brought migrant Central American laborers to the same Southern cities that were the birthplace of Jim Crow in Douglass's day and that were more recently national signifiers of the black and white civil rights conflict. By the 1990s, Atlanta and Houston had become home to rapidly expanding communities of both legal and illegal immigrants from Mexico, Panama, the Dominican Republic, Guatemala, and El Salvador. Nashville, Mobile, and other mid-sized Southern cities were, in some ways, newer versions of New Orleans and Charleston, marked by polylingual, transnational, and economic connections to a global South running from Southeast Asia to Africa to Latin America.[3] But couldn't something similar be said of New Orleans in the 1850s, with its substantial Cuban expatriate community, its Caribbean textures, and its *filibusteros?* And by importing coolies or free immigrants from Cuba, California, or China, weren't postbellum planters attempting to fashion a precursor to today's "Wal-Mart bracero program"?[4] When Jack Welch, former CEO of General Electric, suggests that "ideally, you'd have every factory on a barge," so that companies could take advantage of looser labor regulations, doesn't he sound a lot like Eliza McHatton, who left the prospect of emancipation behind to find slavery somewhere else?[5]

Perhaps the country has come full circle. Or perhaps there is a continuous thread here, binding the old master class of the Americas with today's globe-trotting executives. So much of the story told here is about agriculture, the harvest of cane, cotton, and coffee, which continues to the present day. The struggle to bring white immigrants to the South as labor persisted through 1900. Efforts to recapture the gang work of black slave labor without the lash persisted and became more elaborate and successful through the last days of Jim Crow. When the federal minimum wage was instituted in 1938, agricultural workers were excluded from the expanding social contract, an exclusion that reflected the power of emerging agribusiness corporations and the racial disenfranchisement of pickers and cutters. With this exception in place, sugar cane cultivation continued to produce labor regimes that mimicked or reproduced slavery. Where machines were impossible—for instance, in cane cultivation on Florida's lakeside muck—a few larger firms procured desperate, Depression-era black labor to cut cane on a grand scale. But as word spread of the abuses of the maturing sugar industry in the South (e.g., forced confinement, debt peonage, and poor wages), recruiters were forced to travel farther and farther across the South to find willing workers, often tricking black men into a job that held no prospect of any wage at all.[6] By 1942, the federal government had issued an indictment of "Big Sugar" for conspiring to reproduce slavery in central Florida. Even while the nation marveled over the twinkling and charming simplicities of *Gone with the Wind,* yearning for the glorious past of the Confederacy, complete with Southern belles, dashing rogues, and trustworthy mammies and slaves, portions of the Deep South had returned to a system of unpaid forced labor and bondage.[7]

One year later, Big Sugar—much like the postbellum South—turned some of its attention outward and began to use Jamaican, Barbadian, and Dominican cane cutters, bringing several thousand West Indians, who were easier to control, to Florida each year through an immigration loophole provided by the Department of Agriculture. It was easier and cheaper, Big Sugar had learned, to harvest the ready labor of the impoverished and dependent Caribbean, desperate for any sort of wage under any sort of circumstances, than to hire black Americans, who were free to move to Northern cities or to find better work somewhere else. It was also easier, at first, to mistreat workers from the Caribbean: as noncitizens in the United States on temporary visas, Jamaicans, Barbadians, Guatemalans, and Mexicans could be silently penned up at night, worn down to the bone by their day's travail (they often fell asleep while still fully dressed). The rumor was that these workers handled a cane knife better than did American blacks; that their long fingers could hold and wield the knife better, surer, and faster; and that their time in the "tropics" made them less likely to fade in the heat of the summer. Needing work, they volunteered for the job, lining up to interview for it and willingly subjecting themselves to the same perverse physical inspections, tasking, and gang work habits that would have greeted any slave captured in Africa or any coolie tricked aboard a ship. Best of all, these imported workers could be made to leave when their work was done, which was a simple but profound "improvement" on indentured servitude, slavery, and even sharecropping. "We want," said Walter Parker of U.S. Sugar, "a mix of man and machine," a phrase that could have been ripped from any number of nineteenth-century sources about the Chinese.[8] It was possible to head south in the year 2000, to arrive at an agribusiness town, and to journey backward in time, finding a labor system built on racial premises not so different from what one might have found along the Mississippi River in 1859 or along the Demerara in 1870. Like slaves and coolies, these men and women were (and are) "nobodies"; and, as was the case in the age of the American Mediterranean, the United States is utterly dependent on their unfree, "slavery-like" labor for the proper functioning of the democracy.[9]

The plight of agricultural labor is just one small part, though, of a larger cultural narrative that is harder to comprehend. Indeed, there are other sorrowful echoes of the old connections in the recent devastation visited on New Orleans and Georgetown, Guyana, two eighteenth-century way stations along the outer edges of the Caribbean and Gulf of Mexico, both located where, all things being equal, no permanent settlement should ever have been established. At the dawn of the nineteenth century, Georgetown was the mainland sugar colony of the British West Indies and the export hub of Demerara, nestled just below sea level, where the wide, slow river turned the ocean a rich, milk-chocolate brown; the city was utterly dependent for its survival on aging Dutch drainage systems. New Orleans was, likewise, the oft-exchanged entrepôt of the French and Spanish empires, clinging to the banks of the unpredictable Mississippi River some few miles from the Gulf of Mexico, surrounded by high levees and sprawling sugar estates and touched by the approach of the Anglo-American imperium. In 2005, when the flood waters rose and lingered for days, weeks, and months, Georgetown and New Orleans—crime-ridden, neglected cities, home to hundreds of thousands of poor people of African descent, in-sufficiently protected by their betters and left to fend for themselves—were returned to their forgotten origins as backward outposts of cash-crop agriculture, located on a specific site for no reason other than to facilitate the rapid transfer of sugar out and slaves and coolies in. "New Orleans is situated like a bowl, with surrounding water kept away by levees," one letter to a Guyanese newspaper put it in September of that year. "Virtually the same can be said of Georgetown and its immediate environs. New Orleans is below sea level. Ditto for our capital. The economy of New Orleans has been on the skids for years, and the social existence of a significant portion of the population can more appropriately be described as surviving rather than living." "Ditto," the writer continued, "also for the circumstances of the populace in our own little green bowl."[10] Georgetown had been flooded for months earlier that year. When the poorer and blacker sections of New Orleans were flooded during Hurricane Katrina in the September that followed, Guyana's minister of public works, Tony Xavier, returned a set of pumps to U.S. ambassador Rolland Bullen. Pumps that had been "about two weeks too late" for Georgetown would, in a grim tragedy, be too late to help New Orleans as well.[11] In Georgetown, these parallels and associations were often discussed. This was not so in New Orleans.

There are hints of the old American Mediterranean in the destruction of these two cities. There are traces of the old exchanges of "revolutionary commodities" in the sordid parallelisms of Mardi Gras and Carnival; in sex trade tourism to Miami, Santo Domingo, and Havana; and in the emergence of a new national trade in immigrant bodies and sex slaves through shipping lanes, ports, and railroads. There are traces of it everywhere. But we do not wish to remember, to see, or to hear.

On the final page of F. Scott Fitzgerald's *The Great Gatsby*, Nick Carraway, the midwestern narrator, ponders the great delusion that lay at the heart of the republic's belief that it had transcended its own history. "Sprawled out on the sand" and "brooding on the old, unknown world," Nick stares out across Long Island Sound, until out of the dark blurs and soft whirls of the night and moonlight he begins to make out the shoreline as it once was, as it had once "flowered" for "Dutch sailors' eyes," inspired "the last and greatest of all human dreams," and brought mankind "face to face for the last time in human history with something commensurate to his capacity for wonder." At that moment, Carraway understands that the confident, future-oriented modernism of New York and Gatsby is a wrong-headed fiction. It is the New World past—what D. H. Lawrence, writing two years earlier, had named the "grinning, unappeased, aboriginal demons" of conquest and settlement, slavery and racism—that matters most. Still, Carraway has little faith that his lonely epiphany would be shared by his fellow moderns. "Tomorrow," he sighs, "we will run faster, stretch out our arms farther." The future matters more than the past, or at least that was what the moderns thought, and that was what many supposed was the difference between the United States and the rest of the world. "So we beat on," he muses finally, "boats against the current, borne back ceaselessly into the past." The story of the postbellum planter class and the emergence of Jim Crow is connected to, and reflective of, a bigger New World context, one that binds together Georgetown and New Orleans. As such, it deserves to be resurrected as a part of "our" past—our past as Southerners; as citizens of the United States; as the descendents of settlers, slaves, and immigrants; and as human beings caught up in the maelstrom of contact between the New World and the Old. We cannot will this away simply by reaching for "the green light, the orgastic future that year by year recedes before us."[12] For too long, we have assumed that the borders of the South were literal expressions of the only distinctions that mattered. And we do not wish to know that the truth might be otherwise. But the story of the slaveholding South in the age of emancipation is, Edouard Glissant writes, a history that "travels with the sea."[13] It takes us away from shore, into the American Mediterranean. So, too, does our present set of circumstances.

Notes

Introduction

1. The phrase comes from Raymond Williams, *The Long Revolution* (1961; reprint, London: Hogarth Press, 1992), 41.
2. William Faulkner, *Absalom, Absalom!* (1936; reprint, New York: Vintage, 1990), 193–200.
3. Edouard Glissant, *Faulkner, Mississippi,* trans. Barbara Lewis and Thomas C. Spear (Chicago: University of Chicago Press, 1999), 83.
4. Faulkner, *Absalom, Absalom!,* 27.
5. Glissant, *Faulkner, Mississippi,* 111. Also see John T. Matthews, "This Race Which Is Not One: The 'More Inextricable Compositeness' of William Faulkner's South," in *Look Away: The U.S. South in New World Studies,* ed. Jon Smith and Deborah Cohn (Durham, NC: Duke University Press, 2004), 201–226.
6. The title of this book is derived from a reading of the sources, but it also owes something to a very different work of history: Lester D. Langley, *Struggle for the American Mediterranean: United States–European Rivalry in the Gulf-Caribbean, 1776–1904* (Athens: University of Georgia Press, 1976).
7. On the circumstances of emancipation in the nineteenth century and the attendant sense of crisis across the Americas, see David Brion Davis, *Inhuman Bondage: The Rise and Fall of Slavery in the New World* (New York: Oxford University Press, 2006); and Thomas Holt, *The Problem of Freedom: Race, Labor, and Politics in Jamaica and Britain, 1832–1938* (Baltimore: Johns Hopkins University Press, 1992).
8. Walter D. Mignolo, "Coloniality at Large: The Western Hemisphere in the Colonial Horizon of Modernity," *CR: The New Centennial Review* 1.2 (2001): 35.

9. Benedict Anderson, *Imagined Communities: Reflections on the Origin and Spread of Nationalism* (New York: Verso, 1991), 63.

10. Vera M. Kutzinski, "Borders and Bodies: The United States, America, and the Caribbean," *CR: The New Centennial Review* 1.2 (2001): 66.

11. Joseph Roach, *Cities of the Dead: Circum-Atlantic Performance* (New York: Columbia University Press, 1996), 4–5.

12. My thanks to Claire Fox for putting it just like this in her commentary on an early version of Chapter 1. See Fox, "Commentary: The Transnational Turn and the Hemispheric Return," *American Literary History* 81.3 (Fall 2006): 641. Readers interested in the growing literature on the South as a part of the Americas can turn to Smith and Cohn, eds., *Look Away!*; John Lowe, ed., *Bridging Southern Cultures: An Interdisciplinary Approach* (Baton Rouge: Louisiana State University Press, 2005); and the special issue "Global Contexts, Local Literatures: The New Southern Studies," ed. Kathryn McKee and Annette Trefzer, *American Literature* 78.4 (December 2006): 677–845.

13. The phrase "hemispheric engagements" is taken from Caroline F. Levander and Robert S. Levine, eds., *Hemispheric American Studies* (New Brunswick, NJ: Rutgers University Press, 2007), 3. For this reevaluation, we can draw on the work of the past decades by scholars of African American history, who have uncovered the strangely parallel story of civil rights and human rights protests in the Cold War era. See especially Ifeoma Kiddoe Nwankwo, *Black Cosmopolitanism: Racial Consciousness and Transnational Identity in the Nineteenth Century* (Philadelphia: University of Pennsylvania Press, 2005), as well as Kevin K. Gaines, *African American in Ghana: Black Expatriates in the Civil Rights Era* (Chapel Hill: University of North Carolina Press, 2006); Mary Dudziak, *Cold War Civil Rights: Race and the Image of American Democracy* (Princeton, NJ: Princeton University Press, 2000); Brenda Gayle Plummer, ed., *Window on Freedom: Race, Civil Rights, and Foreign Affairs, 1945–1988* (Chapel Hill: University of North Carolina Press, 2003); Penny Von Eschen, *Race against Empire: Black Americans and Anticolonialism* (Ithaca, NY: Cornell University Press, 1997); and Penny Von Eschen, *Satchmo Blows Up the World: Jazz Ambassadors Play the Cold War* (Cambridge, MA: Harvard University Press, 2005).

14. Eugene D. Genovese, *The World the Slaveholders Made: Two Essays in Interpretation* (New York: Vintage Books, 1971), 107, 111.

15. Kenneth Stampp, *The Peculiar Institution: Slavery in the Antebellum South* (New York: Knopf, 1956), 21.

16. J. H. Elliot, *Do the Americas Have a Common History?* (Providence, RI: John Carter Brown Library, 1998), 41.

17. C. Vann Woodward, *The Burden of Southern History* (Baton Rouge: Louisiana State University Press, 1960), 19, 21, 22.

18. Genovese, *The World the Slaveholders Made*, 95, 101.

19. James Oakes, *The Ruling Race: A History of American Slaveholders* (New York: Random House, 1982); Steven Hahn, "Class and State in

Postemancipation Societies: Southern Planters in Comparative Perspective," *American Historical Review* 95 (February 1990): 75–98.

20. Holt, *The Problem of Freedom.*
21. "Other Souths" is from Peter Kolchin, *A Sphinx on the Land: The Nineteenth-Century South in Comparative Perspective* (Baton Rouge: Louisiana State University Press, 2003), 74.
22. Herbert Klein, *Slavery in the Americas: A Comparative Study of Virginia and Cuba* (Chicago: University of Chicago Press, 1967), vii. For other classic examples of the comparative history of race relations, see David Brion Davis, *The Problem of Slavery in Western Culture* (Ithaca, NY: Cornell University Press, 1967); John Cell, *The Highest Stage of White Supremacy* (New York: Oxford University Press, 1982); Carl N. Degler, *Neither Black nor White: Slavery and Race Relations in Brazil and the United States* (1971; reprint, Madison: University of Wisconsin Press, 1986); George M. Fredrickson, *White Supremacy: A Comparative Study in American and South African History* (New York: Oxford University Press, 1981); Peter Kolchin, *Unfree Labor: American Slavery and Russian Serfdom* (Cambridge, MA: Harvard University Press, 1982).
23. See Frederick Cooper, "Back to Work: Categories, Boundaries, and Connections in the Study of Labour," in *Racializing Class, Classifying Race: Labour and Difference in Britain, the USA, and Africa,* ed. Peter Alexander and Rick Halpern (New York: St. Martin's Press, 2000), 213–235; Sven Beckert, "From Tuskeegee to Togo: The Problem of Freedom in the Empire of Cotton," *Journal of American History* 92.2 (September 2005): 498–526; Ann Laura Stoler, "Tense and Tender Ties: the Politics of Comparison in North American and (Post)Colonial Studies," *Journal of American History* 88 (2001): 829–865; Matthew Guterl and Christine Skwiot, "Atlantic and Pacific Crossings: Race, Empire, and 'the Labor Problem' in the Late Nineteenth Century," *Radical History Review* 91 (Winter 2005): 40–61.
24. Rebecca J. Scott, *Degrees of Freedom: Louisiana and Cuba after Slavery* (Cambridge, MA: Harvard University Press, 2005), 5.

1. The American Mediterranean

1. Virginia Tatnall Peacock, *Famous American Belles of the Nineteenth Century* (Philadelphia: J. B. Lippincott, 1901), 102.
2. Eliza Chinn McHatton-Ripley, *Social Life in Old New Orleans, Being Recollections of My Girlhood* (New York: D. Appleton, 1912), 86; Ida Raymond, *Southland Writers: Biographical and Critical Sketches of Living Female Writers of the South* (Philadelphia: Claxton, Revson, and Haffelfinger, 1870), 680.
3. James Drake, *"Beautiful Isle"* (Louisville: D. P. Faulds, 1850); T. P. O'Connor, *My Beloved South* (New York: G. P. Putnam's Sons, 1914), 251.
4. Peacock, *Famous American Belles,* 111.

5. Frances Gibson Satterfield, *Madame Le Vert: A Biography of Octavia Walton Le Vert* (Edisto, SC: Edisto Press, 1987), 74, 100.

6. Michael O'Brien, *Conjectures of Order: Intellectual Life and the American South, 1810–1860,* 2 vols. (Chapel Hill: University of North Carolina Press, 2004), 1:24.

7. McHatton-Ripley, *Social Life in Old New Orleans,* 86.

8. Madame Octavia Walton Le Vert, *Souvenirs of Travel,* 2 vols. (Mobile, AL: S. H. Goetzel, 1857), 1:1.

9. Robert E. May, "Reconsidering Antebellum Women's History: Gender, Filibustering, and America's Quest for Empire," *American Quarterly* 57 (December 2005): 1162.

10. Le Vert, *Souvenirs,* 1:289. The term *off-white* is taken from the title of Maria DeGuzmán's *Spain's Long Shadow: The Black Legend, Off-Whiteness, and Anglo-American Empire* (Minneapolis: University of Minnesota Press, 2005).

11. Le Vert, *Souvenirs,* 1:318.

12. Edward Bryan, *The Rightful Remedy: Addressed to the Slaveholders of the South* (Charleston, SC: Walker and James, 1850), 78.

13. Ambrosio Gonzales to Harriet Rutledge Elliot, January 20, 1856, Elliot and Gonzales Family Papers, Southern Historical Collection, Wilson Library, University of North Carolina at Chapel Hill (hereafter EGP).

14. See Mary Boykin Chesnut's comments in *Mary Chesnut's Civil War,* ed. C. Vann Woodward (New Haven, CT: Yale University Press, 1981), 143.

15. The reference is to Tacitus's portrait of his father-in-law, in *The Agricola and the Germania,* trans. H. Mattingly (New York: Penguin Books, 1948), book 1.

16. Ambrosio Gonzales to Harriet Rutledge Elliot, February 22, 1856, EGP.

17. For more on Gonzales, see Antonio Rafael de la Cova, *Cuban Confederate General: The Life of Ambrosio Jose Gonzales* (Columbia: University of South Carolina Press, 2003).

18. Ambrosio José Gonzales, *Manifesto on Cuban Affairs Addressed to the People of the United States* (New Orleans: Printed at the Daily Delta, 1853), 5.

19. O.D.D.O., *The History of the Late Expedition to Cuba* (New Orleans: Printed at the Daily Delta, 1850), 59, 5.

20. Carlos Butterfield, *United States and Mexico Mail Steamship Line* (New York: Johnson and Browning, 1859), 7, 8.

21. Gerald Horne, *The Deepest South: The United States, Brazil, and the African Slave Trade* (New York: New York University Press, 2007), 114, 127.

22. Louis A. Pérez, *On Becoming Cuban: Identity, Nationality, and Culture* (New York: HarperCollins, 1999), 22, and, more broadly, 16–27.

23. For a wonderful collective portrait of this Caribbean world, see *Atlantic Port Cities: Economy, Culture, and Society in the Atlantic World, 1650–1850,* ed. Franklin W. Knight and Peggy K. Liss (Knoxville: University of Tennessee Press, 1991).

24. "Havana, or, Havannah," in *A Cyclopedia of Commerce and Commercial Navigation,* ed. J. Smith Homans and J. Smith Homans Jr. (New York: Harper and Brothers, 1858), 949.

25. John S. Thrasher, *Preliminary Essay on the Purchase of Cuba* (New York: Derby & Jackson, 1859), 14.

26. "Havana, or, Havannah," *Cyclopedia of Commerce,* 951.

27. William Henry Hurlbert, *Gan-Eden, or, Pictures of Cuba* (Boston: J. P. Jewett, 1854), 101.

28. Pike Map, Williams Research Center, Historical New Orleans Collection.

29. Walter Johnson, *Soul by Soul: Life Inside the Antebellum Slave Market* (Cambridge, MA: Harvard University Press, 1999), 1.

30. Entry for December 29, 1854, in *Queen of the South, New Orleans, 1853–1862: The Journal of Thomas K. Wharton,* ed. Samuel Wilson Jr. (New Orleans and New York: Historic New Orleans Collection and the New York Public Library, 1999), 59.

31. "New Orleans," *Cyclopedia of Commerce,* 1417. Also see Adam Rothman, *Slave Country: American Expansionism and the Origins of the Deep South* (Cambridge, MA: Harvard University Press, 2005), 73–117.

32. Joseph G. Treagle Jr., "Creoles and Americans," in *Creole New Orleans: Race and Americanization,* ed. Arnold R. Hirsch and Joseph Logsdon (Baton Rouge: Louisiana State University Press, 1992), 131–185.

33. George W. Williams, *Sketches of Travel in the Old and New Worlds* (Charleston, SC: Walker, Evans, and Cogswell, 1871), 5, 1, 19, 25.

34. Robert May, *The Southern Dream of a Caribbean Empire, 1854–1861* (Baton Rogue: Louisiana State University Press, 1973), 37.

35. Williams, *Sketches of Travel,* 20.

36. Ibid., 40.

37. Rothman, *Slave Country.*

38. William W. Freehling, *Road to Disunion* (New York: Oxford University Press, 1990), 424.

39. "Speech of John A. Quitman, of Mississippi, on the Powers of the Federal Government with Regard to the Territories: Delivered during the Debate on the President's Annual Message, in the House of Representatives, December 18, 1856," reprinted in *Life and Correspondence of John A. Quitman,* 2 vols., ed. J. F. H. Clairborne (New York: Harper & Brothers, 1860), 2:333.

40. Robert E. May, *John A. Quitman: Old South Crusader* (Baton Rouge: Louisiana State University Press, 1985), 238. More generally, see May, *Manifest Destiny's Underworld: Filibustering in Antebellum America* (Chapel Hill: University of North Carolina Press, 2002).

41. James Oakes, *The Ruling Race: A History of American Slaveholders* (New York: Vintage, 1982), 79.

42. Callie to Emmie, March 28, 1857, EGP.

43. Callie to William, September 8, 1858, EGP.

44. May, *John A. Quitman,* 237.

45. John S. Thrasher, *Cuba and Louisiana: Letter to Samuel J. Peters, Esq.* (New Orleans: Picayune Print, 1854), 7–8.

46. Thomas W. Wilson, *The Island of Cuba in 1850* (New Orleans: Printing Office of "La Patria," 1850), 5–6, 9.

47. Maturin M. Ballou, *History of Cuba, or, Notes of a Traveller in the Tropics* (Boston: Phillips, Sampson, and Co., 1854), 225.

48. The quoted wording comes from the title of Robert May's classic work, *The Southern Dream of a Caribbean Empire, 1854–1861* (Baton Rouge: Louisiana State University Press, 1973).

49. Rodrigo Lazo, *Writing to Cuba: Filibustering and Cuban Exiles in the United States* (Chapel Hill: University of North Carolina Press, 2005), 7.

50. Count A. de Gobineau, *The Moral and Intellectual Diversity of Races,* trans. Henry Hotz (Philadelphia: J. P. Lippincott, 1855), 194–195; Gobineau, *Essai sur l'inégalité des races humaines* (Paris: Editions Pierre Belfond, 1967), 849; Reginald Horseman, *Josiah Nott of Mobile: Southerner, Physician, and Racial Theorist* (Baton Rogue: Louisiana State University Press, 1987), 204–205; William Stanton, *The Leopard's Spots: Scientific Attitudes toward Race in America, 1815–59* (Chicago: University of Chicago Press, 1960), 174–175.

51. Here, I am grateful to Ruth Hill for sharing some of her forthcoming work on the separation of the United States from the Americas.

52. Richard Henry Dana, *To Cuba and Back: A Vacation Voyage* (London: Smith, Elder, and Co., 1859), 227–228, 230.

53. Ibid., 255.

54. Lazo, *Writing to Cuba,* 155, 154.

55. Dana, *To Cuba and Back,* 237.

56. Kirsten Silva Gruesz, *Ambassadors of Culture: The Transamerican Origins of Latino Writing* (Princeton, NJ: Princeton University Press, 2001).

57. J. Milton Mackie, *From Cape Cod to Dixie and the Tropics* (New York: G. P. Putnam, 1864), 157–158, 167.

58. Anthony Trollope, *The West Indies and the Spanish Main* (Leipzig: Bernhard Tauchnitz, 1860), 114–115.

59. Nathaniel Parker Willis, *Health Trip to the Tropics* (New York: Charles Scribner, 1853), 361.

60. James Phillippo, *The United States and Cuba* (London: Pewtress, 1857), 303, 306.

61. Amelia M. Murray, *Letters from the United States, Cuba and Canada* (New York: G. P. Putnam, 1857), 267.

62. Fredrika Bremer, *The Homes of the New World; Impressions of America,* 2 vols. (New York: Harper & Brothers, 1854), 2:387, 654, 442. For more on the "tropical South," see Ronald G. Walters, "The Erotic South: Civilization and Sexuality in American Abolitionism," *American Quarterly* 25.2 (May 1973): 177–201; and Alfred N. Hunt, *Haiti's Influence on Antebellum America: Slumbering Volcano in the Caribbean* (Baton Rouge: Louisiana State University Press, 1988).

63. John S. C. Abbott, *South and North, or, Impressions Received during a Trip to Cuba and the South* (New York: Abbey & Abbott, 1860), 54, 64.

64. Steven Hahn, "Class and State in Postemancipation Societies: Southern Planters in Comparative Perspective," *American Historical Review* 95 (February 1990): 75.

65. "Free Negroes in Jamaica," *De Bow's Review* (July 1860): 90; Edward B. Rugemer, "The Southern Response to British Abolitionism: The Maturation of Proslavery Apologetics," *Journal of Southern History* 60.2 (May 2004): 221–248.

66. Martin Delany, *Blake, or the Huts of America* (Boston: Beacon Press, 1971), 305.

67. Thomas Roderick Dew, "The Abolition of Negro Slavery" (1832), in *The Ideology of Slavery: Proslavery Thought in the Antebellum South, 1830–1860*, ed. Drew Gilpin Faust (Baton Rouge: Louisiana State University Press, 1981), 25.

68. David Herbert Donald, "The Proslavery Argument Reconsidered," *Journal of Southern History* 37.1 (February 1971): 4.

69. Dew, "The Abolition of Negro Slavery," 24.

70. Dana, *To Cuba and Back,* 238.

71. Benjamin Hunt, *Remarks on Hayti as a Place for Settlement of Afric-Americans, and on the Mulatto in the Race for the Tropics* (Philadelphia: T. B. Pugh, 1860), 36.

72. J. D. B. De Bow, "The Non-Slaveholders of the South," *De Bow's Review* (January 1861): 75.

73. Thomas R. R. Cobb, *An Inquiry into the Law of Negro Slavery in the United States of America, to Which Is Prefixed an Historical Sketch of Slavery* (Savannah: W. Thorne Williams, 1858), 52.

74. George Fitzhugh, *Sociology for the South, or, the Failure of Free Society* (Richmond: A. Morris, 1854), frontispiece.

75. Ibid., 260.

76. Trollope, *The West Indies and the Spanish Main,* 90–91.

77. John Bigelow, *Jamaica in 1850; or, the Effects of Sixteen Year's Freedom on a Slave Colony* (New York: G. P. Putnam, 1851), 74.

78. Trollope, *The West Indies and Spanish Main,* 91.

79. David Nicholls, *From Dessalines to Duvalier: Race, Colour, and National Independence in Haiti* (1979; reprint, New Brunswick, NJ: Rutgers University Press, 1996), 83.

80. Virginia Trist to Nicholas Trist, December 4, 1834, Trist Papers, Southern Historical Collection, University of North Carolina at Chapel Hill.

81. Willis, *Health Trip to the Tropics,* 260, 267.

82. Hunt, *Remarks on Hayti.*

83. "Hayti," *New York Times,* September 21, 1859; "Free Negroes Leaving for Hayti," *New Orleans Picayune,* January 15, 1860; Nicholls, *From Dessalines to Duvalier,* 82–85.

84. See, for instance, Alfred N. Hunt, *Haiti's Influence.* More broadly, see Brenda Gayle Plummer, *Haiti and the United States: The Psychological Moment* (Athens: University of Georgia Press, 1992).

85. C. L. R. James, *The Black Jacobins: Toussaint L'Ouverture and the San Domingo Revolution* (New York: Random House, 1963), 68; Laurent Dubois, *Avengers of the New World: The Story of the Haitian Revolution* (Cambridge, MA: Harvard University Press, 2005).

86. "Letter from Hayti," *New York Times,* March 6, 1860. The quote is from Henry David Thoreau, "The Last Days of John Brown," reprinted in Carl Bode, ed., *The Portable Thoreau* (New York: Viking Press, 1977), 676.

87. "The Haytians and John Brown: Letter from John Brown, Jr., to President Geffrard," *New York Times,* August 8, 1860.

88. David Reynolds, *John Brown, Abolitionist: The Man Who Killed Slavery, Sparked the Civil War, and Seeded Civil Rights* (New York: Alfred A. Knopf, 2005), 109–110.

89. David Walker, *An Appeal in Four Articles; Together with a Preamble to the Coloured Citizens of the World, but in Particular, and Very Expressly, to Those of the New World,* reprinted in *Classical Black Nationalism: From the American Revolution to Marcus Garvey,* ed. Wilson Jeremiah Moses (New York: New York University Press, 1996), 77.

90. William Wells Brown, "History of the Haitian Revolution," reprinted in *Pamphlets of Protest: An Anthology of Early African American Protest Literature, 1790–1860,* ed. Richard Newman, Patrick Rael, and Phillip Lapansky (New York: Routledge, 2001), 253.

91. Hunt, *Haiti's Influence,* 101, 98–101.

92. Ibid., 88–92.

93. Frederick Douglass, "Toussaint L'Ouverture," *Fredrick Douglass's Paper,* September 4, 1851.

94. Delany, *Blake,* 3.

95. Robert S. Levine, *Martin Delany, Frederick Douglass, and the Politics of Representative Identity* (Chapel Hill: University of North Carolina Press, 1997), 191–199.

96. Delany, *Blake,* 305.

97. Hunt, *Haiti's Influence,* 111, 114, 120, 130, 141–142.

98. D. J. McCord, "The Practical Effects of Emancipation, Part II," *De Bow's Review* (May 1855): 595. See also, for example, Elizor Wright, *The Lesson of St. Domingo, or, How to Make the War Short and the Peace Righteous* (Boston: A. Williams, 1861).

99. James, *Black Jacobins,* 84.

100. James Achille de Caradeuc, *Memoirs of the de Caradeuc Family* (privately published, 1931), 18, De Caradeuc Family Papers, Southern Historical Collection, Wilson Library, University of North Carolina at Chapel Hill (hereafter DCP).

101. William Faulkner, *Absalom, Absalom!* (1936; reprint, New York: Vintage, 1990), 28.

102. Tribute by nephew Thomas della Torre, "James Achille and Elizabeth Ann de Caradeuc," in James Achille de Caradeuc, *Memoirs,* 38, DCP.

103. A. De Caradeuc, *Grape Culture and Wine Making in the South, with a Description of the Best Varieties of Grapes for the Vineyard; Soils; Aspect,*

Preparation of the Grounds, Planting, &c. (Augusta, GA: D. Redmond, 1858), 6.

104. James Achille de Caradeuc, "Diary, 1863–1865," entry labeled "Our Country!!! July & Augt. 1865," DCP.
105. Diary entry, "SIGNS OF THE TIMES (NOV. 1865)," DCP.

2. The White Republic of the Tropics

1. "The New Confederacy," *New York Times*, February 11, 1861.
2. Ibid.; "He Wants to Be Let Alone," *New York Times*, May 4, 1861.
3. "Scott's great snake." Entered according to Act of Congress in the year 1861 by J. B. Elliott of Cincinnati, Maps Division, Library of Congress at http://lcweb2.loc.gov (accessed March 25, 2007).
4. Allen Tate, *Jefferson Davis, His Rise and Fall* (1929; reprint, Nashville: J. S. Sanders & Co., 1998), 46.
5. Hamilton Eckenrode, *Jefferson Davis: President of the South* (New York: Macmillan, 1923), 11.
6. Admitting that the Confederacy was a nation has long been a problem. For many, it seems to implicitly sanction the South's claim to cultural distinctiveness and to therefore suggest that secession was simply an act of what we would today call "self-determination." Most historians, then, have preferred to suggest that there was little practical difference between the North and the South, especially in political culture and social life, and that the wartime South struggled to quickly invent a national culture where none had existed before. "The Southerner as American" has, then, become a well-recognized trope, an agreed-upon point of departure for all manner of opinions. "The Southerner," C. Vann Woodward noted, "is obviously American as well as Southern." Emory Thomas, author of a history of "the Confederate nation," notes the deliberate attempt to wrap Southern nationalism around the question of "self-determination," but merely establishes that the South was a sort of breakaway regional republic, composed of Americans rebelling against America. Drew Gilpin Faust, the leading historian of Southern nationalism during the war, equates the struggle to create a nation with creation itself, calling into question the success of the Confederacy. "Southern commentators," Alice Fahs writes, dispelling the myth of Southern distinctiveness, "repeatedly asserted that their wartime literature was essentially different from the literature of the North—despite all evidence to the contrary." And in her work on the rapid construction of Confederate nationalism, Anne Sarah Rubin describes the overlapping and separated loyalties to the South and to the United States as a matter of "the local" and "the national." The question here, of course, is not whether the South was a nation but whether notions of "regionalism" and "nationalism" can possibly contain the cosmopolitan mindset of the Old South, with its slaveholding worldview that sprawled well beyond the borders of the United States. C. Vann Woodward, *The Burden of Southern History* (Baton Rouge: Louisiana State University Press, 1968), xii; Emory Thomas, *The Confederate Nation: 1861–1865* (New

York: Harper Torchbooks, 1979), 105, 5; Drew Gilpin Faust, *The Creation of Confederate Nationalism: Ideology and Identity in the Civil War South* (Baton Rouge: Louisiana State University Press, 1988), 6; Alice Fahs, *The Imagined Civil War: Popular Literature of the North and South, 1861–1865* (Chapel Hill: University of North Carolina Press, 2001), 9; Anna Sarah Rubin, *A Shattered Nation: The Rise and Fall of the Confederacy, 1861–1868* (Chapel Hill: University of North Carolina Press, 2005), 2.

7. The phrase is from Benedict Anderson, *Imagined Communities: Reflections on the Origin and Spread of Nationalism* (London: Verso, 1983), 151.

8. Italics in the original. Eli N. Evans, *Judah P. Benjamin: The Jewish Confederate* (New York: Free Press, 1988), xi.

9. Entries for February 13, 1862, and January 18, 1864, in *Mary Chesnut's Civil War*, ed. C. Vann Woodward (New Haven, CT: Yale University Press, 1981), 288, 542.

10. Don E. Fehrenbacher, *Slavery, Law, and Politics: The Dred Scott Case in Historical Perspective* (New York: Oxford University Press, 1981), 3, 185, 251–252, and passim.

11. *Speech of Hon. J. P. Benjamin, of LA., Delivered in Senate of the United States on Tuesday, March 11, 1868. Slavery Protected by the Common Law of the New World. Guaranteed by Constitution. Vindication of the Supreme Court of the U.S.* (Washington, DC: Gideon, 1858), 4, 10.

12. Fehrenbacher, *Slavery, Law, and Politics*, 252.

13. Robert Douthat Meade, *Judah P. Benjamin: Confederate Statesman* (1943; reprint, Baton Rouge: Louisiana State University Press, 2001), 46. William C. Davis, in the foreword to the new edition of Meade's 1943 biography, notes that there were "unusual circumstances" surrounding Benjamin's birth, a reference, it seems, to the mere fact that such a prominent Confederate could be born outside of the South. Davis, "Foreword," in Meade, *Judah P. Benjamin*, xi. Meade himself simply described Benjamin as "exotic" and "mysterious." Meade, *Judah P. Benjamin*, 3.

14. Meade, *Judah P. Benjamin*, 5.

15. Ibid., 44.

16. See, for instance, Judah P. Benjamin, "Louisiana Sugar," *De Bow's Review* (November 1846): 313–331; Judah P. Benjamin, "Advances of Agricultural Sciences," *De Bow's Review* (January 1848): 44–58; Judah P. Benjamin, "Soleil's Sacchrometer," *De Bow's Review* (April 1848): 357–365. The world of the "Sugar Masters" is carefully rendered in Richard Follett, *The Sugar Masters: Planters and Slaves in Louisiana's Cane World, 1820–1860* (Baton Rouge: Louisiana State University Press, 2005).

17. David Potter, *The Impending Crisis, 1848–1861* (New York: Harper & Row, 1976), 177–198.

18. In this, Southern expansionism—with its fear of slave rebellion and its vision of national or regional greatness—was quite consistent with what Michael Hunt has noted were the staple features of U.S. foreign policy from settlement through the Cold War. See Hunt, *The Ideology of U.S. Foreign Policy* (New Haven, CT: Yale University Press, 1988).

19. Rollin G. Osterweis, *Romanticism and Nationalism in the Old South* (New Haven, CT: Yale University Press, 1949), 174–176; Robert May, *The Southern Dream of a Caribbean Empire, 1854–1861* (Baton Rouge: Louisiana State University Press, 1973), 156–157.

20. Cited in Meade, *Judah P. Benjamin*, 74.

21. Michael A. Morrison, *Slavery and the American West: The Eclipse of Manifest Destiny and the Coming of the Civil War* (Chapel Hill: University of North Carolina Press, 1997), 12 and passim. Also see Michael Dunning, "Manifest Destiny and the Trans-Mississippi South: Natural Laws and the Extension of Slavery into Mexico," *Journal of Popular Culture* 35 (Fall 2001): 111–127; May, *Southern Dream of a Caribbean Empire*; Adam Rothman, *Slave Country: American Expansionism and the Origins of the Deep South* (Cambridge, MA: Harvard University Press, 2005).

22. Jefferson Davis, "Speech in Atlanta," in *Papers of Jefferson Davis*, 11 vols., ed. Lydia Lasswell Christ (Baton Rouge: Louisiana State University Press, 1985–), 7:44 (hereafter *PJD*).

23. Davis to Anna Ella Carroll, March 1, 1861, *PJD*, 7:65.

24. William H. Holcombe, "A Separate Nationality, or the Africanization of the South," *Southern Literary Messenger* (February 1861): 82.

25. "Jefferson Davis to the Confederate Congress, January 12, 1863," in *Jefferson Davis, Constitutionalist: His Letters, Papers, and Speeches*, 10 vols., ed. Dunbar Rowland (Jackson: Mississippi Department of Archives and History, 1923), 5:403 (hereafter *JDC*); Joseph T. Durkin, *Confederate Navy Chief: Stephen R. Mallory* (1954; reprint, Birmingham: University of Alabama Press, 2005), 5.

26. George E. Buker, *Blockaders, Refugees, and Contrabands: Civil War on Florida's Gulf Coast, 1861–1865* (Tuscaloosa: University of Alabama Press, 1993); Hamilton Cochran, *Blockade Runners of the Confederacy* (Tuscaloosa: University of Alabama Press, 1958).

27. Durkin, *Confederate Navy Chief*, 158–159.

28. Letter from M. M. Kimmey, November 4, 1862, in *Diary and Correspondence of Salmon P. Chase*, ed. George S. Denison (Washington, DC: American Historical Association, 1903), 526.

29. William Alexander to Montgomery Blair, January 13, 1863, in *Private and Official Correspondence of Gen. Benjamin F. Butler, during the Period of the Civil War*, 5 vols. (Springfield, MA: Plimpton Press, 1917), 2:629; James W. Daddyman, *The Matamoros Trade: Confederate Commerce, Diplomacy, and Intrigue* (Newark: University of Delaware Press, 1983); Patrick Kelly, "Los Algodones (the Time of Cotton): War, Rebellion, and Trade along the Texas-Mexican Border, 1855–1875," unpublished manuscript in author's possession.

30. Cf. William Lederer and Eugene Burdick, *The Ugly American* (New York: W. W. Norton, 1999).

31. Joseph A. Fry, *Dixie Looks Abroad: The South and U.S. Foreign Relations, 1789–1973* (Baton Rouge: Louisiana State University Press, 2002), 79–83;

Frank Owsley, *King Cotton Diplomacy: Foreign Relations of the Confederate States of America* (1931; reprint, Chicago: University of Chicago Press, 1959).

32. John Stuart Mill, *The Contest in America* (Boston: Little, Brown, 1862), 29.

33. Donald S. Frazier, *Blood and Treasure: Confederate Empire in the Southwest* (College Station: Texas A&M University Press, 1995).

34. Kathryn Abbey Hanna, "The Roles of the South in the French Intervention in Mexico," *Journal of Southern History* 20 (February 1954): 10.

35. Fry, *Dixie Looks Abroad*, 99.

36. John S. Preston to Jefferson Davis, February 25, 1865, *JDC*, 6:485.

37. John Thomas Pickett to Don Manuel Maria De Zamacona y Francisco Zarco, September 16, 1861, reprinted in the *Hispanic American Historical Review* 2 (1919): 611–617.

38. Michael Chevalier, *France, Mexico, and the Confederate States,* trans. William Henry Hurlbert (New York: C. B. Richardson, 1863), 15.

39. Thomas Schoonover, "Napoleon Is Coming! Maximilian Is Coming? The International History of the Civil War in the Caribbean Basin," in *The Union, the Confederacy, and the Atlantic Rim,* ed. Robert E. May (Lafayette, IN: Purdue University Press, 1995), 101–130; James Morton Callahan, *Diplomatic History of the Confederacy* (1901; reprint, New York: Frederick Ungar, 1964), 202–206.

40. Callahan, *Diplomatic History of the Confederacy*, 77, 98, 124, 168, 207.

41. Robert Toombs to Charles Helm, July 22, 1861, and Judah P. Benjamin to John Slidell, May 9, 1863, both in *A Compilation of the Messages and Papers of the Confederacy, Including Diplomatic Correspondence, 1861–1865,* 2 vols., ed. James D. Richardson (Nashville: United States Publishing Co., 1905), 2:48, 484.

42. Pierre Adolph Rost to R. M. T. Hunter, March 21, 1862, and Robert Hunter to William Yancy, Pierre Adolph Rost, and A. Dudley Mann, August 24, 1861, both in *A Compilation of Messages and Papers of the Confederacy*, 2:204, 74.

43. On Cubans and the Civil War and especially on Gonzales, see Antonio Rafael de la Cova, *Cuban Confederate Colonel: The Life of Ambrosio José Gonzales* (Columbia: University of South Carolina Press, 2003). The story of Loreta Janeta Velazquez—presented as "fact or fiction"—is wonderfully discussed in Jesse Alemán, "Authenticity, Autobiography, and Identity: *The Woman in Battle* as a Civil War Narrative," in *The Woman in Battle: The Civil War Narrative of Loreta Velazquez, Cuban Woman and Confederate Soldier,* ed. Jesse Alemán (1876; reprint, Madison: University of Wisconsin Press, 2003), ix–xli. The clippings file and the letter to P. T. Beauregard, dated April 17, 1861, are in the Elliot and Gonzalez Family Papers, Southern Historical Collection, Wilson Library, University of North Carolina at Chapel Hill.

44. Franklin W. Knight, *The Caribbean: The Genesis of a Fragmented Nationalism* (New York: Oxford University Press, 1990), 159–160.

45. Anderson, *Imagined Communities*, 53–54.

46. "New Orleans—the Athens of the South," *Southern Literary Messenger* (April 1861): 312, 313.

47. Faust, *Creation of Confederate Nationalism*, 8.

48. Robert E. Bonner, *Colors and Blood: Flag Passions of the Confederate South* (Princeton, NJ: Princeton University Press, 2002), passim.

49. Anderson, *Imagined Communities*, 62.

50. Alfred H. Guernsey, "Jefferson Davis and the Confederacy," *Appleton's Journal* 11 (August 1881): 172.

51. Varina Davis, *Jefferson Davis: Ex-President of the Confederate States of America; A Memoir by His Wife*, 2 vols. (New York: Belford, 1890), 1:179.

52. Anderson, *Imagined Communities*, 151.

53. Varina Davis, *Jefferson Davis*, 2:18–19; William J. Cooper Jr., *Jefferson Davis, American* (New York: Vintage, 2000), 70–95.

54. Thomas Reade Rootes Cobb to Marion Lumpkin Cobb, February 9, 1861, in *The Correspondence of Thomas Reade Rootes Cobb, 1860–1862*, ed. Augustus Longstreet Hull (Washington, DC: Southern History Association, 1907), 80.

55. Mary Ashton Rice Livermore, *The Story of My Life, or, the Sunshine and Shadow of Seventy Years* (Hartford: A. D. Worthington, 1897), 463.

56. Jefferson Davis, *The Rise and Fall of the Confederate Government*, 2 vols. (New York: D. Appleton, 1881), 1:260.

57. "Can we not," David Potter once wondered, "ask whether the difference between Union and Confederate political performance was not as great or greater as economic disparities—whether in fact the discrepancy in ability between Abraham Lincoln and Jefferson Davis was not as real and as significant as the inequality in mileage between the Union and Confederate railroad systems?" In Potter's critical portrait, Davis fails as a Southerner and becomes the man who quite deliberately lost, so to speak, the "Lost Cause." "There is no real evidence," Potter concludes, "in all the literature that Davis ever at any one time gave extended consideration to the basic question of what the South would have to do to win the war." David M. Potter, *The South and the Sectional Conflict* (Baton Rouge: Louisiana State University Press, 1968), 267, 283. Also see Brian Dirck, *Lincoln and Davis: Imagining America, 1809–1865* (Lawrence: University Press of Kansas, 2001). For a long time, historians described the South as a premodern and provincial place. The Civil War was, in this conception, a strange consequence of the "deeper level of consciousness," where Southerners were dimly aware of "the anachronism of Negro slavery" and were troubled "by the need to defend it in an egalitarian society." William Taylor, *Cavalier and Yankee: The Old South and American National Character* (1957; reprint, New York: Harper Torchbooks, 1969), 297. For a great correction to this argument, see Michael O'Brien, *Conjectures of Order: Intellectual Life and the American South, 1810–1860* (Chapel Hill: University of North Carolina Press, 2003). Also see Drew Gilpin Faust, *A Sacred Circle* (Baltimore: Johns Hopkins University Press, 1977). More re-

cently, in another variant on this theme, it has become popular to label the Civil War "revolutionary" only when one speaks from a Northern perspective, as if the creation of the Confederacy was merely a "counterrevolution," the deeply conservative act of terribly conservative men. On the absence of revolutionary intent in the South, see, for instance, David Brion Davis, *Inhuman Bondage: The Rise and Fall of Slavery in the New World* (New York: Oxford University Press, 2006), 298, and James M. McPherson, *Battle Cry of Freedom* (New York: Oxford University Press, 2003), 234.

58. Varina Davis, *Jefferson Davis*, 1:413.
59. Faust, *Creation of Confederate Nationalism*, 27.
60. Varina Davis, *Jefferson Davis*, 2:36.
61. Jefferson Davis, "Inaugural Address," in *The Messages and Papers of Jefferson Davis and the Confederacy*, 2 vols., ed. Allan Nevins (New York: Chelsea House, 1966), 1:36.
62. Alexander Stephens, "Speech Delivered on the 21st March, 1861, in Savannah, Known as 'The Corner-Stone Speech,' reported in the Savannah Republican," in *Alexander H. Stephens, in Public and Private: With Letters and Speeches, before, during, and since the War*, ed. Henry Cleveland (Philadelphia: National Publishing Co., 1886), 718, 719, 721.
63. Alexander Stephens, "Speech before the Virginia Secession Convention," April 23, 1861, in *Alexander H. Stephens*, 735, 739.
64. Mark Neely, Harold Holzer, and Gabor Boritt, *The Confederate Image: Prints of the Lost Cause* (Chapel Hill: University of North Carolina Press, 2000), 13–15.
65. Varina Davis, *Jefferson Davis*, 2:19.
66. Bonner, *Colors and Blood*, 111–112.
67. Faust, *Creation of Confederate Nationalism*, 26.
68. Taylor, *Cavalier and Yankee*, 262.
69. "Secession and Reconstruction," *New York Times*, January 21, 1861.
70. Stephens, "Speech Delivered on the 21st March, 1861," 721.
71. "Constitution of the Confederate States," in *Messages and Papers of Jefferson Davis*, 1:51.
72. Stephens, "Speech before the Virginia Secession Convention," 743.
73. Holcombe, "A Separate Nationality," 82, 85.
74. Stephens, "Speech Delivered on the 21st March, 1861," 728.
75. "Northern Mind and Character," *Southern Literary Messenger* (November 1860): 345, 349, 347; Faust, *Creation of Confederate Nationalism*, 10–11; Richie Watson, " 'The Difference of Race': Antebellum Race Mythology and the Development of Southern Nationalism," *Southern Literary Journal* 35.1 (2002): 1–13.
76. *Punch*, cited in Fry, *Dixie Looks Abroad*, 91.
77. Davis, "To the Confederate Congress, January 12, 1863," *JDC*, 5:409.
78. Charles B. Dew, *Apostles of Disunion: Southern Secession Commissioners and the Causes of the Civil War* (Charlottesville: University Press of Virginia, 2001), 40–41, 80–81.

79. "Remarks of Jefferson Davis on the Special Message on Affairs in South Carolina, January 10, 1861," *JDC*, 5:30.
80. Faust, *Creation of Confederate Nationalism*, 70, 63–71; Diane Sommerville, *Rape and Race in the Nineteenth-Century South* (Chapel Hill: University of North Carolina Press, 2004); Anne Sarah Rubin, *A Shattered Nation: The Rise and Fall of the Confederacy, 1861–1868* (Chapel Hill: University of North Carolina Press, 2005), 100–102; Dew, *Apostles of Disunion*.
81. Richard G. Doty, "The Color of Money: Background and Commentary," in *Confederate Currency; the Color of Money: Images of Slavery in Confederate and Southern States Currency*, ed. John W. Jones (West Columbia, SC: New Directions Publishing, 2002), 43, 39–43.
82. Reproduced in *Confederate Currency*, 64, 66.
83. Edward A. Pollard, "Hints on Southern Civilization," *Southern Literary Messenger* (April 1861): 310.
84. John Michael Vlach, *The Planter's Prospect: Privilege and Slavery in Plantation Paintings* (Chapel Hill: University of North Carolina Press, 2002), 109.
85. Bonner, *Colors and Blood*, 106.
86. Vlach, *Planter's Prospect*, 113–190.
87. Davis to Smith, March 25, 1865, *PJD*, 11:461; Bruce Levine, *Confederate Emancipation: Southern Plans to Free and Arm Slaves during the Civil War* (New York: Oxford University Press, 2006), 95, 103–108, 161.
88. Neely, Holzer, and Boritt, *Confederate Image*, 184–185.
89. Note, "May 2," *PJD*, 11:579–580; Davis, "Speech at Macon," September 22, 1864, *PJD*, 11:62.
90. Andrew F. Rolle, *The Lost Cause: The Confederate Exodus to Mexico* (Norman: University of Oklahoma Press, 1965), 38–49.
91. "Jefferson Davis," *New York Times*, May 28, 1865.
92. Jefferson Davis, *A Short History of the Confederate States of America* (New York: Belford, 1890), 503.
93. Roy Franklin Nichols, "United States vs. Jefferson Davis," *American Historical Review* 31.2 (January 1926): 283, 266–284; Cooper, *Jefferson Davis*, 577–610; David K. Watson, "The Trial of Jefferson Davis: An Interesting Constitutional Question," *Yale Law Journal* 24.8 (June 1915): 669–676.
94. Jefferson Davis to Varina Davis, March 13, 1866, in *Jefferson Davis: Private Letters, 1823–1899*, ed. Hudson Strode (New York: Harcourt, Brace, and World, 1966), 239.
95. Gerrit Smith, "Gerrit Smith on the Bailing of Jefferson Davis" (Peterboro, NY, 1867), in the Pamphlet Collection, Special Collections, Syracuse University Library.
96. "The Plea for Davis," *Harper's Weekly* (June 24, 1865): 386–387
97. "Treason Made Easy and Respectable," *New York Times*, May 23, 1867.
98. "Horace Greeley and Jefferson Davis," *The Nation* (May 1867).

99. "Maximilian and Jefferson Davis," *New York Times,* July 17, 1867; "The Fate of Maximilian," *New York Times,* July 19, 1867. Davis's case was cited as a precedent at Maximilian's proceedings. See Frederic Hall, *Life of Maximilian I, Late Emperor of Mexico, with a Sketch of the Empress Carlotta* (New York: J. Miller, 1868), 236.

100. Varina Davis, *Jefferson Davis,* 2:803.

101. One wartime traveler felt uncomfortable honeymooning at the Hotel Cubano, despite its "comfortable apartments," precisely because it was the "head-quarters of the Secessionists." He chose to stay in his room during his stay. William David Stuart, *Memoir of William David Stuart* (Philadelphia, 1865), 39.

102. "Testimonial to Jefferson Davis in Louisiana," *New York Times,* January 28, 1868.

103. Varina Davis, *Jefferson Davis,* 2:805; Cooper, *Jefferson Davis,* 615–618; "The Davis Family—Lease of Plantation to Negroes," *New York Times,* December 2, 1866.

104. The notion of a hybrid South comes from John T. Matthews, "This Race Which Is Not One: The More 'Inextricable Compositeness' of William Faulkner's South," in *Look Away! The U.S. South in New World Studies,* ed. Jon Smith and Deborah Cohn (Durham, NC: Duke University Press, 2004), 201–226.

105. Eliza Chinn McHatton-Ripley, *From Flag to Flag* (New York: D. Appleton, 1896), 132.

106. Thomas, *Confederate Nation,* 305–306.

107. Jubal Early to T. L. Rosser, May 10, 1866, reprinted in William D. Hoyt Jr., "New Light on Jubal Early after Appomattox," *Journal of Southern History* 9.1 (February 1943): 115, 116.

108. MacKinlay Kantor, *If the South Had Won the Civil War* (1967; reprint, New York: Tor Books, 2001), 97, 100.

109. *C.S.A.: Confederate States of America,* dir. Kevin Wilmott (Hodcarrier Films, 2004).

110. Howard Means, *C.S.A.* (New York: William Morrow, 1998).

111. Harry Turtledove, *How Few Remain* (New York: Del Rey, 1998), and *The Guns of the South* (New York: Del Rey, 1992), 560.

112. Roger Ransom, *The Confederate States of America: What Might Have Been* (New York: W. W. Norton, 2005).

113. "Diary of Eliza Frances Andrews, April, 1865," in *The War-Time Journal of a Georgia Girl, 1864–1865,* ed. Spencer B. King Jr. (New York: Appleton-Century-Crofts, 1908), 392.

114. May, *Southern Dream of a Caribbean Empire,* 257.

3. The Promise of Exile

1. W. W. Legaré, "Circular Letter," dated August 1, 1867, in the South Caroliniana Library, University of South Carolina. Also see "Notice," *Daily Clarion,* June 22, 1865.

2. James L. Rourk, *Masters without Slaves: Southern Planters in the Civil War and Reconstruction* (New York: W. W. Norton, 1977), 123–124.

3. C. L. R. James, "From Toussaint L'Ouverture to Fidel Castro," an appendix in *Black Jacobins: Toussaint L'Ouverture and the San Domingo Revolution* (1938; reprint, New York: Vintage, 1989), 409.

4. Gerald Horne, *The Deepest South: The United States, Brazil, and the African Slave Trade* (New York: New York University Press, 2007), 2. Also see Laura Jarnagin Pang, "Social Networking and Atlantic Capitalism in the Nineteenth Century," unpublished manuscript in author's possession.

5. On McCollam, see J. Carlyle Sitterson, "The McCollams: A Planter Family of the Old and New South," *Journal of Southern History* 6.3 (August 1940): 347–360; Rourk, *Masters without Slaves*, 128–130.

6. Entry for June 6, 1866, in "The Brazilian Diary of Andrew McCollam," Southern Historical Collection, University of North Carolina, Andrew McCollam Papers, subseries 2.1, folder 44 (hereafter "Brazilian Diary").

7. Entries for July 5 and July 14, 1866, "Brazilian Diary."

8. Entries for July 14, July 17, August 4, and August 29, 1866, "Brazilian Diary."

9. Carl N. Degler, *Neither Black Nor White: Slavery and Race Relations in Brazil and the United States* (1971; reprint, Madison: University of Wisconsin Press, 1988), esp. 207–264.

10. It was only a short while before McCollam was in Havana, Cuba, staying at the Saint Isabel Hotel. "Havana," he wrote, "is all life." He spent the next day visiting the market and then, in the evening, at a bullfight—though he found it too gruesome and "cruel" to enjoy. Entry for February 25, "Brazilian Diary."

11. Entries for September 19, 1866, February 25, March 2, March 3, and March 12, 1867, "Brazilian Diary."

12. Rollin G. Osterweis, *The Myth of the Lost Cause, 1865–1900* (New York: Anchor Books, 1973), 8. Also see Clement Eaton, *The Waning of the Old South Civilization, 1860–1880s* (Athens: University of Georgia Press, 1968); *The Confederados: Old South Immigrants in Brazil*, ed. Cyrus B. Dawsey and James M. Dawsey (Tuscaloosa: University of Alabama Press, 1995); Eugene C. Harter, *The Lost Colony of the Confederacy* (Jackson: University Press of Mississippi, 1985); William Clark Griggs, *The Elusive Eden: Frank McMullan's Confederate Colony in Brazil* (Austin: University of Texas Press, 1987); Donald C. Simmons Jr., *Confederate Settlements in British Honduras* (Jefferson, NC: McFarland, 2001).

13. "From Brazil," *New York Times*, December 3, 1865.

14. See, for instance, "Southern Emigration: Brazil and British Honduras," *De Bow's Review* (December 1867): 537–545.

15. Charles Willis Simmons, "Racist Americans in a Multi-racial Society: Confederate Exiles in Brazil," *Journal of Negro History* 67.1 (Spring 1982): 34–39; Harter, *Lost Colony of the Confederacy*; Griggs, *The Elusive Eden*; Dawsey and Dawsey, *The Confederados*.

16. Senator Westcott of Florida, *Congressional Globe* (30:1), appendix, 608.

17. *Speech of Hon. E. W. Chastain, of Georgia, on the Acquisition of Cuba, in Reply to the Speech of Mr. Boyce, of South Carolina, Delivered in the House of Representatives, Feb. 17, 1855* (Washington, DC: A. O. P. Nicholson, 1855), 14. Also see Basil Rauch, *American Interest in Cuba: 1848–1855* (New York: Columbia University Press, 1948); Juan A. Sánchez Bermúdez, "La Pretensiones Anexionistas de los Estados Unidos en Cuba Colonial," *Islas* 64 (1979): 43–63.

18. Samuel L. Walker, *Cuba and the South* (n.p., 1854), 3; *The Commercial Guide or Merchant's Manual, Comprising All the Most Important Information Required by Merchant's Shipowners, and Others, Transacting Business with the Island of Cuba* (Havana, 1861).

19. Though she later published her memoirs under a different name—as Eliza Chinn McHatton-Ripley—I have referred to her in this chapter by her married name in this era, Eliza McHatton.

20. "Chinese Servants," *New Orleans Times,* February 11, 1871.

21. Eliza Chinn McHatton-Ripley, *Social Life in Old New Orleans: Being Recollections of My Girlhood* (New York: D. Appleton, 1912), 43.

22. See Drew Gilpin Faust, *Mothers of Invention: Women of the Slaveholding South in the American Civil War* (New York: Vintage, 1996).

23. Physical description given on Eliza's travel visa, dated November 2, 1870, in the McHatton Family Papers, Hargrett Rare Book and Manuscript Library, University of Georgia (hereafter MFP).

24. "Chinese Servants."

25. Eliza Chinn McHatton-Ripley, *From Flag to Flag: A Woman's Adventures and Experiences in the South during the War, in Mexico, and in Cuba* (1888; reprint, New York: D. Appleton, 1896), 12, 22.

26. Diary of Henry McHatton, dated 1870, which contains a family genealogy, and the affidavit of James McHatton, February 15, 1872, both in MFP.

27. McHatton-Ripley, *Social Life in Old New Orleans,* 192.

28. Eliza Frances Andrews, from her diary of May of 1865, in *The War-Time Journal of a Georgia Girl, 1864–1865,* ed. Spencer B. King Jr. (New York: Appleton Press, 1908), 198.

29. Eliza McHatton to Mrs. R. H. Chinn, August 28, 1862, MFP.

30. "Four Hundred Wagonloads of Negroes," *New York Herald,* November 20, 1862.

31. Balance sheet for the Arlington plantation, 1861, and the affidavit of James McHatton, February 15, 1872, both in MFP. Also see Andrew Rolle, *The Lost Cause: The Confederate Exodus to Mexico* (Norman: University of Oklahoma Press, 1992).

32. Italics in original. McHatton-Ripley, *Flag to Flag,* 83.

33. "Dictation of Richard Chinn, Solano County, 1888," Bancroft Library, University of California, Berkeley.

34. Rolle, *The Lost Cause,* 31.

35. McHatton-Ripley, *Flag to Flag,* 123.

36. Ibid., 119, 150. Zell's age is impossible to verify, though it is clear that some-time during their stay in Cuba, he turned twenty years old. See ibid., 291.

37. Emphasis in original. Eliza McHatton to Anna Chinn, October 31, 1864; Eliza McHatton to Anna Chinn, February 21, 1865; James Hewett and J.H.P. Aldersbery to Eliza McHatton, April 8, 1865; and R. Atkinson to Eliza McHatton, April 21, 1865, all in MFP.

38. McHatton-Ripley, *Flag to Flag,* 132.

39. McHatton-Ripley, *Social Life in Old New Orleans,* 287–292.

40. "The Situation," *New York Herald,* May 18, 1865.

41. McHatton-Ripley, *Flag to Flag,* 126.

42. Draft version of *From Flag to Flag* and diary of Henry McHatton, 1870, both in MFP.

43. McHatton-Ripley, *Flag to Flag,* 150.

44. Eliza McHatton to unknown, October 15, 1870, MFP.

45. McHatton-Ripley, *Flag to Flag,* 151.

46. Ibid., 152.

47. Ibid., 149–150, 155, 163–165, 166.

48. Franklin Knight, *Slave Society in Cuba during the Nineteenth Century* (Madison: University of Wisconsin Press, 1970), 29. On the specific demo-graphic and economic transformations engendered in Cuba by this "sugar revolution," see Knight, *Slave Society in Cuba,* 25–84; and Louis Pérez, *Cuba: Between Reform and Revolution* (New York: Oxford University Press, 1995), 70–103.

49. Mark Anthony De Wolf to Joseph Seymour, November 30, 1838, De Wolf Papers, Rhode Island Historical Society, box 5, series I, folder 241.

50. Joseph John Gurney, *A Winter in the West Indies, Described in Familiar Letters to Henry Clay, of Kentucky* (London: John Murray, 1840), 209.

51. William Green, *British Slave Emancipation: The Sugar Colonies and the Great Experiment, 1830–1865* (Oxford: Clarendon Press, 1976), 261–293; Alan H. Adamson, *Sugar without Slaves: The Political Economy of British Guiana, 1838–1904* (New Haven, CT: Yale University Press, 1972), 41–56; Thomas C. Holt, *The Problem of Freedom: Race, Labor, and Politics in Ja-maica and Britain, 1832–1938* (Baltimore: Johns Hopkins University Press, 1992).

52. On these advances and transformations, see especially Manuel Moreno Fraginals, *El ingenio: Complejo económico social cubano del azúcar,* 3 vols. (Havana: Editorial de Ciencias Sociales, 1978), condensed and translated as Moreno Fraginals, *The Sugarmill: The Socioeconomic Complex of Sugar in Cuba* (New York: Monthly Review Press, 1976); Laird W. Bergad, *Cuban Rural Society in the Nineteenth Century: The Social and Economic History of Monoculture in Matanzas* (Princeton, NJ: Princeton University Press, 1999), 107–114; Hugh Thomas, *Cuba, or, The Pursuit of Freedom* (1971; reprint, New York: Da Capo Press, 1998), 120–125; and Louis A. Pérez Jr., *Winds of Change: Hurricanes and the Transformation of Nineteenth-Century Cuba* (Chapel Hill: University of North Carolina Press, 2001).

53. Miguel Barnet, *Biography of a Runaway Slave,* trans. W. Nick Hill (1966; reprint, Willimantic, CT: Curbstone Press, 1994), 101.

54. "Planting in Cuba," *Home & Hearth,* August 20, 1870.

55. Chinese coolies had been harvesting guano off the Peruvian coast since the 1850s. According to the report, misfiled in the MFP as "soil analysis," Eliza and James had the guano analyzed in 1870, after several years in Cuba, at the New Jersey State Agricultural College. Also see McHatton-Ripley, *Flag to Flag,* 253.

56. McHatton-Ripley, *Flag to Flag,* 233, 254, 162.

57. The census of 1841 listed 418,211 whites, 436,495 slaves, and 152,838 free people of color. See Duvon Clough Corbitt, *A Study of the Chinese in Cuba, 1847–1947* (Wilmore, KY: Asbury College, 1971), 2.

58. Robert L. Paquette, *Sugar Is Made with Blood: The Conspiracy of La Escalera and the Conflict over Slavery in Cuba* (Middletown, CT: Wesleyan University Press, 1988), 81–103, 209–232.

59. Mary Turner, "Chinese Contract Labour in Cuba, 1847–1874," *Caribbean Studies* 14.2 (July 1974): 71; Duvon Clough Corbitt, "Immigration in Cuba," *Hispanic American Historical Review* 22 (May 1942): 302.

60. Corbitt, *A Study of the Chinese in Cuba,* 4; Arthur F. Corwin, *Spain and the Abolition of Slavery in Cuba, 1817–1886* (Austin: University of Texas Press, 1967), 86.

61. According to Thomas Skidmore, Brazil did not suffer from the same level of acute labor shortage. Hence, the question of bringing in Chinese coolies was not an issue there until the moment of abolition in the 1870s, and even then the question was resolved in the negative—there would be no broad-based Chinese immigration to Brazil. The "controversy over Chinese immigration," he writes, "forced many Brazilians" to unite behind "a strong commitment to a progressively whiter Brazil." Thomas Skidmore, *Black into White: Race and Nationality in Brazilian Thought* (1974; reprint, Durham, NC: Duke University Press, 1993), 24–27, quote on 27.

62. Cited in Moreno Fraginals, *El ingenio,* 1:273.

63. Evelyn Hu-Dehart, "Race Construction and Race Relations: Chinese and Blacks in Nineteenth Century Cuba," unpublished manuscript in author's possession.

64. William H. Robertson to William L. Marcy, August 6, 1855, in "Report of the Secretary of State, in Compliance with a Resolution of the Senate of April 24, Calling for Information Relative to the Coolie Trade," *Senate Documents, 1st & 2nd Session, 34th Congress, 1855–1856* (Washington, DC: A. O. P. Nicholson, 1856), 15:3.

65. McHatton-Ripley, *Flag to Flag,* 155.

66. The details of the voyage come from the Captain Thomas R. Pillsbury Papers, Stephen Phillips Memorial Library, Penobscot Maritime Museum, Searsport, Maine (hereafter PP). This collection contains much of the legal documentation of the trip along with Pillsbury's correspondence and "Log

Book of Ship Forest Eagle of incidents appertaining to the Emigrants from Macao to Havana, 500 in number. Reported by John O. Shaw, Coolie Master" (n.d., handwritten). My thanks to John Arrison of the Penobscot Marine Museum for bringing this collection to my attention.

67. "March 13th," in Shaw, "Log Book," PP.

68. See Shaw, "Log Book," passim, in PP.

69. Turner, "Chinese Contract Labour in Cuba," 66–81.

70. Knight, *Slave Society in Cuba,* 116.

71. Hu-Dehart, "Race Construction and Race Relations."

72. Ibid.; Knight, *Slave Society in Cuba,* 116–118. As Knight documents, traveler Antonio Gallenga had noted during his visit to Cuba that it was often heard that one was off to "buy a chino." See Antonio Gallenga, *Pearl of the Antilles* (London: Chapman & Hall, 1873), 88.

73. Lui A-jui, quoted in *The Cuba Commission Report: A Hidden History of the Chinese in Cuba,* ed. Denise Helly (1876; reprint, Baltimore: Johns Hopkins University Press, 1993), 89.

74. "Chinese Servants."

75. One historian has remarked, "Slaves on efficient modern plantations with steam-driven mills were treated more inhumanely than those on the old oxen-driven mills: they were confined to menial and manual labour; and they were regarded and treated as economic rather than human units." Corwin, *Spain and the Abolition of Slavery in Cuba,* 109–110.

76. Ramón Sagra, *Cuba en 1860, o sea cuadro de sus adelantos en la población, la agricultura, el comercio y las rentas públicas, suplemento a la primera parte de la historia política y natural de la isla de Cuba* (Paris: L. Hachette y Cia, 1863), 43–44.

77. The classic example is *Practical Rules for the Management and Medical Treatment of Negro Slaves in the Sugar Colonies, by a Professional Planter* (London: J. Barfield, 1811).

78. Italics in original. William H. Robertson to William L. Marcy, September 3, 1855, in "Report of the Secretary of State," 4; Hu-Dehart, "Race Construction and Race Relations."

79. McHatton-Ripley, *Flag to Flag,* 175.

80. Richard J. Levis, *Diary of a Spring Holiday in Cuba* (Philadelphia: Porter & Coates, 1872), 35.

81. C. D. Tyng, *The Stranger in the Tropics; Being a Handbook for Havana and a Guide Book for Travellers in Cuba, Puerto Rico, and St. Thomas* (New York: American News, 1868), 66–67.

82. Charles Jackson to Eliza McHatton, December 11, 1873, and Charles Jackson to Eliza McHatton, November 2, 1874, both in MFP.

83. Anonymous, *Rambles in Cuba* (New York, 1870), 9.

84. Eliza McHatton to Robert and Anna, August 26, 1866, MFP.

85. "Chinese Servants."

86. George Barclay, *"Little Cuba"; or, Circumstantial Evidence. Being a True Story of Love, War, and Startling Adventures* (Philadelphia: Barclay, 1873).

87. Michael H. Hunt, *Ideology and U.S. Foreign Policy* (New Haven, CT: Yale University Press, 1987); Kristen Hoganson, *Fighting for Manhood: How Gender Politics Provoked the Spanish-American and Philippine-American Wars* (New Haven, CT: Yale University Press, 1998).

88. Samuel Hazard, *Cuba with Pen and Pencil* (Hartford: Hartford Publishing Co., 1871), 149.

89. Ibid., 162.

90. Ibid., 168. There is a sketch of this characterization on 212.

91. "Chinese Servants"; "Planting in Cuba."

92. Autobiographical draft, "Chinese Murder," MFP.

93. "Chinese Servants."

94. McHatton-Ripley, *Flag to Flag*, 177.

95. Ibid., 180.

96. Rebecca J. Scott, *Slave Emancipation in Cuba: The Transition to Free Labor, 1860–1889* (Princeton: Princeton University Press, 1985), 31–32.

97. The debate between Rebecca Scott and Manuel Moreno Fraginals over technological modernization and "free" immigrant labor is aptly and lucidly summed in Hu-Dehart, "Chinese Coolie Labour in Cuba in the Nineteenth Century," 78–83.

98. Scott, *Slave Emancipation in Cuba*, 33, 33–34.

99. McHatton-Ripley, *Flag to Flag*, 172.

100. Ibid., 173.

101. Charles Jackson to Eliza McHatton, September 22, 1873, MFP.

102. McHatton-Ripley, *Flag to Flag*, 174.

103. Helly, *Cuba Commission Report*, 49.

104. Ibid., 55.

105. Barnet, *Biography of a Runaway Slave*, 43. The *Commission Report* likewise suggests a relatively high rate of suicide both in Cuba and on the voyage overseas from China; see Helly, *Cuba Commission Report*, 43–47, 99–103.

106. Helly, *Cuba Commission Report*, 101.

107. Thomas, *Cuba*, 188.

108. W. M. L. Jay [Woodruff], *My Winter in Cuba* (New York: E. P. Dutton, 1871), 222; Hu-Dehart, "Race Construction and Race Relations"; Knight, *Slave Society in Cuba*, 116–118.

109. R. H. Chinn to Eliza McHatton, September 17, 1874, MFP.

110. McHatton-Ripley, *Flag to Flag*, 178.

111. R. H. Chinn to Eliza McHatton, July 23, 1874, MFP.

112. R. H. Chinn to Eliza McHatton, July 9, 1874, MFP.

113. Henry McHatton to Eliza McHatton, June 10, 1875, MFP.

114. Reviewer's comment, describing McHatton's memoir, "From Flag to Flag," *The Globe*, April 6, 1889, in file named "Clippings, Reviews of Flag to Flag," in MFP.

115. R. H. Chinn to Eliza McHatton, May 24, 1874, MFP.

116. R. H. Chinn to Eliza McHatton, September 9, 1874, MFP.

117. McHatton-Ripley, *Flag to Flag*, 293.
118. Ibid.
119. Turner, "Chinese Contract Labour in Cuba," 78.
120. James McHatton to Eliza McHatton, November 12, 1867, MFP.
121. Ada Ferrer, *Insurgent Cuba: Race, Nation, and Revolution, 1868–1989* (Chapel Hill: University of North Carolina Press, 1999), 4.
122. "Diary, 1886 Dec 23–1887 Jan 18," Special Collections and University Archives, Jean and Alexander Heard Library, Vanderbilt University, Nashville.
123. McHatton-Ripley, *Flag to Flag*, 128.
124. Horne, *Deepest South*, 220, 241–243.
125. McHatton-Ripley, *Social Life in Old New Orleans*, 292.
126. McHatton-Ripley, *Flag to Flag*, 210.
127. Eliza mentions this detail about Zell in *Flag to Flag*, 295. But letters from him do not appear to have been preserved in the McHatton Family Papers.
128. "August 1877," Diary of Henry McHatton, MFP.
129. McHatton-Ripley, *Social Life in Old New Orleans*, 211.
130. "Chinn's Plantation," Alfred R. Waud Collection, Historic New Orleans Collection, New Orleans; "Louisiana Intelligence," *New Orleans Daily Crescent*, April 10, 1866; "Sugar Plantations," *New Orleans Genesis* 3.10 (March 1964): 120–129; West Baton Rouge Genealogical Society, *West Baton Rouge Families* (Ft. Worth, TX: Landmark Press, 1999), 132, 134.
131. Eliza McHatton to Henry McHatton, September 17, 1876; Eliza McHatton to Henry McHatton, February 16, 1876; and "Chinese Murder," all in MFP.
132. McHatton-Ripley, *Flag to Flag*, 295.
133. "From Flag to Flag," *The Literary News* (January 1889): 11, and "Recent Publications," *New Orleans Picayune*, March 3, 1889, both in file named "Clippings, Reviews of Flag to Flag," in MFP.

4. The Labor Problem

1. Ira Berlin, *Slaves without Masters: The Free Negro in the Antebellum South* (New York: Pantheon, 1975), 381–395.
2. This phrase comes from Henry Sterne, *A Statement of Facts, Submitted to the Right Hon. Lord Glenelg, His Majesty's Principal Secretary for the Colonies* (1837; reprint, New York: Negro Universities Press, 1969), vi.
3. James Williams, *Narrative of Events since the First of August, 1834, by James Williams, an Apprenticed Labourer in Jamaica* (London: John Haddon, 1837), 3, 5.
4. Ibid., 5, 13.
5. Ibid., 23.
6. The details of Williams's life are taken from Diana Paton, "Introduction," in James Williams, *A Narrative of Events, since the First of August, 1834, by James Williams, an Apprenticed Labourer in Jamaica* (1837; reprint,

Durham, NC: Duke University Press, 2001), xiii–xlvi. Sturge's use of "indolent" in reference to Williams is discussed on p. xliv.

7. James M. Phillippo, *Jamaica, Its Past and Present State* (1842; reprint, London: Dawsons of Pall Mall, 1969), 170–171.

8. William Laurence Burn, *Emancipation and Apprenticeship in the British West Indies* (London: Jonathan Cape, 1937); William Green, *British Slave Emancipation: The Sugar Colonies and the Great Experiment, 1830–1865* (Oxford: Clarendon Press, 1976); Thomas C. Holt, *The Problem of Freedom: Race, Labor, and Politics in Jamaica and Britain, 1832–1938* (Baltimore: Johns Hopkins University Press, 1992).

9. R. R. Madden, *A Twelvemonth's Residence in the West Indies, during the Transition from Slavery to Apprenticeship* (1835; reprint, Westport, CT: Negro Universities Press, 1970), 39.

10. Anthony Trollope, *The West Indies and Spanish Main* (Leipzig: Bernhard Tauchnitz, 1860), 74.

11. William G. Sewell, *The Ordeal of Free Labor in the British West Indies* (London: Sampson, Low, Son, & Co., 1862), 169.

12. William B. Gravely, "The Dialectics of Double Consciousness in Black American Freedom Celebrations, 1808–1863," *Journal of Negro History* (Winter 1982): 304–305. Douglass is quoted on p. 304.

13. James M. McPherson, "Was West Indian Emancipation a Success? The Abolitionist Argument during the American Civil War," *Caribbean Studies* 4.2 (1964): 30.

14. Sewell, *Ordeal of Free Labor,* 230–243, 260–276; McPherson, "Was West Indian Emancipation a Success?" 26–34. These arguments echoed earlier refutations of the "decline of the planter class" idea by the British antislavery movement. See Thomas Clarkson, *Not a Labourer Wanted for Jamaica* (London: Thomas Ward & Co., 1842).

15. "The Southern Staples," *Daily Picayune,* August 29, 1865.

16. "The Status of the Freedmen," *Daily Clarion,* November 12, 1865.

17. Sterne, *A Statement of Facts,* v.

18. These parallels are discussed in Eric Foner, *Nothing but Freedom: Emancipation and Its Legacy* (Baton Rouge: Louisiana State University Press, 1983), 8–38. The standard treatment of the black codes is Theodore Branter Wilson, *The Black Codes of the South* (University: University of Alabama Press, 1965).

19. "Southern Staples."

20. "The Future of the Negro," *Daily Clarion,* August 17, 1865.

21. Christopher G. Memminger to Andrew Johnson, September 4, 1865, in *The Papers of Andrew Johnson,* ed. Paul H. Bergeron (Knoxville: University of Tennessee Press, 1991), 9:25. For more on the influence of West Indian apprenticeship on postbellum Southern attitudes, see Foner, *Nothing but Freedom,* 49–51; Eric Foner, *Reconstruction: America's Unfinished Revolution, 1863–1877* (New York: Harper & Row, 1988), 201–202; Vernon Lane Wharton, *The Negro in Mississippi, 1865–1890* (Chapel Hill: University of North Carolina Press, 1947), 93.

22. On this issue, see especially Amy Dry Stanley, *From Bondage to Contract: Wage Labor, Marriage, and the Market in the Age of Slave Emancipation* (Cambridge: Cambridge University Press, 1998).

23. Leon Litwack, *Been in the Storm So Long: The Aftermath of Slavery* (New York: Vintage, 1980), 399, 400. On the powerful desire for land, see also Foner, *Reconstruction*, 104–106.

24. Carl Schurz to Andrew Johnson, August 29, 1865, in *Advice after Appomattox: Letters to Andrew Johnson, 1865–1866*, ed. Brooks D. Simpson, Leroy P. Graf, and John Muldowney (Knoxville: University of Tennessee Press, 1987), 113; Carl Schurz, *The Condition of the South: Extracts from the Report of Major-General Carl Schurz of the States of South Carolina, Georgia, Alabama, Mississippi, and Louisiana* (Philadelphia, 1865), 7–8.

25. See, for example, Susan Dabney Smedes, *Memorials of a South Planter* (1887; reprint, Jackson: University of Mississippi Press, 1981), 237, 240; John T. Trowbridge, *The Desolate South, 1865–1866* (1866; revised and abridged, New York: Duell, Sloan and Pearce, 1956), 190, 197–198.

26. "Southern Staples."

27. Quoted in James L. Roark, *Masters without Slaves: Southern Planters in the Civil War and Reconstruction* (New York: W. W. Norton, 1977), 115.

28. "The Labor Question," *Daily Clarion*, 1865.

29. Letter reprinted in F. W. Loring and C. F. Atkinson, *Cotton Culture and the South* (Boston: A. Williams and Co., 1869), 14.

30. Pete Daniel, "The Metamorphosis of Slavery, 1865–1900," *Journal of American History* 66.1 (June 1979): 93.

31. This is Thomas C. Holt's elegant summary of an argument made by C. Vann Woodward; see Holt, " 'An Empire over the Mind': Emancipation, Race, an Ideology in the British West Indies and the American South," in *Region, Race, and Reconstruction: Essays in Honor of C. Vann Woodward*, ed. J. Morgan Kousser and James M. McPherson (New York: Oxford University Press, 1982), 285.

32. Evans's speech is reprinted in Appendix 14 of Schurz, *Condition of the South*, 65.

33. W. E. B. Du Bois, *Black Reconstruction in America, 1860–1880* (1935; reprint, New York: Athenaeum, 1992), 133. Also see Hans L. Trefousse, *Carl Schurz: A Biography* (Knoxville: University of Tennessee Press, 1982).

34. Carl Schurz to Frederick Althaus, June 25, 1965, in *The Intimate Letters of Carl Schurz, 1841–1869*, ed. Joseph Schafer (Madison: State Historical Society of Wisconsin, 1928), 340.

35. Schurz to Frederick Althaus, June 25, 1965, in *Intimate Letters*, 340.

36. Carl Schurz to Charles Sumner, June 5, 1865, in *Speeches, Correspondence, and Political Papers of Carl Schurz*, 6 vols., ed. Frederick Bancroft (New York: G. P. Putnam, 1913), 1:259.

37. Schurz, *Condition of the South*, 2.

38. Trefousse, *Carl Schurz*, 153–154.

39. Schurz, *Condition of the South*, 13.

40. Ibid., 22.
41. Ibid., 21.
42. Ibid., 21–22.
43. James L. Roark, *Masters without Slaves*, 200.
44. Schurz, *Condition of the South*, 27.
45. William C. Harris, *Presidential Reconstruction in Mississippi* (Baton Rouge: Louisiana State University Press, 1967), 25–26.
46. "Letter from Mississippi," *Daily Picayune*, November 25, 1865.
47. Carl Schurz to "Mrs. Schurz," in *Speeches, Correspondence, and Political Papers*, 1:268–269.
48. Holt, "An Empire over the Mind," 294.
49. "Labor Regulations," *Daily Clarion*, June 21, 1865; Foner, *Reconstruction*, 164–167.
50. Wilson, *The Black Codes of the South*, 57.
51. Schurz, *Condition of the South*.
52. Stanley, *From Bondage to Contract*, 38–45, especially 43–44.
53. Holt, "An Empire over the Mind," 289. Also see Thomas Holt, *The Problem of Freedom: Race, Labor, and Politics in Jamaica and Britain, 1832–1938* (Baltimore: Johns Hopkins University Press, 1992); Diana Paton, *No Bond but the Whip: Punishment, Race, and Gender in Jamaican State Formation, 1780–1870* (Durham, NC: Duke University Press, 2004), 83–120.
54. Holt, *Problem of Freedom*; Stanley, *From Bondage to Contract*, 36–37.
55. Willie Lee Rose, *Rehearsal for Reconstruction: The Port Royal Experiment* (1964; reprint, New York: Vintage Books, 1967).
56. Entries for March 23 and April 5, in Susan Walker, *The Diary of Miss Susan Walker, March 3rd to June 6th, 1862,* ed. Sherwood Henry Noble (Cincinnati: Historical and Philosophical Society of Ohio, 1912), 26, 27.
57. "Message of the Governor in Relation to the Freedmen, & c.," November 20, 1865, in the appendix of the *Journal of the Senate of the State of Mississippi, October, November, and December Sessions of 1865* (Jackson, MS: J. J. Shannon, 1866), 44.
58. Rosanne Currarino, "Labor Intellectuals and Labor Question: Wage Work and the Making of Consumer Society in America, 1873–1905" (Ph.D. diss., Rutgers University, 1999); William Leach, *Land of Desire: Merchants, Power, and the Rise of a New American Culture* (New York: Vintage, 1994); Jackson Lears, *Fables of Abundance: A Cultural History of Advertising in America* (New York: Basic Books, 1994).
59. "The Regulation of Labor," *Daily Picayune*, December 21, 1865.
60. "How to Have the South Peopled and Cultivated," *Daily Picayune*, July 29, 1865.
61. The businessman's comments originally appeared in the *Mobile Daily Times*, as cited in the *Daily Picayune*, October 6, 1865.
62. "The Freedmen in the Interior," *Daily Picayune*, December 1, 1865.
63. Entry for December 23, 1865, diary of J. B. Moore (1860–1874), Alabama Department of Archives and History, Montgomery, Alabama.

64. "News Miscellany," *Daily Picayune,* December 6, 1865.

65. Reprinted in *Daily Picayune,* December 1, 1865.

66. Du Bois, *Black Reconstruction in America,* 67.

67. Litwack, *Been in the Storm So Long,* 322–323 and passim.

68. Schurz, *Condition of the South,* 15.

69. Entry for Saturday, September 16, 1865, General Josiah Gorgas, "Diary, 1863–1865," Alabama Department of Archives and History, Montgomery, Alabama.

70. "How to Make Free Labor Profitable," *Daily Clarion,* August 8, 1865.

71. Carl Schurz, *The Reminiscences of Carl Schurz,* 3 vols., ed. Frederic Bancroft and William A. Dunning (New York: McClure, 1908), 3:191.

72. Trefousse, *Carl Schurz,* 158–159; Schurz, *Reminiscences,* 189–200.

73. Cited in Harris, *Presidential Reconstruction,* 52.

74. *Constitution of the State of Mississippi, as Amended, with the Ordinances and Resolutions Adopted by the Constitutional Convention, August, 1865* (Jackson, MS: E. M. Yerger, 1865), 44; Harris, *Presidential Reconstruction,* 54.

75. Schurz, *Condition of the South,* 33–34.

76. *Journal of the Proceedings and Debates in the Constitutional Convention of the State of Mississippi, August 1865* (Jackson, MS: E. M. Yerger, 1865), 165; "The Convention," *Daily Clarion,* August 21, 1865.

77. *Proceedings and Debates in the Constitutional Convention of the State of Mississippi, August 1865,* 137–138.

78. Lawrence J. Friedman, "The Search for Docility: Racial Thought in the White South, 1861–1917," *Phylon* 31.3 (1970): 314.

79. "Governor's Inaugural Address," in *Journal of the Senate of the State of Mississippi, October, November, and December Sessions of 1865,* 16.

80. "Texas—Condition of the Planters—Advice to Them," *New Orleans Crescent,* October 20, 1865.

81. "Negro Vagrants in New Orleans," *Natchez Democrat,* October 31, 1865.

82. Sarah R. Espy, entries for June 3 and July 13, 1865, "Private Journal, 1859–1868," Alabama Department of Archives and History, Montgomery, Alabama.

83. Steven Hahn, *A Nation under Our Feet: Black Political Struggles in the Rural South from Slavery to the Great Migration* (Cambridge, MA: Harvard University Press, 2003), 138–139; Steven Hahn, " 'Extravagant Expectations' of Freedom: Rumor, Political Struggle, and the Christmas Insurrection Scare of 1865 in the American South," *Past & Present* 157 (November 1997): 122–158.

84. "A St. Domingo Predicted," *Daily Picayune,* August 1, 1865.

85. See the entry for November 1, 1865, in the *Journal of the Senate of Mississippi,* 96.

86. Wilson, *Black Codes of the South,* 71.

87. Franklin Knight, *The Caribbean: The Genesis of a Fragmented Nationalism* (New York: Oxford University Press, 1990), 282.

88. On the Morant Bay rebellion, see Holt, *Problem of Freedom*, 265–309; Green, *British Slave Emancipation*, 381–392.

89. Bernard Semmel, *The Governor Eyre Controversy* (London: MacGibbon & Kee, 1962), 15.

90. Edward Bean Underhill, *The Tragedy of Morant Bay: A Narrative of the Disturbances in the Island of Jamaica, 1865* (1895; reprint, Freeport, NY: Books for Libraries Press, 1971), 110.

91. Foner, *Nothing but Freedom*, 30.

92. "The Negro Outbreak in Jamaica," *Daily Picayune*, November 28, 1865.

93. "The Insurrection in Jamaica," *New Orleans Daily Crescent*, November 9, 1865.

94. "The Jamaica Insurrection," *Daily Picayune*, November 19, 1865. Also see "Important from the West Indies," *Daily Picayune*, November 23, 1865.

95. "Mississippi Intelligence," *New Orleans Daily Crescent*, October 31, 1865.

96. "The Jamaican Insurrection," *Vicksburg Daily Journal*, December 13, 1865.

97. "The Uprising in Jamaica," *New Orleans Daily Crescent*, January 18, 1866.

98. "Why Emancipation Failed in the British Colonies," *Daily Picayune*, November 4, 1865.

99. Harris, *Presidential Reconstruction*, 139; Wilson, *Black Codes of the South*, 66–71; Peter W. Bardaglio, *Reconstructing the Household: Families, Sex, and the Law in the Nineteenth-Century South* (Chapel Hill: University of North Carolina Press, 1995), 162–163.

100. Paton, *No Bond but the Whip*, 87.

101. Christopher Waldrep, "Substituting Law for the Lash: Emancipation and Legal Formalism in a Mississippi County Court," *Journal of American History* 82.4 (March 1996): 1425–1451; Wilson, *Black Codes of the South*, 68–72. On convict leasing, see Alex Lichtenstein, *Twice the Work of Free Labor: The Political Economy of Convict Labor in the New South* (London: Verso Press, 1996).

102. See the debate over "An Act to confer civil rights upon freedmen" on November 24, 1865, in *Journal of the Senate of Mississippi*, 229–232. The amendment in question is discussed on p. 231.

103. Waldrep, "Substituting Law for the Lash," 1436. Also see Christopher Waldrep, *Roots of Disorder: Race and Criminal Justice in the American South, 1817–80* (Urbana: University of Illinois Press, 1998), 101–108.

104. Waldrep, "Substituting Law for the Lash"; Waldrep, *Roots of Disorder*, 98–99.

105. *Chicago Tribune*, December 1, 1865, cited in Harris, *Presidential Reconstruction*, 141.

106. Appendix 29 in Schurz, *Condition of the South*, 83.

107. "A Model Report," *New Orleans Daily Crescent*, January 9, 1866.

108. Holt, *Problem of Freedom*, 274–276; Green, *British Slave Emancipation*, 396–397.

109. George M. Fredrickson, *White Supremacy: A Comparative Study in American and South African History* (New York: Oxford University Press, 1981), 235 and passim.
110. "Coolies in the West Indies," *Daily Picayune*, September 2, 1865.
111. "The Coolie Question," *Daily Picayune*, November 7, 1865.
112. Schurz, *Condition of the South*, 21.

5. Latitudes and Longitudes

1. Whitelaw Reid, *After the War: A Tour of Southern States, 1865–1866* (New York: Moore, Wilstach, and Baldwin, 1866), 562.
2. "Many masters," Susan Walker remembered, "told their slaves the Yankees would take them and send them to Cuba." Susan Walker, entry for March 1862, in *The Journal of Miss Susan Walker, March 3rd to June 6th, 1862*, ed. Henry Noble Sherwood (Cincinnati: Historical and Philosophical Society of Ohio, 1912), 22.
3. Gerald Horne, *The Deepest South: The United States, Brazil, and the African Slave Trade* (New York: New York University Press, 2007), 107–127.
4. Albert S. White, "Report: Emancipation and Colonization," House of Representatives, 37th Cong., 2d sess., Report no. 148, to accompany HR 576 (printed on July 16, 1862), 16; William Seraille, "Afro-American Emigration to Haiti during the American Civil War," *The Americas* 35.2 (October 1978): 185–200.
5. Reid, *After the War*, 563.
6. Anthony Trollope, *The West Indies and the Spanish Main* (Leipzig: Bernhard Tauchnitz, 1860), 138.
7. Adam Adamson, *Sugar without Slaves: The Political Economy of British Guiana, 1838–1904* (New Haven, CT: Yale University Press, 1972); Hugh Tinker, *A New System of Slavery: The Export of Indian Labor Overseas, 1830–1920* (New Haven, CT: Yale University Press, 1974).
8. Toto Mangar, "The Hopetown Experiment: An Aspect of Chinese Immigration in Nineteenth-Century British Guiana," unpublished manuscript in author's possession.
9. Moon-Ho Jung, *Coolies and Cane: Race, Labor, and Sugar in the Age of Emancipation* (Baltimore: Johns Hopkins University Press, 2005).
10. Denise Helly, "Introduction," in *The Cuba Commission Report: A Hidden History of the Chinese in Cuba* (Baltimore: Johns Hopkins University Press, 1993), 10.
11. Lucy M. Cohen, *Chinese in the Post–Civil War South: A People without a History* (Baton Rouge: Louisiana State University Press, 1984), 68–69, 74, 77, 80, 143.
12. Jung, *Coolies and Cane*, 5, 225.
13. Madhavi Kale, *Fragments of Empire: Capital, Slavery, and Indian Indentured Labor in the British Caribbean* (Philadelphia: University of Pennsylvania

Press, 1998), 5. Kale makes a distinction between histories of "labor migration" and histories of "imperial labor reallocation," a distinction on which the foundation for this chapter lies.

14. "Another Arrival of Swiss Immigrants," *Charleston Daily Courier,* July 12, 1869; "Chinese Labor for the Southern States," *Charleston Daily Courier,* July 12, 1869.

15. "Coolies for Charleston," *Charleston Daily Courier,* August 24, 1869; "The Coolies," *Charleston Daily Courier,* August 30, 1869.

16. William Lawton, *An Essay on Rice and Its Culture, Read before the Agricultural Congress, Convened at Selma, Alabama, December 5, 1871* (Charleston, SC: Walker, Evans, and Cogswell, 1871), 10–11.

17. Francis Butler Simkins and Robert Hilliard Woody, *South Carolina during Reconstruction* (Chapel Hill: University of North Carolina Press, 1932), 186–223.

18. "The Mobile Riot," *Charleston Daily Courier,* August 7, 1869.

19. William Johnstone to unknown, February 7, 1869, James Ritchie Sparkman Papers, South Caroliniana Library, University of South Carolina (hereafter JRS).

20. George M. Fredrickson, *The Black Image in the White Mind: The Debate over Afro-American Character and Destiny* (New York: Harper & Row, 1971), 187–188, 153–164. On the broader characteristics of the literature on racial decline, see Patrick Brantlinger, *Dark Vanishings: Discourse on the Extinction of Primitive Races, 1800–1930* (Ithaca, NY: Cornell University Press, 2003).

21. "Trollope's West Indies," *Charleston Daily Courier,* May 25, 1869.

22. J. C. Delavigne, "The Labor Question," *De Bow's Review* (February 1870): 167–173.

23. E. Philips to James Philips, October 27, 1865, James Jones Philips Papers (#972), series 1, folder 3, General and Literary Manuscripts, Wilson Library, University of North Carolina at Chapel Hill.

24. *Natchez Democrat,* December 28, 1865.

25. "Cotton and Labor," *Natchez Democrat,* November 18, 1865.

26. "Communicated," *Natchez Democrat,* December 16, 1865.

27. *Natchez Democrat,* December 28, 1865.

28. Quoted in Reid, *After the War,* 417.

29. John T. Trowbridge, *The Desolate South, 1865–1866: A Picture of the Battlefields and of the Devastated Confederacy* (1866; revised and abridged, New York: Duell, Sloan and Pearce, 1956), 204.

30. William Lawton to the editors of the *New York Journal of Commerce,* July 17, 1869, JRS.

31. William Lawton to Robert Mure, July 19, 1869, JRS.

32. "News from Havana," *Daily Picayune,* July 6, 1865.

33. "The Coolies," *Daily Picayune,* October 22, 1865.

34. Cohen, *Chinese in the Post–Civil War South,* 53, 51–54. On the Chinese in the South more generally, see Jung, *Coolies and Cane;* James W. Loewen,

The Mississippi Chinese: Between Black and White (1971; reprint, Prospect Heights, IL: Waveland Press, 1988), 9–31; Robert Seto Quan, *Lotus among the Magnolias: The Mississippi Chinese* (Jackson: University of Mississippi Press, 1982); Ronald Takaki, *Strangers from a Different Shore: A History of Asian Americans* (New York: Penguin Books, 1989), 94–95.

35. See Lucy M. Cohen, "George W. Gift, Chinese Labor Agent in the Post–Civil War South," *Chinese America: History and Perspectives* (1995): 157–178.

36. Cohen, *Chinese in the Post–Civil War South*, 93.

37. *Savannah Republican,* July 16, 1870, cited in Cohen, *Chinese in the Post–Civil War South*, 97; Sylvia H. Krebs, "John Chinaman and Reconstruction Alabama: The Debate and the Experience," *Southern Studies* 21 (1982): 379–381.

38. Cohen, *Chinese in the Post–Civil War South*, 17.

39. Both in Walton Look Lai, *The Chinese in the West Indies: A Documentary History* (Barbados: University of the West Indies Press, 1998), 114, 115–119.

40. For a general overview, see Alexander Saxton, *The Indispensable Enemy: Labor and the Anti-Chinese Movement in California* (1971; reprint, Berkeley: University of California Press, 1995); and Najia Aarim-Heriot, *Chinese Immigrants, African Americans, and Racial Anxiety in the United States, 1848–1882* (Urbana: University of Illinois Press, 2003).

41. See, for instance, *"Chinaman or White Man, Which?" A Reply to Father Buchard by Rev. O. Gibson, Delivered in Platt's Hall, San Francisco, Friday Evening, March 14, 1873* (San Francisco: Alta California Printing House, 1873). The phrase "criminally cheap labor" is from p. 8. Rosanne Currarino, "Labor Intellectuals and Labor Question: Wage Work and the Making of Consumer Society in America, 1873–1905" (Ph.D. diss., Rutgers University, 1999); Robert G. Lee, *Orientalism: Asian Americans in Popular Culture* (Philadelphia: Temple University Press, 1999), 15–82.

42. Currarino, "Labor Intellectuals and Labor Question," chapter 4, p. 6.

43. Saxton, *The Indispensable Enemy;* David R. Roediger, *The Wages of Whiteness: Race and the Making of the American Working Class* (New York: Verso Press, 1991), 179–180.

44. James H. Hammond, "Speech on the Admission of Kansas, under the Lecompton Constitution, Delivered in the Senate of the United States, March 4, 1858," in *Selections from the Letters and Speeches of the Hon. James H. Hammond, of South Carolina* (1866; reprint, Spartansburg, SC: The Reprint Co., 1978), 318.

45. Aarim-Heriot, *Chinese Immigrants*, 121–122; Cohen, *Chinese in the Post–Civil War South*, 22–45; Jung, *Coolies and Cane*, 81–82.

46. Jung, *Coolies and Cane*, 92.

47. Cohen, *Chinese in the Post–Civil War South*, 66–71; Steven E. Anders, "The Coolie Panacea in the Reconstruction South: A White Response to Emancipation and the Black 'Labor Problem'" (M.A. thesis, Miami University of Ohio, 1973), 78–100.

48. Andrew Gay to Edward Gay, August 13, 1870, Edward Gay and Family Papers, Louisiana State University Special Collections, Hill Memorial Library, Baton Rouge, LA (hereafter GP).

49. Samuel Cranwill to Edward Gay, September 3, 1870, GP.

50. Cohen, *Chinese in the Post–Civil War South,* 117–131; John C. Rodrigue, *Reconstruction in the Cane Fields: From Slavery to Free Labor in Louisiana's Sugar Parishes, 1862–1880* (Baton Rouge: Louisiana State University Press, 1991), 137.

51. J. K. Vance, "Report on Chinese Immigration," in *Proceedings of the Immigration Convention, Held at the Academy of Music, Charleston, South Carolina, on the 3rd, 4th, and 5th of May, 1870* (Charleston, SC: Walker, Evans, and Cogswell, 1870), 78.

52. Ibid., 78–79.

53. "Foreign Items," *New Orleans Daily Crescent,* May 21, 1866.

54. See " 'Chinese Cheap Labor' in Louisiana" and "Sketches in Louisiana," in the Alfred R. Waud Collection, Historical New Orleans Collection, New Orleans, LA.

55. "Gen. Lee on Chinese Immigration," *De Bow's Review* (May–June 1870): 498. Also see "Incongruity of Population Not Desirable," *De Bow's Review* (July 1870): 580.

56. William M. Burwell, "Science and the Mechanic Arts against Coolies," *De Bow's Review* (July 1869): 557–571; Cohen, *Chinese in the Post–Civil War South,* 63, 69.

57. Jeffrey Moran, "Chinese Labor for the New South," *Southern Studies,* New Series 3.4 (1992): 290–291; Cohen, *Chinese in the Post–Civil War South,* 82–86; Lee, *Orientals,* 65–66.

58. J. W. Alvord, *Letters from the South, Relating to the Condition of the Freedmen, Addressed to Major General O. O. Howard* (Washington, DC: Howard University Press, 1870), 9.

59. Cited in "Incongruity of Population Not Desirable," 580.

60. William Lawton to James R. Sparkman, August 2, 1869, JRS.

61. "John Chinaman Has Come," *St. Louis Republican,* reprinted in the *Charleston Daily Courier,* January 6, 1870.

62. Hattie Elliot to Mama, November 11, 1867, Elliot and Gonzales Family Papers, Southern Historical Collection, Wilson Library, University of North Carolina at Chapel Hill (hereafter EGP).

63. Unknown to "my dear Emmie," late April 1866, EGP.

64. William Elliot to his mother, April 15, 1866, EGP.

65. Mamie Elliot to Mama, February 29, 1868, EGP; Anne H. Elliott to Harriet Gonzales, November 28, 1866, EGP.

66. Hattie Elliot to Mama, October 28, 1868, EGP.

67. Johnnie Elliot to Mother, March 23, 1867, EGP.

68. Hattie Elliot (?) to Emmie, March 9, 1867, EGP.

69. Ralph Elliot to his mother, February 8, 1866, EGP.

70. Hattie Elliot to Mother, May 19, 1867, EGP.

71. Hattie Elliot to Mama, [May 1869,] EGP.

72. Mary Elliot to Mother, October 23, 1869, EGP.

73. William A. Green, *British Slave Emancipation: The Sugar Colonies and the Great Experiment, 1830–1865* (New York: Oxford University Press, 1975), 261–293; Brackette F. Williams, *Stains on My Name, War in My Veins: Guyana and the Politics of Cultural Struggle* (Durham, NC: Duke University Press, 1990), 143–144; Rebecca J. Scott, *Slave Emancipation in Cuba: The Transition to Free Labor, 1860–1899* (Princeton, NJ: Princeton University Press, 1985), 213, 216; Jeffrey Lesser, *Negotiating National Identity: Immigrants, Minorities, and the Struggle for Ethnicity in Brazil* (Durham, NC: Duke University Press, 1999), 13–39.

74. Frederick Trautmann, ed., *Travels on the Lower Mississippi, 1879–1880: A Memoir by Earnst von Hesse-Wartegg* (Columbia: University of Missouri Press, 1990), 212.

75. Joel Williamson, *After Slavery: The Negro in South Carolina during Reconstruction, 1861–1877* (1965; reprint, New York: W. W. Norton, 1975), 118–119.

76. Williamson, *After Slavery*.

77. On the general air of desperation in the earliest efforts to get white immigrants to the South, see Bert James Loewenberg, "Efforts of the South to Encourage Immigration, 1865–1900," *South Atlantic Quarterly* 33 (1934): 363–385. James S. Pike reported that African American congressmen in South Carolina were immediately aware that European immigration was "intended to overslaugh and crowd out the blacks." See James S. Pike, *The Prostrate State: South Carolina under Negro Government* (New York: D. Appleton, 1874), 55; E. C. Cabell, "White Emigration to the South," *De Bow's Review* (January 1866): 93.

78. Frederick Law Olmsted, *A Journey in the Seaboard Slave States in the Years 1853–1854, With Remarks on Their Economy*, 2 vols. (New York: G. P. Putnam's Sons, 1904), 1:101.

79. See especially David T. Gleeson, *The Irish in the South, 1815–1877* (Chapel Hill: University of North Carolina Press, 2001); Christopher Silver, "Immigration and the Antebellum Southern City: Irish Working Class Mobility in Charleston, South Carolina, 1840–1860" (M.A. thesis, University of North Carolina at Chapel Hill, 1975).

80. J. Floyd King to Lin Caperton, December 29, 1865, Thomas Butler King Papers (#1252), Manuscripts Department, Wilson Library, University Library of the University of North Carolina at Chapel Hill, series 1.8, folder 441 (hereafter TBK).

81. Thomas C. Holt, " 'An Empire over the Mind': Emancipation, Race, and Ideology in the British West Indies and the American South," in *Region, Race, and Reconstruction: Essays in Honor of C. Vann Woodward*, ed. J. Morgan Kousser and James M. McPherson (New York: Oxford University Press, 1982), 315–348; Robert Higgs, *Competition and Coercion: Blacks in the American Economy* (Cambridge, MA: Harvard University Press, 1977); Leon Litwack, *Been in the Storm So Long: The Aftermath of Slavery* (New York: Alfred A. Knopf, 1979).

82. J. Floyd King to Lin Caperton, January 1, 1866, TBK.

83. J. Floyd King to Lin Caperton, January 18, 1866, TBK.

84. J. Floyd King to Mallery Page King, January 18, 1866, TBK.

85. J. Floyd King to Lin Caperton, February 13, 1866, TBK.

86. J. Floyd King to Georgia Smith, February 19, 1866, TBK.

87. J. Floyd King to Mallery Page King, January 18, 1866, and J. Floyd King to Lin Caperton, February 13, 1866, both in TBK.

88. Cf. Robert Somers, *The Southern States since the War, 1870–1871* (London: Macmillan, 1871), 74, 123. Also see Cohen, *Chinese in the Post–Civil War South,* 93.

89. *Daily Columbus Enquirer,* June 20, 1866, cited in E. Merton Coulter, *The South during Reconstruction, 1865–1877* (Baton Rouge: Louisiana State University Press, 1947), 105.

90. Trowbridge, *The Desolate South,* 203.

91. Coulter, *The South during Reconstruction,* 104. Also see Eric Foner, *Reconstruction: America's Unfinished Revolution, 1863–1877* (New York: Harper and Row, 1988), 213–214.

92. Carl Schurz, *The Condition of the South: Extracts from the Report of Major-General Carl Schurz of the States of South Carolina, Georgia, Alabama, Mississippi, and Louisiana* (Philadelphia, 1865), 23–24.

93. "Georgia," *New York Times,* November 15, 1866.

94. Robert H. Woody, "The Labor and Immigration Problem of South Carolina during Reconstruction," *Mississippi Valley Historical Review* 18.2 (September 1931): 198.

95. "South Carolina," *New York Times,* February 16, 1869.

96. Woody, "The Labor and Immigration Problem," 196–199.

97. "Mr. Lawton's Remarks," *Proceedings of the Immigration Convention,* 9.

98. Jung, *Coolies and Cane,* 163–180. More broadly, see Rowland Bertoff, "Southern Attitudes towards Immigration," *Journal of Southern History* 17 (1951): 336–338.

99. "Alabama, Its Inducements to Immigrants," *De Bow's Review* (April 1868): 356.

100. *South Carolina: A Home for the Industrious Immigrant. Published by the Commissioner of Immigration* (Charleston, SC: Joseph Walker's, 1867).

101. Woody, "The Labor and Immigration Problem," 202–203; Bertoff, "Southern Attitudes towards Immigration," 336–337.

102. Woody, "The Labor and Immigration Problem," 203–204.

103. "The Action of the Convention," *Charleston Daily Courier,* May 7, 1870.

104. J. D. B. De Bow, "The Future of the South," *De Bow's Review* (January 1866): 13–14.

105. "Letter from M. F. Maury," *Proceedings of the Immigration Convention,* 11.

106. Coulter, *The South during Reconstruction,* 105.

107. Thomas Spence, *The Settler's Guide in the United States and British North American Provinces* (New York, 1862), iii.

108. For some sense of the history of the South as a "tropical" space, see Ronald Walters, "The Erotic South: Civilization and Sexuality in American Abolitionism," *American Quarterly* 25.2 (May 1973): 177–201; Natalie J. Ring, "Inventing the Tropical South: Race, Region, and the Colonial Model," *Mississippi Quarterly* (Fall 2003): 619–632. On the general idea that tropical spaces were unhealthy for Europeans, see Philip D. Curtin, *Death by Migration: Europe's Encounters with the Tropical World in the Nineteenth Century* (Cambridge: Cambridge University Press, 1989). On the common themes of the regional literature that sought to court immigrants to the United States, see Merle Curti and Kendall Birr, "The Immigrant and the American Image in Europe, 1860–1914," *Mississippi Valley Historical Review* 37.2 (1950): 203–230.

109. "A Home for the Immigrant—State of South Carolina," in *Proceedings of the Immigration Convention*, 14, 15.

110. "Report on Education," in *Proceedings of the Immigration Convention*, 52.

111. "Report on the Flora of the State," in *Proceedings of the Immigration Convention*, 74.

112. Foner, *Reconstruction*, 213.

113. Krebs, "John Chinaman and Reconstruction Alabama," 381.

114. Gavin Wright, *Old South, New South: Revolutions in the Southern Economy Since the Civil War* (New York: Basic Books, 1986), 75–76.

115. Cohen, *Chinese in the Post–Civil War South*, 68.

116. "The Labor Question," *De Bow's Review* (August 1868): 783.

117. Cf. "In Lieu of Labor," *De Bow's Review* (July–August 1867): 69–83; "Southern Railroad Policy," *De Bow's Review* (September 1868): 841–843; "Sorgo Mills and Evaporators," *De Bow's Review* (July 1868); "Railroad Policy for the South," *De Bow's Review* (July 1868): 607–611; "Knagg's Process of Cane Sugar-Making," *De Bow's Review* (June 1868): 567–569; Oscar Zanetti and Alejandro García, *Sugar and Railroads: A Cuban History*, trans. Franklin W. Knight and Mary Todd (Chapel Hill: University of North Carolina Press, 1998); T. Guilford Smith, *Report of the Mineral Lands and Resources of the Alabama & Chattanooga Railroad Company* (Troy, NY: Wm. H. Young and Blake, 1871).

118. Wright, *Old South, New South*, 75, 17–31.

119. Philip D. Curtin, *The Rise and Fall of the Plantation Complex: Essays in Atlantic History* (Cambridge: Cambridge University Press, 1998), 196. Also, witness Robert Somers's description of the backwardness of Louisiana sugar production: Somers, *Southern States since the War*, 228–231. Two prominent Southern historians write that "Southern leaders . . . built their transportation system colonial style; it bound the staple-producing plantation districts to the ports and largely bypassed the upcountry." Eugene Genovese and Elizabeth Fox Genovese, *Fruits of Merchant Capital* (New York: Oxford University Press, 1983), 50.

120. G. Pillsbury to J. V. Alvord, January 10, 1870, reprinted in J. W. Alvord, *Letters from the South Relating to the Condition of Freedmen Addressed to*

Major General O. O. Howard (Washington, DC: Howard University Press, 1870), 11.

121. Coulter, *The South during Reconstruction,* 107; Williamson, *After Slavery,* 119.

122. In a different context, this point is made by historian Rick Halpern. See Halpern, "Solving the 'Labour Problem': Race, Work, and the State in the Sugar Industries of Louisiana and Natal, 1870–1910," *Journal of South African Studies* 30.1 (March 2004): 19–40.

123. David M. Oshinsky, *Worse than Slavery: Parchman Farm and the Ordeal of Jim Crow Justice* (New York: Free Press, 1996), 44.

124. *La Rue Cases Nègres,* directed by Euhzan Palcy (NEF Diffusion, 1983).

125. David Blight, *Race and Reunion: The Civil War in American Memory* (Cambridge, MA: Belknap Press, 2002); Gaines M. Foster, *Ghosts of the Confederacy: Defeat, the Lost Cause, and the Emergence of the New South, 1865–1913* (New York: Oxford University Press, 1988); Kirk Savage, *Standing Soldiers, Kneeling Slaves: Race, War, and Monument in Nineteenth-Century America* (Princeton, NJ: Princeton University Press, 1997); John Michael Vlach, *The Planter's Prospect: Privilege and Slavery in Plantation Paintings* (Chapel Hill: University of North Carolina Press, 2002).

126. Frederick Douglass, "Parties Were Made for Men, Not Men for Parties," an address delivered in Louisville, Kentucky, on September 25, 1883, in *The Frederick Douglass Papers. Series One: Speeches, Debates, and Interviews,* ed. John W. Blassingame and John R. McKivigan (New Haven, CT: Yale University Press, 1992), 5:100.

Epilogue

1. Christopher Lasch, *The Revolt of the Elites, and the Betrayal of Democracy* (New York: W. W. Norton, 1995), 5.

2. I am borrowing here from the title of Leon Fink's excellent *The Maya of Morganton: Work and Community in the Nuevo New South* (Chapel Hill: University of North Carolina Press, 2003).

3. In 2003, one newspaper columnist could note with dripping sarcasm that Miami was home to more right-wing Latin American ex-dictators than any other city in the world. Naomi Klein, "Latino Politics, Miami Beached," *Globe & Mail,* October 23, 2003. See, for instance, Rakesh Kochhar, Roberto Suro, and Sonya Tafoya, "The New Latino South: The Context and Consequences of Rapid Population Growth," report prepared for the Pew Hispanic Center, July 26, 2005.

4. Juan Gonzalez, "Down This Dead-End Road Before," *Daily News* (New York), January 8, 2004.

5. Quoted in Jeff Cowie, *Capital Moves* (Ithaca, NY: Cornell University Press, 1999).

6. At one point, German prisoners of war were used to cut cane; they found the labor so oppressive that at least one committed suicide. On the German

prisoners of war, see "Five Recent Cases with Slavery Convictions," *Palm Beach Post*, December 7, 2003.

7. Alec Wilkenson, *Big Sugar: Seasons in the Cane Fields of Florida* (1989; reprint, New York: Vintage, 1990), 5–6; Risa Goluboff, " 'Won't You Please Help Me Get My Son Home?' Peonage, Patronage, and Protest in the World War II Urban South," *Law & Social Inquiry* 24 (Fall 1995): 777–806; Cindy Hahamovitch, *The Fruits of Their Labor: Atlantic Coast Farmworkers and the Making of Migrant Poverty, 1870–1945* (Chapel Hill: University of North Carolina Press, 1997); Alex Lichtenstein, *Twice the Work of Free Labor: The Political Economy of Convict Labor in the New South* (London: Verso Press, 1996).

8. Quote from "Machines Displacing Foreign Sugar Cane Cutters in Florida," *Washington Post*, December 30, 1991. Also see "Way of Life for Jamaican Cane Cutters in Jeopardy," *Houston Chronicle*, January 5, 1992. On the prevalence of slavery in present-day Florida, see "Five Recent Cases with Slavery Convictions"; "Farm Boss Sentenced for Slavery," *St. Petersburg Times*, September 22, 1999; "Big Sugar Displays a Plantation Mentality," *St. Petersburg Times*, October 10, 1996.

9. John Bowe, *Nobodies: Modern American Slave Labor and the Dark Side of the New Global Economy* (New York: Random House, 2007).

10. "The Breach in the Dam in New Orleans and the Resultant Floods Hold a Lesson for Us," *Stabroek News*, September 5, 2005.

11. "Wednesday Ramblings," *Stabroek News*, September 7, 2005.

12. F. Scott Fitzgerald, *The Great Gatsby* (1925; reprint, New York: Scribner's, 1980); D. H. Lawrence, *Studies in Classic American Literature* (New York: Thomas Seltzer, 1923).

13. Edouard Glissant, *Faulkner, Mississippi*, trans. Barbara Lewis and Thomas C. Spear (1996; reprint and translation, Chicago: University of Chicago Press, 1999), 29.

Acknowledgments

Colleagues at three different institutions have offered me critically important help with this project. At Washington State University, José Alamillo, Kelly Ervin, Linda Heidenreich, Alex Kuo, Epifanio San Juan Jr., Theresa Schenk, and Heather Streets were immensely supportive. A New Faculty Seed Grant from Washington State University allowed me to get started quickly. At Brown University, Bill Simmons and Evelyn Hu-DeHart were early champions of this book, as were Jim Campbell and Bob Lee. At Indiana University, my colleagues and graduate students in African American and African Diaspora Studies, in American Studies, and in the College of Arts and Sciences were generous to a fault. I am most especially indebted to John Bodnar, Claude Clegg, Deborah Cohn, Kon Dierks, Valerie Grim, Trica Keaton, Sarah Knott, Vivian Halloran, Michael McGerr, Marissa Moorman, Khalil Muhammad, Amrita Myers, Steve Stowe, Kirsten Sword, and Kumble Subbaswamy. Support from the College Arts and Humanities Institute and the Office of the Vice President for Research was critically important. Laila Amine, Cynthia Gwynne Yaudes, Kellie J. Hogue, and Danille Christensen were fabulous research assistants. Joshua Nadal and Eric Plaag were my eyes on the spot. Paula Cotner, our American Studies administrative assistant, made everything go smoothly.

I was lucky to get fellowships from the Center for the Study of Race and Ethnicity in America, Brown University; the Library Company of Philadelphia; and the Gilder Lehrman Center for the Study of Slavery, Resistance, and Abolition, Yale University; and a Bernadotte Schmitt Grant from the American Historical Association.

Many others were enthusiastically supportive, appropriately skeptical, or constructively critical, including John G. Arrison of the Stephen Phillips Memorial Library, Penobscot Marine Museum; and Ed Blum, James T. Campbell, Glenda Gilmore, Candice Goucher, Nancy Hewitt, Matthew Frye Jacobson, Winthrop Jordan, Caroline Levander, Robert Lee, Robert Levine, Charlie McGovern, and Diana Williams. The anonymous reviewers for Harvard University Press, for the *Radical History Review*, for *American Literary History*, and for the *Journal of World History* deserve praise for their generous, lengthy, and well-intentioned skewerings.

In the end, the progress and completion of this book were helped along by some very good friends. Michael Adas always seemed to know what I was doing before I did and told me about it in just the right way. Finis Dunaway helped this project along by reading the whole thing closely and gently steering me in the right directions. Jim Gatewood and I shared a beer every Tuesday night for a year to work out some of the kinks. Jennifer Roth Gordon was a stalwart companion, a genius planner, and a great life critic. Katie Lofton was an inspirational (and supremely fast) reader and critic. Rosanne Currarino nearly deserves coauthorship, as she read every word of this, sometimes in paragraph form and sometimes as a whole, and walked me through the good and the bad. Debbie Cohn always asked about the book, nudging me to talk about it and introducing me to the literary crowd. Vivian Halloran gamely tolerated my talking about this in class, even when it clearly did not match up with what we were supposed to be discussing. Pat McDevitt brought me to Buffalo to give a talk and share encouragement. Kim Brodkin and Rick Jobs let me sleep on their blow-up mattress in Portland. Todd Uhlman was a good friend, and knew when I was not willing to talk about it. At a pivotal moment, Michael McGerr wisely suggested that a slower pace might give me a better perspective. He was right. Christine Skwiot shared her sharp wit and her brilliant and forthcoming work on Cuba and Hawaii. David Levering Lewis, my mentor and friend, cheered me on as I neared the finish line. Former graduate student friends and new Indiana University colleagues Khalil Muhammad and Amrita Myers shared coffee as we pushed our parallel projects to completion. To these friends—and all others—I can only say: I owe you a lot.

At Harvard University Press, Kathleen McDermott was present at the beginning, the middle, and the end. She was a dream.

At some very dark moments, family was often a lifeline to a better state of mind. My uncle, Bill Jordan, my brother-in-law, Hugh

Hamilton, and my mother, Sheryl Guterl all read the book in draft and shared their thoughts. Sandra Latcha kept me on the straight and narrow and lovingly pushed me to get this done even as she insisted on attentive fatherhood and partnership. Our children, Robert and Maya, did not exist when this book was conceived. As the writing progressed and the manuscript got longer and I got more involved, they had very little patience with me, my computer, or anything else related to this book. Their innocent demands—manifested in the insistent tugging of pants, in the repeated pressing of the off button on my keypad, and, more recently, in the frequent asking of questions—were, in the end, simultaneously endearing, frustrating, and motivational. For more reasons than one, then, I dedicate the book to them and, as always, to Sandi.

Index